Joann Schladale and Therese Langan's
Stop It! A Practical Guide for Youth Violence Prevention

It's complicated. That is the truth about intractable social problems and violence prevention is no different. Schladale and Langan embrace that complexity, addressing issues from birth control, to parenting, relationship-building, racial and economic disparities with a thoughtful, challenging and practical evidence-based approach to the problem. This is an invaluable contribution to the literature that belongs on all of our bookshelves.

Steven Bengis, Executive Director
New England Adolescent Research Institute

Schladale and Langan have captured succinctly the essence of adolescent violence prevention approaches. Stop It! will expedite the understanding and implementation of education and interventions aimed at increasing success and safety for youth.

Gail Ryan, Director
Kempe Perpetration Prevention Program
University of Colorado School of Medicine

Schladale and Langan have delivered a book that is a tool for professionals, paraprofessionals, volunteers and families involved in this very important issue. Peppered with real life stories and written for everyone, this will become a "go to resource" on everyone's shelf.

As a sexuality educator, I especially appreciate the discussion on sexual health and the role it can play in addressing youth violence. The sections on advocacy and the trauma outcome process are a must read for everyone involved in the issue and are keys in understanding how to effectively address prevention.

Finally, the format of the recommendations and resources at the end of each chapter provide an easy place to get started quickly—a must for all of us who never have enough time and resources.

Triste Brooks, President & CEO
Planned Parenthood of Greater Northern New Jersey

Stop It!

A Practical Guide for
Youth Violence Prevention

Joann Schladale & Therese Langan

ISBN 978-0-615-59998-4

Library of Congress Cataloging-in-Publication Data has been applied for.

Resources for Resolving Violence, Inc.
28 Marshview Drive
Freeport, ME 04032
www.resourcesforresolvingviolence.com

Parkside Family Counseling, LLC
738 South Main Street, Suite 201
Adrian, MI 49221
www.parksideforfamiles.com

*Violence is a most widespread means of entertainment
and also a tremendous business,
both in terms of weapons sales and entertainment industries.*

Overcomingviolence.org

Dedications

This is for my husband, John,
whose support appears to know no bounds.

And for Poseidon, who discovered Athena.

Joann

To my parents, Emma & Jack,
for giving my sisters and I the essential ingredients
of a healthy childhood;
for taking care of all the details and worries of parenting,
so we could go about the business of growing up.

Therese

Contents

[Handwritten annotations:] 28-29 Touch • *34- • -41 • Do this! • 52 This Works • P.48 • To Do List.... -53 • Trama -68 • 69- Evidence Based • Sou...ces 75 • Treatment • ★ Conclusion→ 94 • 95 Resources

Section Three: Other Important Things

Foundation

We want everyone to have a clear understanding of our approach to this complex challenge.

Our mission is to create a practical, user-friendly, research-based guide for youth violence prevention.

The purpose of this book is to:
- Help all youth attain a life free of violence in order to maximize human potential, health, and well being.
- Instill hope and provide a clearly defined path to a productive, connected, and law-abiding lifestyle for youth not yet convinced that a non-violent lifestyle is possible for everyone.
- Provide a research-based foundation for caregivers and service providers to guide youth along such a path.

Our vision is a book on youth violence prevention based on positive youth development. It is a practical, visually fun, and sometimes funny research-based guide for caregivers and service providers.

Philosophy for Youth Violence Prevention

Violence Is Never the Answer. Youth learn to be non-violent by the example of adults who live peacefully.

Respect: All interaction is based on thoughtful consideration for basic human rights and dignity.

Quest for Excellence: All youth violence prevention is based on a community's commitment to success for all youth. Such a commitment promotes safety and security for everyone.

Efficiency: All services are designed and delivered in the most cost-effective manner. Efficiency is measured through the relationship of cost to outcomes. Successful outcomes are achieved through optimal use of resources.

Ecology: Family and community are central to life experience. Youth violence prevention optimally occurs in a youth's natural environment.

Diversity: Respect for differences in families is paramount. Support is given without regard for gender, race, ethnicity, sexual orientation, religion, nationality, culture, and financial status.

Community Education: Educating youth, parents and caregivers, service providers from law enforcement, schools, recreational organizations, faith communities, courts, social service agencies, and mental health organizations about youth violence prevention is an important step toward successfully achieving long-term outcomes.

Individualized Approach: All support is based on the individual and collective strengths and needs of each youth and family.

Hope: Hope is central to future success. All youth violence prevention is intended to instill hope.

Relationships: Youth development takes place within the context of relationships. Youth violence prevention can take hold when it occurs with nonjudgmental genuine support and empathy.

Healing: Healing is the ability to embrace and celebrate life through attention to physical, social, psychological, and spiritual needs. When violence has occurred, intervention is guided by the belief that youth can heal from pain caused by violence. Healing is the basis for leading productive and fulfilling lives by learning to manage pain in ways that do not cause harm.

Resilience: When violence has occurred, youth have the ability to bounce back from adversity.

Successful Outcomes: All youth violence prevention is based upon research. Desired outcomes are established through elements of optimum youth development.

Prevention Continuum: Primary, secondary, and tertiary prevention are provided within a broad range of community organizations.

Core Values

Every member of a community deserves to be safe. Physical and emotional safety are the foundation for optimal human development. Regardless of whether or not people have experienced violence, been victimized, or perpetrated acts of violence, they have a right to live safely.

Violence hurts people. Concern for victims and their needs for justice, respect, healing, empowerment, and ongoing safety must be the guiding principle and driving force that informs all prevention efforts.

Youth can change. When youth behave violently, research shows that effective treatment can prevent future violence.

Youth violence prevention is guided by current research. The scientific study of youth violence prevention is relatively new and constantly advancing. Best practices need to be updated as new findings are validated.

Effective prevention is holistic in character. Youth involved in violence should not be defined by such behavior. Approaching youth as complex individuals addresses needs that may seem removed from the issue of violence. By addressing these needs, prevention can contribute to the long-term success and development of youth as valuable members of a community.

Collaboration enhances youth violence prevention. Collaboration among service providers, families, schools, social services, courts, etc., enhances community safety, as it allows youth to be connected with family, friends, and community life. These efforts can prevent future violence.

Youth violence prevention is informed by cultural competence. Prevention is more successful when based on the strengths, needs, cultural uniqueness, and perspectives of youth and families.

Adults involved in youth violence prevention demonstrate competency in current best practices. All service providers receive specialized training on youth violence prevention.

Our Stories

Joann

November 28, 1999. The phone rings. Standing in the kitchen I glance at the oven clock; it's just 7:22 a.m. Early for a weekend call. It's my sister, "Brother's been stabbed." Me, "Is he okay?" Silence. "Is he alive?" "Yes, they've just taken him into the operating room. A kid stabbed him 25 times." I'm reeling...

A 15-year-old, who had been caught before breaking into Brother's car, was trying again when Brother heard him from his bedroom window. He went down the stairs from his apartment to tell the kid to get out of there. The boy lunged out of Brother's van declaring "I'm gonna kill you!" He then repeatedly stabbed my brother while my brother tried to get away. I'm thinking "who did the kid really want to kill? What's going on in this kid's life that makes him want to kill someone?"

Brother made it to a neighbor's; the police and emergency medical team provided a life-saving response and got him to the hospital.

That's my story. It's a story told over and over in this country. It's much more brutal than it sounds but I'll spare you details.

At that time I'd been working in youth violence prevention for about 18 years. It was the first time my family experienced violence intimately. I hope it's the last. Each of us can help increase the odds that it will be.

Therese

Being a foster parent to older adolescents is a mix of parenting and mentoring. The young people that I fostered didn't have parents that could take care of them at that time in their lives but they weren't naïve children. They had been surviving the best they knew how, running the streets, fighting for fun, and/or becoming involved in illegal or otherwise undesirable pastimes. These detrimental patterns of behavior brought the young men into the foster care system. They all had complicated family lives and were not receiving the support they needed at home at that time in their lives to move toward success. They could have survived on the streets without much trouble if they had to. Instead they were looking for a safe environment and genuine care and guidance to get through the end of adolescence and into adulthood. They picked me as much as I picked them. Ivan, Reggie, Regi, and Donell all wanted the chance to begin their adult lives focused on success. I became a foster parent because I like teenagers, and guiding them through this last stage of their youth was something I wasn't scared to do.

Ivan was the first foster son and he and his foster dad, Drew, became part of my family when Ivan was 19 years old. Ivan adopted me as his mother. It took Ivan a little longer to get ready to be an adult. He needed more time to be a child because he didn't get a full turn his first time around. Now, Ivan is a working man. He and his girl friend are raising their three children and he is helping raise her oldest daughter. He is a good father, in tune with his children. It took him a while but he has grabbed onto the responsibility with both hands.

Reggie was raised by his grandma until she died. He went into foster care, a group home, and then the plan was to move to an independent living program. Reggie wanted to graduate from high school and said that he didn't see himself making it if he didn't have someone to get him out of bed in the morning during his senior year. Independent living meant living on his own with minimal support during his senior year of high school. He said it wouldn't work. My friend Drew and I listened. Reggie and Ivan lived as brothers. Reggie lived with us, graduated from high school, and went into the Marines. He left the Marines early to come home and raise his son.

Regi thrived on positive attention and reassurance that he was a good person. He was a musician and a thinker. He was a loving human being who always made the people he met feel important. He was murdered on December 10, 1994. His killers were never brought to justice. Regi never got the opportunity to raise his son or make his music.

Donell is a talented athlete who needed a supportive place to live so he could play basketball while finishing high school. He earned a college basketball scholarship, was a student-athlete for four years and has nearly completed his college degree. He gets along with everyone he meets, and people are drawn to him. He'd give you the last dollar he has if he thinks you needed it more, even if it's a dollar I gave him!!

Donell never wanted his biological family to get the impression that he thought he was better than them and he never lost the pang he had in his heart to be with his family. He couldn't stand being away from them, and he couldn't be with them and still do right by himself. He is incarcerated and will be for another few years. His story is still unfolding. He is a wonderful young man with supportive people in his life who believe in him. When he gets the chance to dictate his own life again someday, he has the ability to make a worthwhile mark on society.

My connections with Ivan, Reggie, Regi, and Donell were the first time I, my family and close friends experienced so intimately the destructive possibilities that can occur when risk factors for violence stack up in young lives. The experiences of these four young men, their stories of complicated childhoods and teenage survival, happen all across America. Being involved in these young men's lives was a tough learning experience. But it was also an experience filled with hope. That is what made every bit of being a foster parent worthwhile.

Introduction

Why do we need a book about youth violence prevention? Don't we have enough information already? There's a lot of information about it on the Internet.

Evidence about what stops violence is changing. Interventions are being evaluated for cost effectiveness and outcomes. There is a lot of easily available information from people with a variety of perspectives. This book is necessary to bring together sound research on youth violence prevention into a clearly defined, comprehensive approach for community safety.

According to the United Nations Office on Drugs and Crime (Harrendorf, Heiskanen & Malby, 2011), the United States holds the dubious distinction of being the most violent industrialized country on the planet. While juvenile crime is dropping, it remains a problem in many communities. A commitment to end all youth violence requires thoughtful assessment of the complex challenges remaining. Even with downward trends, a need still exists to explore solutions for vulnerable populations such as those of minority background and all youth growing up in poverty.

When searching for information on youth violence, it is difficult to find an integrated approach for successful youth violence prevention in a variety of settings, and the programs that do exist often focus only on youth who are already behaving violently. Resources usually provide conclusions and recommendations for policy change. Seldom are the resources written for the parents and other hard-working folk who directly interact with youth on a day-to-day basis in the settings where the youth live.

Juvenile crime is decreasing (Finkelhor, 2009). Can't we just celebrate our good fortune and keep up the good work? We certainly can, but it's not that simple. Youth violence prevention is multi-faceted. Involving families in successful problem solving, youth mentoring, anti-bullying efforts, and improved policing all influence the decline in youth violence. These are ongoing efforts that require constant attention in order to maintain successful outcomes.

It is important to note that youth violence has been reduced simply through birth control (Levitt & Dubner, 2005). Since 1973, access to legal abortions has allowed women to prevent unwanted pregnancies. Unwanted children are more likely to experience violence, both as victims and perpetrators (Cochran, Mayer, Carr, Cayer, McKenzie & Peck, 2012). Yet, birth control and abortion have seldom been connected with youth violence prevention.

Current research suggests that a non-violent life can begin at birth. This offers hope and guidance to parents and professionals embarking on a journey with the next generation. It also offers new ideas for youth already experiencing violence. This information is available, and we want you to have it.

Communities intent on providing safety and protection for everyone must address youth violence. Media sensationalism about this subject often creates mixed messages, and concerned adults may be at a loss about what to believe. While some media appears to promote violence, others create a false sense of fear when information does not accurately represent solid research.

Gender attitudes about male behavior, such as "boys will be boys," can inhibit prevention and adequate intervention. Male toughness norms continue to promote harmful aggression.

Unequal distribution of wealth and resources creates an increasing divide between the "haves" and the "have nots." Mahatma Gandhi once said, "Poverty is the greatest form of violence." Adequately addressing all of these concerns requires thoughtful consideration and action.

While children's services are everywhere, not all provide an evidenced-based response to the problem of youth violence. Many communities struggle to address the challenges effectively.

Stop It! is a practical and research-based guide for caregivers and service providers. The goal is to make prevention easier, more successful, and fun. Yes, fun! Playful solutions to serious problems can enhance motivation for change.

The purpose of this book is to provide strategies for:
- Leading all youth toward productive, connected, and law-abiding lifestyles.
- Helping all parents understand the importance of taking a stand against all types of violence.

- Stopping youth violence.
- Applying a clearly defined, structured approach for community-wide prevention.
- Providing easy ways to share research on youth violence prevention.
- Promoting evidence-based interventions for successful outcomes.
- Instilling hope in all youth, including those not convinced, that a non-violent lifestyle is possible for everyone.
- Addressing challenges in a playful way — because this work is tough and can sap the ever-lovin' life out of awesome people who dedicate themselves to making a difference in the lives of children!

This book is for everyone concerned about youth violence, and for everyone whose job impacts children and teens. This includes, but is not limited to:

- Parents interested in preventing violence in the lives of their children.
- Child welfare workers in protective services, case management, and foster care.
- Mental health and medical practitioners serving youth in any setting.
- Juvenile justice personnel such as probation officers, judges, attorneys, detention staff, law enforcement, prosecutors, and court service workers.
- Employees in child-serving agencies such as schools, religious organizations, and treatment programs.
- Community organizers, public and private administrators, legislators, and local and state coalition members addressing youth violence.
- Anyone whose loved ones are at risk of being victimized, and/or at risk of behaving violently.

Preventing youth violence is tremendously hard work! People struggle every day with inadequate support and resources. We want to help everyone work more effectively so the hard work pays off.

This is an exciting time for youth violence prevention! Even though economic restrictions and ineffective policies create undue stress on service delivery, current research provides a wealth of information about successful efforts that are cost effective. *Stop It!* has been written to help provide this information in a practical and accessible way.

The first section of the book, entitled *What Works*, describes challenges and solutions for creating a successful approach to youth violence prevention. Chapter 1, *Working Together for Community Safety*, provides a conceptual framework for community collaboration and communication. Chapter 2, *Growing Up Physically, Emotionally, and Sexually Healthy*, describes critical developmental issues that clarify the context in which all prevention occurs. Chapter 3 provides *The Facts, Ma'am, Just the Facts: Research That Informs Services* through integration of research findings into a comprehensive whole.

Section Two, *How to Stop It*, combines current research and literature in a clearly defined, structured approach. Many parents are deeply committed to raising respectful children but have been unable to do so. Parents have hopes and dreams for their children and want what's best for them. But circumstances can dash such hopes and dreams and increase the potential for youth violence. Historically families of youth behaving violently have been blamed and referred to in pathological and disrespectful ways. Accepting delinquent behavior as a symptom of an overstressed family allows for greater wisdom and understanding, which may promote successful outcomes.

Chapter 4, *Connecting with Kids and Families*, and Chapter 5, *Assessing Family Strengths and Needs*, focus on how to engage youth and families in order to maximize understanding of their situation and how to formulate recommendations for intervention. Such information guides Chapter 6, *Working Toward Success* and Chapter 7, *Stopping Violence for Good*. These chapters integrate research on successful approaches to stop harm and promote lifelong success.

Section Three, *Other Important Things*, has three chapters. Chapter 8, *Everyone's Not the Same: Addressing Uniqueness in Families*, addresses how to best support uniqueness in youth and family members impacted by violence. Chapter 9, *When All Else Fails...Out of Home Placement*, addresses the importance of integrating evidence-based best practices for business administration of programs focusing on youth violence prevention. Finally, Chapter 10, *Taking Good Care of Ourselves* promotes self-care while addressing the impact of youth violence. Preventing youth violence is not for the faint of heart! It is often thankless and gut-wrenching, and is known to be a field of high burnout, resulting in staff turnover and a lack of continuity of care for families that need safety and stability the most.

Tina Turner recorded a song entitled "What's Love Got To Do With It?"

It is easy to answer that question in reference to youth violence prevention. Love has everything to do with it! Years ago Joann heard the Reverend Jesse Jackson say that children living in violence suffer from a love deficit disorder. He added that these children also suffer from a dream deficit disorder. Violence makes love go awry. When loves goes awry humans are vulnerable to behaving desperately. This book was written with great love. Our passion and love for our work, and the families we serve, sustain us every day.

Joann Schladale   Therese Langan
Freeport, Maine   Ann Arbor, Michigan

What Works

Chapter 1

Working Together for Community Safety

*Never doubt that a small group of thoughtful committed
citizens can change the world; indeed,
it is the only thing that ever does.*

Margaret Mead

Overview

Youth violence reveals itself in so many ways. Some young people harm
others while some harm themselves. Still others behave violently to both
themselves and others. Sometimes the violence remains secret, while at
other times it is exposed and stopped. Violence can easily become a destructive habit. But youth violence can be prevented before it ever occurs, and it
can be stopped if it has already happened. Before communities can prevent
youth violence, however, information about the problem and a common
language for addressing it are needed. This chapter identifies and defines

important key terms relating to youth violence; provides information about the prevalence of the problem; and describes a conceptual framework for community collaboration and communication. Successful intervention creates lifelong change and alters a youth's future. This chapter is designed to show how caregivers and service providers can work together to address violence in ways that support youth in becoming valued and productive family and community members.

Objectives

By the end of this chapter we hope you will be able to:
- Define youth violence and youth violence prevention and identify factors that influence both.
- Understand challenges in taking a stand against youth violence.
- Identify youth and community needs to achieve safety for everyone.
- Create a system of effective communication and collaboration for prevention.

Definitions of Key Terms

Violence

Violence is any behavior involving intention to hurt, damage, or kill someone or something. This book defines youth violence as intentional harm committed by any person under the age of 18 or 21, depending on legal age as defined by state statute. It includes harm to self or others.

Youth violence includes a broad range of behavior. Types of violence involve, but are not limited to: bullying, harassment, hazing, verbal abuse, emotional abuse, physical assault, sexual assault, destruction of property, arson, murder, self-harm, and suicide. Additionally, violence includes anything that meets a criminal code in juvenile justice statutes. Individuals, groups, or formal gangs commit violence. Sometimes it is impulsive and sometimes it is planned, or premeditated.

Young people who behave violently are a very diverse group. Violent youth involved in the juvenile justice system are categorized as delinquents. Yet many violent youth brought to the attention of authorities never enter the juvenile justice system. These youth are served through child welfare, the mental health system, schools, or private treatment agencies. It is important to note that a small but increasing percentage of youth violence is perpetrated by females (Cauffman, 2008).

Harm to self constitutes violence. Delinquency in no way encompasses all youth violence, particularly self-inflicted harm. Some youth are at greater

> Violence is the intentional use of physical force or power, threatened or actual, against oneself, another person, or against a group or community, that either results in or has a high likelihood of resulting in injury, death, psychological harm, maldevelopment or deprivation.
>
> *World Health Organization*

risk of behaving violently through self-harm or suicide. Self-harm is not necessarily a step on the path to suicide. Many youth who cause harm to self have not found healthy ways to manage pain in their lives and benefit from simply learning healthy coping skills.

Prevention

Prevention involves a broad range of interventions; this book describes many research-based approaches to preventing youth violence. Literature on the topic identifies three types of prevention, but does not always call them the same thing. The Institute of Medicine (Mrazek & Haggarty, 1994) created the following categories:

- *Universal* prevention attempts to stop violence from ever happening in the general population.
- *Selective* prevention focuses on groups believed to be at risk of behaving violently.
- *Indicated* prevention provides interventions when violence has occurred.

Other sources simply identify the different types numerically (Ryan, Leversee & Lane, 2010), the terms below are used throughout the book because they may be easier to remember:

- *Primary* prevention focuses on public education to prevent involvement in any type of violence.

- *Secondary* prevention identifies youth at risk of acting violently and directs specific efforts toward preventing such involvement.
- *Tertiary* prevention aims to stop violence from reoccurring after any acts of harm toward self and/or others.

Youth violence prevention can take place everywhere even without people realizing it. Prevention happens in pre-natal care, and later when a visiting nurse answers questions and offers support to young parents. Prevention occurs when parents read to young children, when a community takes a stand against domestic violence, and when a community support person meets with a family in their home. When energetic school teachers foster curiosity and children get excited about learning, it's happening then too. Prevention occurs in mentoring programs, in organized sports, and in programs that promote the arts. It happens in schools where teen parents have childcare so they can earn their high school diploma. And when trusted adults help young people imagine and pursue their dreams it's happening then also. Youth violence prevention happens all the time!

Cooperation among service providers, families, and all community members guides successful prevention. Assessment, competency development, and treatment can occur with the greatest potential for long-term success when a collaborative process is in place. The stage is set for effective collaboration when communities are clear about the prevalence of youth violence and have a common language for preventing it.

> **Types of Prevention**
>
> **Primary, or Universal:** Public service efforts to keep violence from happening.
>
> **Secondary, or Selective:** Efforts aimed toward at-risk youth before violence happens.
>
> **Tertiary, or Indicated:** Interventions to stop violence from happening again, once it has occurred.

Prevalence of Youth Violence

It is impossible to determine how much youth violence actually occurs because so much of it is overlooked or inaccurately reported. A lot of youth violence is not reported or addressed. Cultural values such as "boys will be boys," "don't be a tattletale," and "don't air our family's dirty laundry" can keep serious violence from being unaddressed for any length of time. Self-inflicted harm such as self-mutilation and suicidal behavior commonly take place secretly and can go undetected until the self-harm becomes fatal.

The available data does not sufficiently address challenges in understanding the true prevalence of youth violence. Even with well-documented statistics, information can be misleading. Disproportionate representation of minorities in the juvenile justice population may indicate blatant inequities in both reporting and response (Piquero, 2008). Girls are appearing in the juvenile justice system at a higher rate than ever, but that information does not necessarily convey self-inflicted violence (Cauffman, 2008).

Economics impact the prevalence of youth violence. Reduced funding for prevention services increases risk for youth violence when vital services are eliminated at any point along the prevention continuum. Poverty directly influences prevalence.

According to the Centers for Disease Control and Prevention (2010), most recent statistics indicate that youth violence is the second leading cause of death for young people between ages 10 and 24 (accidents are the leading cause of death for all children). Approximately 15 young people are murdered every day in America. Over 650,000 youth were treated in emergency rooms for injuries caused by physical assault in 2008. In 2009, 32% of high school students reported being in a physical fight during the previous year and 20% reported being bullied on school property. In 2004, suicide was the third leading cause of death for youth between 10 and 24 years old, and statistics indicate an increase in the incidence of youth suicide since 2004. According to Cornell University's research program on *Self-Injurious Behavior in Adolescents and Young Adults* (2011), 12% to 24% of youth have purposefully caused self-harm and approximately 6% to 8% do so chronically.

Paths leading to youth violence vary greatly and there is no way to predict specific ways a youth may be violent. For example, recidivism, or re-offense rates, indicate that youth who have caused sexual harm are at significantly greater risk of committing non-sexual criminal offenses than of re-offending sexually (Chaffin, Bonner, & Pierce, 2003). Conventional wisdom and media sensationalism promote unnecessary fear by falsely indicating that delinquency is the beginning of a life of crime. However, evidence-based interventions prevent most youth violence from happening again. It is therefore critical that community responses focus on evidence for all types of youth violence and delinquency intervention.

Collaboration

The word *collaboration* gets a lot of press. It's a term often used but not always practiced. Merriam-Webster dictionary's first definition of collaboration is "the act of working with someone to create or produce something." The second definition is "traitorous cooperation with an enemy." When people's values and beliefs collide in a setting that does not support differing ideas or respectful conversation about different points of view, collaboration does resemble traitorous cooperation with an enemy. **Practically speaking, if team members are quick to blame or keep information from each other, the end result is likely to reduce community safety.**

This book defines collaboration as: exchanging information; sharing resources as a means to altering a youth's activities to prevent violence; and enhancing the capacity of everyone involved to create safer communities. Collaboration has to be more than just reporting each team member's efforts. It is a process of integrating all efforts and services provided by all team members over time. **Practically speaking, when a youth needs extra opportunities for success it is important to involve people, such as friends or neighbors, in supporting the youth this way.**

Joseph and his family were preparing for his return home from residential treatment. He needed a high level of supervision from people who wanted to help him succeed. Joseph's community-based therapist began by contacting the family's pastor. The pastor recommended a business man involved in the church's youth group whose youngest child had graduated from high school and who had time and an interest in helping. The therapist also recruited football and wrestling coaches, and a police officer who liked to fish. All could potentially mentor Joseph through shared interests. Involving them as soon as Joseph came home increased the potential for Joseph to feel good about himself and for the men to feel good about helping a teenager before any potential problems occurred.

Successful collaboration is creative and consistent and crosses traditional service lines. A true test of violence prevention is a youth's ability to apply new skills into his or her daily life, and well into the future. This can be enhanced by continuity of care, or the ability of service providers to be involved throughout the full continuum of services. For example, when a youth is in residential treatment, practicing skills necessary for living safely in the community can assist him or her in making a successful transition from residential to community services. When family work is integrated into residential treatment in a meaningful way, going home is easier. Parents are already familiar with changes their son or daughter is making, and parents are making changes right along with their child. As a result, when youth go home, the environment is healthier than when they left. Both residential and community-based service providers have successfully collaborated among themselves and with all family members.

Collaboration is not for the faint of heart! The following example illustrates typical difficulties in collaboration.

> Due to extremely high-risk behavior that included physical and sexual assault, theft, and other criminal offenses, a family had numerous private and public agencies involved at different times for several children. On one occasion staff at a residential program lied, and falsified documents about one child's behavior, in order to get another program to accept the youth for services. Another time, an angry program manager hung up on the service coordinator after yelling about his dissatisfaction with decision making in a team meeting he did not attend. Such experiences create a range of challenges and threaten community safety.

Dedicated collaboration between service providers and parents involves genuine partnership. When home-based service providers support parents' commitment to change, the potential for long-term success is greater. It's very hard to achieve permanent change (think healthy eating!) and not slip back into old unhealthy patterns. If parents don't embrace change, and if the youth and family interaction with the community doesn't change, parents may slip back into accepting old harmful behavior in their teens. When parents allow their child to hang out with other violent youth and stop monitoring homework or chores, unhealthy patterns can resurface and successful outcomes are threatened.

Genuine collaboration involves dedication to a team process of finding out what works and then using it. **Practically speaking, youth are more likely to experience success when they are connected to and supported by their community and the adults involved in the process work together.**

Barriers to Effective Collaboration

Thinking through complex challenges involved in good communication and team building increases the potential for success. Before getting to what works it is important to be clear about those things that can prevent effective collaboration. Barriers include, but are not limited to:

- Conventional wisdom that collaboration is not necessary
- The belief that multi-system coordination is not attainable
- Cutting corners on services and collaboration with a false belief in cost savings
- Inadequate planning
- Lack of defined leadership
- Resistance to research-based practices
- Leaving key people such as parents or teachers out of the process
- Lack of family involvement

- Isolated communities
- Unnecessary competition
- Not valuing differing opinions
- Limitations in funding and resource allocation
- Difficulty changing policies and mindsets
- Overwhelming task assignments
- Too many and/or unorganized meetings
- Fear of things that go bump in the dark, oh, we mean change

Effective Collaboration is:

- A unique process for each community. Urban, suburban, and rural environments present a broad array of challenges, resources, or a lack of resources. Cultural attitudes and diversity are important in accessing services. Attitudes, values, and beliefs influence all collaboration.
- Necessary for gathering and sharing evidence-based information.
- The key to formulating successful plans for youth violence prevention. Each individual involved in a youth's life has a perspective about who a youth is and about his or her potential for success. Professionals can work with people personally involved with youth to bring about comprehensive change in a way that cannot be achieved by anyone individually.
- Developed and can successfully endure through direct, open, and respectful communication. Listening skills involve paying attention to each person as well as respectfully considering how each individual voice adds value to the process. Embracing diverse thought and opinions involves accepting disagreements when a variety of perspectives are expressed. It can be hard work to voice an honest opinion that may be opposed or debated, but respectful and candid discussion is the most viable way to explore potential solutions.
- Necessary for successfully finding the most effective ways to prevent youth violence.

Achieving Effective Collaboration

Genuine communication and collaboration are essential in achieving a strong community-based approach for addressing youth violence prevention. Interagency cooperation focused on youth violence prevention can be successful when professionals from juvenile justice, child welfare, mental health, and schools all partner with families. Many communities are successfully creating partnerships among families, public and private agencies, and other concerned citizens in order to improve communication, eliminate duplication of services, and enhance successful outcomes. Practically speaking, when everyone is involved, open-minded, and respectful, stronger service and safety plans are created and maintained.

Wraparound

Wraparound is a successful model of collaboration based on intensive individualized services for youth with serious and/or complex needs. The National Wraparound Initiative has a website, nwi.pdx.edu, which provides the mission and history of Wraparound as well as a wealth of resources and publications. Community Partners, Inc. (Grealish, 2011) also has a website, www.wraparoundsolutions.com, which provides descriptions and handouts that are guidelines for the implementation of Wraparound. Paperboat.com (Miles & Franz, 2011) contains among other resources, archived articles and presentations about Wraparound. Karl Dennis and Ira Lourie's (2006 book) "Everything is Normal Until Proven Otherwise" shows how putting these Wraparound philosophy into practice really works for families.

Wraparound is a family-driven process of collaboration that addresses all parts of a youth's life. The goal is to help youth be successful in their home and community. Family members, the family's social support network, and service providers jointly address unmet needs through an individualized plan, implementation of the plan, and evaluation of a youth's success over time. The Wraparound process typically includes formal and informal services such as therapy, mentoring, tutoring, and leisure activities. It is implemented uniquely for each family.

Successful collaboration requires continuous evaluation of who should be involved. Each community should have key members who establish and manage the forum through which a formal process for prevention occurs. Additionally, multidisciplinary treatment teams should have responsibility for actively engaging youth, parents (or guardians), and social support network members in activities for youth violence prevention. This is an inclusive, rather than exclusive, process. The more people involved in eliminating youth violence, the greater the potential for successful outcomes.

Concerned service providers should designate an organized entity to lead the development of a community collaborative for youth violence prevention. A steering committee can evaluate the designated community to identify strengths and needs. Recommendations from such an evaluation provide the foundation from which specific efforts begin. Key elements of such an evaluation should include, but are not limited to:

- Identification of service providers
- Current prevention efforts
- Protocols for responding to youth violence
- Gaps in service provision
- Recommendations for enhancing community response

Above all else, explicit, respectful cooperation is the key to successful collaboration. It is also the most exciting way to perform the often grueling and gut-wrenching work of eliminating youth violence. Professionals, youth, and family members working diligently to stop harm can join together in a committed effort to restore victim justice and community safety. When this happens, secrecy and isolation associated with violence are reduced, attachments are formed, and restorative experiences occur. When service providers addressing youth violence prevention agree to participate in a community collaborative, a standardized approach can be developed.

A Unified Response to Youth Violence

Working together for community safety requires a standardized approach for youth violence prevention involving a shared mission, vision, core values, and philosophy of care that guide all service provision. It is critical that all participants contribute to the creation of this information in order to ensure compliance. When an approach is dictated rather than shared, communities risk division and/or noncompliance that may prevent progress and reduce community safety.

Community services should be designed after thoughtful review of the research so they best meet the need for youth violence prevention and are delivered in the most cost-effective way. These services should be available for all youth. A standardized approach promotes fairness in service delivery in order to ensure long-term safety.

When developing a unified response, participants should plan for conflict, and embrace it. Yes, embrace it! It's a normal part of the process. Acknowledging different missions, values, and philosophies as soon as possible can reduce potential conflict. When differences are openly acknowledged early in the collaborative process, effective communication respects varied interests and provides a foundation for honoring diverse thought and action. Some organizations, such as Wraparound, have decision-making protocols; organizations that do not have such protocols can establish them to handle conflict, especially to prevent opposition resulting in deadlock. **Practically speaking, when specific team members appear opposed to, or are clearly against, a suggested plan, listen to them, talk to them, address their concerns about the plan, and adjust the plan when their ideas have merit. When opposition is not considered to have merit, established protocols are vital to manage such conflict.**

A uniform response requires general agreement about what constitutes best practices for harm reduction; commitment to the plan; and motivation to put into practice evidence-based interventions. A uniform response can help educate the public; identify problems through screening and assessment; promote successful interventions; improve effective systems of care; and provide a competent response.

Everyone collaborating should be required to demonstrate how:
- Interventions contribute to harm reduction.
- Relevant service providers are involved in ways that promote successful outcomes.
- Decision making focuses on serving youth and families in the least restrictive setting.

- Evaluation and continuous assessment guide a clearly defined process of service and safety planning throughout all transitions across the full continuum of care.
- Services are cost-effective.

Community Safety

If you treat an individual as he is, he will stay as he is,
but if you treat him as if he were what he ought to be and could be,
he will become what he ought to be and could be.
Johann Wolfgang von Goethe

The primary goal for youth violence prevention is to promote optimum child development so children never behave violently. This issue will be addressed at length in the following chapter on development. Secondary and tertiary prevention require knowledge about factors that prevent violence in vulnerable populations, and how to stop it as soon as any harm comes to light.

All collaboration is based on research relating to:
- Positive youth development
- Core competencies for court involved youth
- Trauma
- Affect regulation (managing emotions)
- Resilience and protective factors
- Best practices for youth violence prevention
- Teen suicide prevention

It is important to base community safety on all relevant research relating to positive youth development, core competencies for court involved youth, trauma, affect regulation, resilience and protective factors, and best practices for youth violence and suicide prevention. It is also important for documents to reflect the state of the research relating to effective screening, evaluation, assessment, and intervention. These topics are addressed at length in Chapter 5.

Successful youth violence prevention involves a holistic, individualized approach based on solid research. *Holistic means all parts of a person's life and includes all physical, social, psychological, and spiritual aspects.* Family sensitive services that embrace strength, competency, resources, and resilience provide the most direct and effective route to successful outcomes. Effective collaboration helps this happen.

Current evidence shows that most effective treatment is based on a nonjudgmental attitude, empathy, genuineness, and warmth, communicated with a sense of hope and expectation for change (Duncan, Miller, Wampold, & Hubble, 2009; Miller & Rollnick, 2002). All of these can be modeled through collaboration. **Practically speaking, if you want to promote community safety, treat kids with respect for who they are, and how they came to be this way. Get to know them, provide hope and clear expectations for change, and provide support along the way. There you have it!**

Effective collaboration reflects all of these same things. If you want to stop youth violence, treat everyone with respect for who they are and how they came to be involved. Get to know them, approach the work with hope and clear expectations for successful outcomes, and provide support when needed.

Treatment Teams

Purpose: Creating a treatment team for each youth involved in secondary or tertiary prevention provides a therapeutic approach based on support, mentorship, and advocacy. Designing an individualized approach to best meet the unique needs of each youth and family places emphasis on discovering and developing strengths and resources. Assessing motivation involves exploring how ready, willing, and able each person is for change throughout the treatment process.

Facilitator: An identified facilitator is determined through collaboration among all team members and may serve throughout the continuum of care or for a specifically designated time. The facilitator collaborates with all team members in matters relating to service planning, therapeutic tasks, and goals. This includes monitoring: progress toward goals; family involvement; social interaction; and responsibilities of all team members. This person is in charge of facilitating team meetings according to an agreed-upon format. The facilitator remains vigilant in identifying the youth's strengths, positive efforts, and successes throughout the collaboration process. This person is often referred to as a case manager.

Membership: Treatment team participation includes, but is not limited to: youth; parents, or guardians; all service providers; designated school personnel; and anyone who provides social support for the youth.

Structure: Treatment team meetings provide a avenue for creating, reviewing, and revising goals with youth, and significant others, in order to assess all violence prevention efforts. Each meeting begins with a youth identifying what is better since the last meeting. This represents a youth's understanding of goals and responsibility for meeting them. Youth are then asked to identify concerns and possible areas for improvement. New goals are established from this conversation and are documented. Any special requests are made, discussed, and decided upon during the meeting. If any information requires further action, it is documented and assigned to a team member for follow-up, with a timeline for completion.

Services occur in a holistic, ecological framework throughout the full continuum of care. Using a family focus that addresses physical, social, psychological, and spiritual elements of therapeutic change increases the possibility for long-term success. Collaboration makes this process easier and increases potential for community safety.

Interventions for youth violence prevention are continually evolving. Research-based studies are emerging in the field and guiding practice. It is vital to acknowledge that advances in research will influence ongoing change in best practices for eliminating harm. Collaboration provides a venue for sharing such vital information.

We are learning that youth can, and most often should be, served in their community, (rather than incarcerated or placed in residential treatment) to maximize health and well being, and to help them grow into productive community members. When youth violence requires intervention, research indicates that most youth do not require incarceration or removal from the community in order to maintain safety (Borduin & Schaeffer,

...affin, Bonner, & Pierce, 2003). Interventions have been found to be more successful when children live at home with their families, as long as safety is monitored and maintained. This important research provides a foundation to best address the needs of these youth, their families, victims, and the community at large. Current research indicates that youth are not only best served at home and in the community, but such intervention is the most cost-effective (Borduin & Schaeffer, 2001; Chaffin, Bonner, & Pierce, 2003; Thornton, Craft, Dahlberg, Lynch, & Baer, 2002). When everyone collaborates, community safety is easier to achieve.

Conclusion

Taking a stand against youth violence is hard but satisfying work. A wide variety of factors influence potential for youth violence, and there isn't a single, clearly defined formula to predict it, or prevent it. Defining youth violence and all terms associated with it can help everyone communicate more clearly about it.

A foundation for community safety can be established and maintained through a uniform approach based on thoughtful communication, collaboration, and action. This begins with identifying youth and community needs to achieve safety for everyone.

A single professional seldom serves youth and families throughout the full continuum of care. Most often these youth and families experience a multitude of child-serving agencies and a diverse array of professionals. The complex nature of youth violence requires thoughtful consideration of each youth's unique life experiences by everyone involved all along the way.

Creating a system of effective communication and collaboration for prevention makes everyone's job easier and more successful. Collaboration promotes cohesion and eases application of evidence-based practices for youth violence prevention.

Recommendations

- Use evidence-based models for youth violence prevention, trauma, and child abuse whenever indicated and possible.
- Create a context of respect, care, and concern for the development of trust in working relationships.
- Share all resources.
- Involve families, teachers, coaches, clergy, and anyone else willing to support these youth in their efforts at harm reduction.
- Embrace distrust, ambivalence, and resistance.
- Allow each youth and family to lead the process.
- Recognize challenges in addressing the pain of violence and abuse.
- Advocate and support all participants in using untapped strengths and resources to prevent future violence.
- Help participants become law-abiding community members.
- Provide ongoing support as indicated.

Dedicated service providers can use the following empirically based factors to enhance collaboration and harm reduction:

- Be genuine.
- Define clear expectations.
- Don't judge.
- Practice empathy.
- Express warmth.
- Exercise patience!
- Provide hope and optimism for a youth's success.
- Give clear instruction and support for truth telling.
- Discuss and explore feelings in an emotionally safe environment.
- Find out about each youth's interests and dreams.
- Help them explore and pursue those interests and dreams.
- Do things kids and families like to do.
- Share any concerns with professionals who can help.
- Promote and have fun!
- Celebrate any success no matter how small, or seemingly insignificant.
- Celebrate yourself, and your colleagues, every day for a job well done!

Resources

Centers for Disease Control and Prevention: www.cdc.gov/violenceprevention

Community Partners, Inc.: www.wraparoundsolutions.com

Cornell Research Programs on Self-Injurious Behaviors: www.crpsib.com

The Future of Children: www.futureofchildren.org

Harvard University: www.developingchild.harvard.edu

Models for Change: www.modelsforchange.net

National Wraparound Initiative: www.nationalwraparoundinitiative.shuttlepod.org or www.nwi.pdx.edu

National Council on Mental Health and Juvenile Justice: www.ncmhjj.com

Office of the Surgeon General: www.surgeongeneral.gov/library/youthviolence

Portland State University Research and Training Center on Family Support and Children's Mental Health: www.rtc.pdx.edu

Resources For Resolving Violence, Inc.: www.resourcesforresolvingviolence.com

Parkside Family Counseling, LLC: www.parksideforfamilies.com

Safe Youth: www.safeyouth.gov

Self Injury: www.selfinjury.com

Stop Bullying Now: www.stopbullyingnow.hrsa.gov

Chapter 2

Growing Up Physically, Emotionally, and Sexually Healthy

It is easier to raise strong children
than to repair broken men.

Frederick Douglass

Overview

Establishing an evidence-based approach for youth violence prevention requires a lot of effort. Successful intervention depends on understanding each youth's everyday life experiences. This chapter offers information necessary for providing children with a foundation for an emotionally healthy life.

Extensive research on child development provides building blocks for health and well-being and is summarized here. This is primary prevention. When children miss any elements of optimum development, they have potential to obtain them through interventions later on. This is secondary and tertiary prevention.

Objectives

By the end of this chapter we hope you will be able to:
- Understand the influence of development and life experiences on youth violence prevention.
- Promote individualized services in order to best meet the developmental needs of all children.

Optimum Child Development

How children are brought up greatly impacts the rest of their lives. Research reveals very important information about what promotes lifelong health and well-being and prevents youth violence. The National Research Council and Institute of Medicine (2001) identifies elements of optimum child development. They are:

- Physical and psychological safety
- Appropriate structure
- Supportive relationships
- Opportunities to belong
- Positive social norms
- Support for efficacy and mattering
- Opportunities for skill building
- Integration of family, school, and community efforts

Originally published in 2001 this information is still relevant. These factors remain the foundation for primary prevention of youth violence. Each one is addressed at length in this chapter.

Physical and Psychological Safety

Physical safety is the condition of being protected from harm.
Psychological safety is an emotional experience of feeling safe and protected from harm.

Safety and stability are the foundation for both secure attachment and for healing trauma. In order to thrive, young children must have a stable and secure base from which to explore life. When this occurs, children learn to take calculated risks and to know they can rely on parents, or caregivers, to provide comfort and nurturing as needed.

Secure attachment comes from the experience of both physical and psychological safety. When physical safety is threatened, psychological safety is too. Yet people can be physically safe while feeling unsafe emotionally.

Physical safety is easier to identify than emotional safety. Assessing a youth's physical proximity to danger indicates his or her level of physical safety. After children witness violence, they can be in a physically safe environment while feeling psychologically unsafe. This is why children removed from violent situations often exhibit symptoms influenced by violence long after it has stopped (Groves, 2002; Kagan, 2004; Stien& Kendall, 2004).

Practically speaking, when children grow up feeling safe, secure, and respected they thrive. When bad things happen and adults respond with care and compassion and adequate services (if necessary), children continue to thrive.

Appropriate Structure

Appropriate structure is ideal organization of a child's daily life. It involves predictable daily activities and timetables allowing for periods of activity and rest that promote physical and emotional growth.

Appropriate structure for children can be a challenge to provide when parents are overworked, underpaid, and required to do more with less in order to provide adequately for their families. Providing elements of optimum child development requires creativity on the parts of parents and community organizations in order to best meet the needs of all children.

One important activity that shows up consistently in research is family dinnertime. When families sit down together on a regular basis for dinner, family connections are strengthened. This is just one example of how seemingly unimportant activities can impact optimum development.

Some children have too little structure in their lives. This can result in boredom, lack of energy, restlessness, and insecurity. Statistics indicating the amount of television American children watch in comparison to children in other countries indicates a frightening lack of structure.

Conversely, many children are over structured in their daily activi

Parents may feel pressure to maintain a fast-paced lifestyle for all family members. Youth may be so over scheduled with extracurricular activities that they have little time for rest, reflection, and/or solitude throughout the day. When adults are over scheduled, they can often do something about it. Children can't, and they may be shuttled from activity to activity with little consideration for what best meets their needs. Both too much structure and too little structure can cause problems in the lives of children.

Problems can occur when parents have unrealistic expectations for structure that do not meet a child's unique needs. For example, punishing a child with attention problems when he or she does not sit still and follow rules, and having no medication or behavioral plan for that child, sets everyone up for failure. All structure should be developmentally appropriate and include predictable routine.

All human beings need both activity and rest. What does this mean? Appropriate structure is different for children based on their personality and needs. It includes quiet time, rest, and solitude in addition to learning, social activities, and body movement. Urie Bronfenbrenner, a world famous specialist in child development, was known to have said that play is children's work. Both structured and unstructured play help children learn explore, create, fantasize, develop competencies, and build self-esteem and autonomy.

> Devon, 14, is in the 8th grade. He is diagnosed with attention problems and is autistic. Even though he takes medication and is receiving home-based therapy his symptoms are not decreasing. Devon's mom continually gives him consequences when his inability to focus causes him to get behind in his schoolwork and misbehave. She is unwilling to help with his homework or supervise him effectively. She stated that she does not want him to become dependent on medication. She believes he has to learn how to behave now without extra support so he will be able to control himself as an adult.

Practically speaking, make sure everyone has lots of time for a balance of activity and rest. Kids should get a good night's sleep of at least eight hours, eat nutritious food, exercise regularly, have quiet time, and time for learning in a variety of ways through schoolwork and play. Adults need this too. When everyone gets these needs met everyone feels better and gets along better.

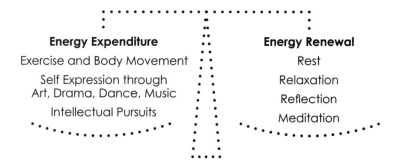

Energy Expenditure	Energy Renewal
Exercise and Body Movement	Rest
Self Expression through Art, Drama, Dance, Music	Relaxation
	Reflection
Intellectual Pursuits	Meditation

Supportive Relationships

Supportive relationships are simply connections with others that promote optimum growth, health, and well-being.

Research from the Centers for Disease Control and Prevention (Thornton, Craft, Dahlberg, Lynch, & Baer, 2002) shows that supportive relationships promote optimum development and prevent harm. They influence everyone's health and well-being. Supportive relationships promote secure attachment and restore safety and security when attachments have been harmed or broken. All adults share responsibility for providing supportive relationships in every child's life.

Practically speaking, all children should have at least three people in their life who provide lifelong unconditional support. None of these people should be paid professionals.

Opportunities to Belong

Opportunities to belong are activities that make it possible for a child to develop a sense of connection and fitting in with a positive group or community.

Opportunities to belong provide a sense of positive connection necessary for children to become responsible and productive community members. Connectedness, or belonging, promotes resilience. *Resilience is the ability to bounce back after something bad happens.*

The first connection children have is to their family. Becoming a family member is their first opportunity to develop attachment, self-esteem, and emotional and physical safety.

Adults must be sensitive to the needs of children and encourage opportunities for participation in cooperative activities. Such activities promote self-esteem and well-being. When children are shy, socially awkward, or suffer from disorders of attachment, they are more likely to feel left out or isolated, especially in settings outside their own homes. When children are bullies, or are being bullied, they too are at risk of not fitting in.

All youth who perceive themselves as different from others may feel vulnerable when trying to establish a sense of belonging. Some, such as children with developmental challenges or physical difficulties, and young people identifying as gay, lesbian, bisexual, or transgendered, are even more at risk of being rejected, harassed or the victims of hate crimes. These issues and more are addressed in Chapter 8. **Practically speaking, everyone needs human connection and a sense of belonging or fitting in. Adults need to make children feel welcome and valued wherever and whoever they are.**

Positive Social Norms

Positive social norms are how society expects people to act and get along. Such behavior promotes respect and law-abiding behavior.

Positive social norms are what make societies work. While many adults talk about pro-social beliefs, their behavior may not always reflect such values. Differences between personal values and ways people act can give children unintended mixed messages.

Adults cause confusion by claiming to promote respect while modeling subtle anti-social behavior such as revenge, racism, sexism, or general disregard for others or the environment. When parents smoke or abuse substances and complain when their teenagers do the same, young people feel unjustly accused and may view the adults as hypocrites.

Practically speaking, positive social norms hold adults responsible for good behavior so we are good role models. This is no small task! It's hard to be good all the time, especially when we're going through tough times or just having a bad day.

Support for Efficacy and Mattering

What the heck is this?

Efficacy is an ability to make things happen. Mattering is the understanding that something is important. Support for efficacy and mattering is a youth's understanding that he or she is important and can impact change.

Human beings need to know they are good at something and that others notice these skills. This concept promotes good decision-making, competence, and confidence. When children are encouraged and supported in using their own resources to solve life challenges they learn to be responsible, work with others, and take good care of themselves.

Such support helps self-esteem blossom. An example of mattering is giving children age-appropriate responsibilities such as picking up after themselves, feeding a family pet, or other household chores. Having responsibility as part of a family is an example of mattering that can bolster self-esteem, self-confidence, and a sense of belonging.

Practically speaking, letting children know they matter and have value, even when they make mistakes or cause harm, is extremely important. It allows them to know they can get support when they mess up and obtain guidance to prevent the problem from happening again. Sometimes adults don't want to do this, particularly if they are hurt or angry about the youth's behavior. Modeling patience and tolerance can go a long way in preventing violence.

Opportunities for Skill Building

Skill building is competency development.

Human beings continually develop skills throughout life. An easy example is learning mathematics. Mastery of addition, subtraction, multiplication, and division is a foundation for successfully learning more advanced subjects such as algebra, geometry, and calculus.

Opportunities for skill building are available in all areas of a child's life, and are sometimes called teachable moments. Children require skill building in a range of areas such as academics, communication, managing emotions, good decision-making, workforce development, and skills for everyday living.

It is important for children to develop skills based on physical and emotional maturity. Trying to teach an average five-year-old calculus usually far exceeds a youngster's ability to master such advanced math. Conversely, holding children back and inhibiting development of very simple, yet important, skills like setting an alarm clock and getting up for school on time can cause problems with development.

Children who are asked to do too much or too little can become overwhelmed and unable to move forward with normal developmental tasks. Overload occurs when children are expected to perform tasks too advanced for their ability, and underload occurs when they are required to do too little. Both cause problems with development.

Practically speaking, children thrive when they learn new skills. Give them lots of opportunities to do so, support their hard work through mentoring and monitoring their progress, and provide corrective feedback when necessary.

Integration of Family, School, and Community Efforts

Integration of family, school, and community efforts is effective coordination of activities among all parts of a child's life in order to optimize health and well-being.

This element of optimum child development highlights the importance of collaboration between everyone involved in a child's life. Interaction among these systems promotes consistent and clear expectations for success. They are important in teaching children how all parts of life are interrelated. Providing consistent messages about expectations for behavior can reduce mixed messages that cause confusion and prevent optimum development.

Elements of optimum child development provide a baseline for understanding and evaluating the needs of all children. Two forms are provided in the Appendix that can help both families and child-serving programs assess their ability to provide these important functions for children.

Practically speaking, children's lives should easily flow between their family, school, and community life. If there are struggles in any or all areas, act fast to get them back in sync.

Maurice, a father of two young children, lives in an urban neighborhood with families having a range of income levels. He met a lot of children and families who his children interact with at school and in the local park. Many parents traveled some distance out of the neighborhood to access summer enrichment programs for their children. Parents with fewer resources were less able to obtain summer programs for their children. Maurice contacted people at a local university with facilities that were unused most of the summer. With minimal effort, he convinced the university to provide space for the positive development of local youth that could have long-term impact on the community. Maurice worked with the university to organize a summer program for recreation, academic, and arts enrichment. What an unsung hero Maurice is for those youth and families!

Developmental Categories

Children develop physiologically, cognitively, emotionally, and morally.

- Physiological development involves all the ways body parts function.
- Cognitive development refers to brain processing that has to do with thinking, reasoning, and remembering.
- Emotional development is brain processing that has to do with feelings.
- Moral development is a person's ability to make good decisions based upon a desire to do the right thing

Culture also plays a tremendous role in development. The potential for experiencing violence is influenced by where children grow up, their race, ethnicity, religion, socio-economic status, and family make-up. All of these categories create a complex web of influence on every child's personal growth.

Touch

Touch is a word seldom mentioned in relation to youth violence, yet touch plays a tremendous role in it. How and what children learn about touch makes a big difference in how they manage their body throughout life. When they receive messages that harmful touch is okay, they come to expect it and are at risk of harming themselves or others in the same way.

Healing, or therapeutic, touch is simply the use of touch to repair harm and restore health. When families use touch in ways that make people feel good, and never use it in anger, children learn well-meaning and kind ways of touching. When touch has been used violently, services must include clear messages about restorative touch and the role it plays in youth violence prevention.

Tasks Involving Touch

Everyone has a basic need to touch and be touched. When touch demonstrates respect, care, and concern for everyone, youth receive consistent and encouraging messages. The first task is creating a family culture where kind and considerate touch is practiced consistently. Letting everyone know how touch influences health and well-being helps everyone understand its importance.

Educating children about different types of touch, and how touch impacts others, provides a foundation for learning and practicing well-meaning touch. Learning that holding hands helps people feel connected and cared for, while hitting hurts and causes people to be fearful, teaches children how to distinguish between nurturing and harmful touch. Witnessing touch like handshakes, pats, hugs, handholding, and high-fives allows a child to consider a range of options for touching.

When adults teach children about touch, it is important to explain and emphasize the importance of choice and protection for self and others. Children can easily learn that harmful touch is a bad choice and they should not do it. They can learn to protect themselves by talking with adults who advise them and help them practice nonviolent ways of managing challenging situations. Children can also learn how to be an active bystander by reporting any harmful touch they witness. Adults can also do this by sharing personal preferences about touch and modeling boundaries that support such preferences. It is most helpful when adults are clear about their own values around touch. Simply telling a child pushing is not okay because it makes people feel uncomfortable can go a long way in helping that child learn about touch and the impact it has on others. Letting a child know how much a parent enjoys sharing hugs because it shows how much they love each other is a great way to promote secure development.

When touch does not involve choice it is abusive. Examples of how the media portrays different kinds of touch can help children learn about it. Youth can learn that how people use touch reflects the type of person they will become. If someone thinks violence such as hitting, kicking or punching is okay they are likely to be considered a trouble maker and get a bad reputation.

It is also important to help children understand connections between touch and emotions. Therapeutic exercises exploring types of touch that elicit a variety of emotions can help children to categorize them and consider decision-making strategies about the use of each. Explaining "the uh-oh feeling" (that gut instinct that tells us when something is wrong) helps youth to develop intuition that can help them to explore safety when they feel potential threat. Helping them to explore how touch involves a range of feelings from physical pleasure and joy to fear and terror can help them understand its complexities.

> Keith was a resident in a community-based group home after a failed foster placement. Staff in the program successfully advocated for Keith to attend the local prom with a friend from his neighborhood. Teens from this group home did not usually attend this type of event and the experience Keith gained from this opportunity far exceeded any artificially contrived substitute activity he might have received in treatment.

Exploring the context of touch also promotes understanding. Defining and discussing privacy, confidentiality, and secrecy can help children learn to differentiate the three. Learning about cultural norms and rituals can inform social skill development and enhance opportunities for respectful touch. Sex education that includes courtship practices helps children consider a wide range of experiences that come with dating. **Practically speaking, when a small child hits, kicks, bites, or scratches for the first time, adults can respond immediately by calmly and kindly telling the**

Touch in Youth Violence Prevention

- Define types of touch and explain differences between touch that helps people feel good and touch that makes people feel uncomfortable, or bad.
- Provide clear expectations and boundaries for touch.
- Explain differences between affection and sensual and sexual touch.
- Clarify differences between privacy, secrecy and surprises, and expectations for not keeping any secrets.
- Respect everyone's privacy by having rules about touch.
- Have a positive, non-punitive plan for responding to harmful touch.
- Exercise patience!

All touch:
- **Is well-meaning, kind, and charitable:** The action reveals thoughtful consideration.
- **Takes place publicly:** It is witnessed by others so any confusion or misunderstanding can be clarified.
- **Is developmentally congruent:** It is appropriate for the child's age, intelligence, and mental capacity.
- **Is based on permission:** The person being touched gives permission before it occurs.
- **Is related to what is going on at the time:** It makes sense in the context in which it occurs
- **Is clearly communicated:** Everyone is able and willing to talk about it.
- **Models good boundaries:** It promotes emotional and physical safety.
- **Provides comfort and promotes health and well being:** It feels good!

---

child to stop it, and explaining that such behavior is unacceptable. They can then direct the child to a positive activity so he or she learns how to easily change behavior.

Children learn a lot about touch from the media. Television, movies, video games, and social media websites all influence values and beliefs about touch. How youth behave while participating in media activities, such as video games, also communicates a great deal about touch. Without monitoring, children are vulnerable to being exposed to images of sexual and violent touch before they can even understand what it is. Many adults are unsure how to communicate with youth about these explicit images, but paying close attention to all messages children receive about touch and communicating openly whenever the topic comes up can go a long way in promoting health and well-being.

Sexual Development

"Sexuality is seldom treated as a strong or healthy force in the positive development of a child's personality in the United States. We are not inclined to believe that our children are sexual or that they should be sexual in any of their behaviors. Although it is difficult to generalize in our pluralistic society, there is typically no permission for normal child sexual experiences. Children are not taught to understand their sexual experiences or to anticipate sexual experiences as enjoyable. Rather, they are taught to be wary of most sexual experiences, both interpersonally and intrapsychically [within a person's mind]." (Martinson, 2010, p. 31)

Child sexual development and sexuality are highly controversial topics in the United States. Sexual health is just one part of youth development. Since it is so controversial, it is addressed separately so it does not get lost or overlooked. American children see sexual behavior in the media, sometimes at a very early age. Yet few youth development programs directly address issues related to sexuality. Lack of awareness, funding restrictions, and fear of controversy are just some of the reasons for these missed opportunities (SIECUS, 2004).

A lack of research on childhood and adolescent sexual development reduces knowledge about the full range of sexual expression, from that which is considered normal to that which is considered problematic or pathological. American values and beliefs greatly impact responses to childhood sexual development. The fluid nature of sexual development and lack of evidence regarding "normal" childhood sexuality hinder greater understanding of sexual development. This controversy is addressed because sexual harm is one type of youth violence, and research shows there are certain sexual values and beliefs that can influence such violence. They are:

- Showing hostility toward women
- Supporting myths about rape, such as victims ask for it, or enjoy it
- Hanging around others who agree with such myths
- Believing there is a lot of conflict between women and men
- Not caring about others, and their feelings
- Heavy drinking
- Casual attitudes about sex
- Having a lot of casual sexual relationships
- Experiencing violence and abuse as children (Abbey, 2005)

Sexual health is "a state of physical, emotional, mental, and social well-being in relation to sexuality; it is not merely the absence of disease, dysfunction, or infirmity. Sexual health requires a positive and respectful approach to sexuality and sexual relationships, as well as the possibility of having pleasurable and safe sexual experiences, free of coercion, discrimination, and violence. For sexual health to be attained and maintained, the sexual rights of all persons must be respected, protected, and fulfilled" (World Health Organization, 2007).

When people strive to adopt the World Health Organization's definition of sexual health, children may develop a greater sense of overall health and well-being. Such an approach respects all elements of child development.

Youth development programs are in an exciting position to help young people understand their sexuality and avoid negative outcomes such as unintended pregnancy and disease. SIECUS, the *Sexuality Information and Education Council of the Unites States*, provides

---

SIECUS Guidelines for
Comprehensive Sexuality Education: Grades K-12
Key Concepts and Topics

Human Development	Relationships	Personal Skills
Reproductive Anatomy & Physiology	Families Values	Knowledge
Reproduction	Friendship	Decision Making
Puberty	Love	Communication
Body Image	Dating	Assertiveness
Sexual Identity & Orientation	Marriage & Lifetime Commitment	Negotiation
Family Life	Raising Children	Looking for Help

Sexual Behavior	Sexual Health	Society & Culture
Sexuality Throughout Life	Contraception	Sexuality & Society
Masturbation	Abortion	Gender Roles
Shared Sexual Behavior	STDs, including HIV	Sexuality & the Law
Abstinence	Sexual Abuse & Religion	Sexuality Diversity
Human Sexual Response	Reproductive Health	Sexuality & the Arts
Fantasy		Sexuality & the Media
Sexual Dysfunction		

---

education and information about sexuality and sexual and reproductive health. Their report *On the Right Track* (2004) indicates that most successful programs designed to reduce sexual risk-taking are those that rely on aspects of positive youth development. Numerous age-appropriate messages, such as "Everyone's body changes at its own pace," "Girls often begin pubertal changes before boys," and "During puberty, emotional changes occur," can help reduce normal sexual confusion.

Do we expect children to learn how to read without teaching them the alphabet? Do we expect children to develop math skills without teaching them how to add and subtract? Do we really expect children to experience sexual health and development without modeling and teaching it to them?

Resilience

Resilience is the ability to bounce back after bad things happen. It provides information vital for understanding youth violence prevention. Personal skills such as courage and strength allow youth opportunities to be successful regardless of difficulties they face.

Henderson, Benard, and Sharp-Light (1996) describe resilience through *protective factors, which are characteristics that can diminish potential for violence, or stop it after it occurs.* Protective factors are both internal (within an individual), and environmental (outside an individual), and should be provided for all children to minimize the possibility of experiencing violence.

Internal Protective Factors

- Feelings of self-worth and self-confidence
- Giving of self in service to others and/or a cause
- Using life skills, including good decision-making, assertiveness, impulse control, and problem-solving
- Sociability/ability to be a friend/ability to form positive relationships
- Sense of humor
- Internal locus of control
- Autonomy/independence
- Positive view of personal future
- Flexibility
- Capacity for and connection to learning
- Self-motivation
- Being good at something/personal competence

Environmental Protective Factors

- Promote close bonds
- Provide high warmth/low criticism style of interaction
- Set and enforce clear boundaries (rules, norms, and laws)
- Encourage supportive relationships with many caring others
- Promote sharing of responsibilities, service to others, required helpfulness (community service)

- Access basic needs of housing, employment, health care, recreation, nutrition, etc.
- Express high, and realistic, expectations for success
- Encourage goal setting and mastery
- Promote pro-social development of values and life skills
- Provide leadership, decision-making, and other opportunities for meaningful participation
- Appreciate the unique talents of each individual

Developmental Vulnerabilities

Exposure to violence
changes the landscape of childhood forever.
Betsy McAlister Groves

While it is critical to understand optimum elements of child development it is equally important to know what vulnerabilities place children at risk of youth violence. The Centers for Disease Control and Prevention (Thornton, et. al., 2002) identify vulnerabilities that place children at risk of behaving violently. These include:

- Poor interaction between parents and children as early as the first year of life
- Emotionally distressed parents involved in anti-social behaviors
- Marital conflict and poor communication
- Parental criminal and violent behavior
- Alcohol and substance abuse
- Child abuse and neglect
- Harsh inconsistent discipline
- Poor parental supervision
- Violent neighborhoods
- Witnessing violence
- Learning problems
- School absenteeism
- Bullying, or being the target of bullying
- Being arrested before age 14

These are critical factors in understanding how to eliminate youth violence. Knowing such important information can inform all elements of prevention. For primary prevention, these are things to prevent violence from happening in the lives of all children. From a secondary and tertiary prevention perspective, these are issues to be addressed as soon as possible in order to prevent vulnerable youth from becoming violent and from preventing recidivism with those youth who have already behaved violently. A checklist of these factors is provided in the Appendix.

In her book *Children Who See Too Much,* Groves (2002) reports that young children exposed to violence:

- Have neither the cognitive nor emotional structure to understand the context of violence.
- Do not understand motives.
- Are more likely to imitate others' violent behavior.
- Have less ability to distinguish reality from fantasy.
- Do not understand that a television story may be pretend.
- Do not understand that media violence is worse than it looks.
- See that violence is frequently rewarded.
- See that violence is funny and acceptable.
- Begin to see the world as a dangerous place.
- Are more likely to live in poverty.
- Are more likely to witness substance abuse.
- Are more likely to experience inequality.
- Are at high risk for developing Post-Traumatic Stress Disorder.

She states that exposure to violence, "includes being the direct victim of violence. It also includes seeing or hearing violence or even knowing of its aftermath" (Groves, 2002, p. 19). She further reports the following effects of witnessing violence on young children:

- Impulsive behavior
- Apathy and desensitization
- Less ability to sequence events in time, or to accurately establish a time frame
- Increased fragmentation of memories

- Anxious anticipation of violence happening again
- High levels of anxiety
- Pervasive pessimism
- Distorted self-appraisal
- Sense of foreshortened future
- Hyper arousal and chronic over-activation of stress response
- Increase in aggressive and impulsive behavior
- Loss of newly acquired developmental skill
- Misattribution of events
- Use of disruption to avoid quiet
- Increased delinquency, anti-social behavior, substance abuse, mental illness
- Post-Traumatic Stress Disorder
- Psychological loss of both parents
- Sense that there is no refuge
- Emotional numbness

Groves (2002) also identifies the following risk factors present in systems of care:
- Adults frequently make assumptions that children think like adults and therefore discount, or ignore, how children see the world.
- There is a dangerous tendency to deny, or minimize, children's experiences. When adults do this, children follow suit.
- Appraisal of these children as callous and uncaring is incorrect. Children respond in the only way that makes sense to them, by attempting to block the violence out of their consciousness.
- When adults do not talk about frightening events, children may believe it is too scary for adults, or that the subject is taboo.

Bad things happen. Violence can be debilitating. When violence has a traumatic effect on children it can alter brain processing and intellectual functioning (Schore, 2003; Stien & Kendall, 2004). Healthy attachment plays an important part in healing trauma. *Attachment is an instinctual biological bond that a child has with significant caregivers.* Secure infant attachment is enhanced when attuned caregivers meet a child's needs. A child learns trust through this process, which produces chemical changes in the brain that influence self-regulation. Human capacity for self-regulation develops through attachment. When secure attachment is threatened, significant chemical changes occur in an infant's brain. When caregivers are not consistently predictable or responsive, infants can fail to develop a capacity to self soothe (Bowlby, 1988; Siegel, 1999; Applegate & Shapiro, 2005).

As youth experience secure relationships, their belief systems can change. When caring adults are good role models and spend time with young people, healing occurs and relationship skills improve. When compassionate adults respond to a child's experience of violence immediately, resilience allows optimum development to continue and negative outcomes are diminished.

Many youth misbehaving through violence toward self and others suffer from complex trauma. The National Child Traumatic Stress Network (NCTSN) provides a wealth of information about treatment services and policies. In addition to the website, www.nctsn.org, the document entitled *Complex Trauma in Children and Adolescents* (Cook, Blaustein, Spinazzola, & van der Kolk, 2003) helps with understanding how trauma and youth violence can be related. The document describes complex trauma as "the dual problem of children's exposure to traumatic events and the impact of this exposure on immediate and long-term outcomes. It refers to children's experiences of multiple traumatic events that occur within the care giving system. Typically, [it] refers to the simultaneous or sequential occurrences of child maltreatment ... that are chronic and begin in early childhood... and often lead to subsequent trauma exposure" (Cook, et. al, 2003, p. 5). Significant childhood trauma occurs through violence.

Research indicates that complex trauma results in a variety of problems, including:
- Self-regulatory, attachment, anxiety, and affective disorders in infancy and childhood
- Addictions, aggression, social helplessness, and eating disorders
- Dissociative, cardiovascular, metabolic, and immunological disorders
- Sexual disorders
- Revictimization

The NCTSN identifies seven primary domains of impairment (Cook, et. al, 2003, p.6):

- Attachment
- Biology
- Affect Regulation
- Dissociation
- Behavioral Regulation
- Cognition
- Self-Concept

In the aftermath of trauma, adult support plays a big part in determining how children adapt to victimization. When adults provide comfort and accurate information, including open and honest answers to questions about the trauma, children are much more likely to experience positive outcomes. According to the NCTSN (Cook, et. al, 2003, p.16), there are three main factors that help adults successfully manage their child's complex trauma:

1. Believing and validating their child's experience
2. Tolerating a child's affect
3. Managing their own emotional responses

"Parents and guardians may see a child's behavioral responses to trauma as a personal threat or provocation, rather than as a reenactment of what happened to the child and a behavioral representation of what the child cannot express verbally" (Cook, et. al, 2003, p. 17). The NCTSN further highlights critical factors for promoting resilience. They are:

- Positive attachment and connections to emotionally supportive and competent adults
- Development of cognitive and self-regulation abilities
- Positive beliefs about one's self
- Motivation to act effectively in one's environment

Four Basic Principles for Strengthening Attachment
National Child Traumatic Stress Network, 2003

1. Create a structured and predictable environment by establishing rituals and routines. This includes behavior management and limit setting.
2. Enhance the caregiver's abilities to "tune in" to the child's affect in order to respond to the affect rather than react to the behavior.
3. Model effective management of intense affect by supporting a child in both labeling and coping with emotional distress. Model adaptive coping.
4. Praise, reinforce, and focus on children doing something positive in order to help a child identify with strengths rather than deficits.

Every human being is unique in so many ways. Understanding each child's development and responding to his or her needs accordingly, provides an opportunity to help children thrive as they mature. When adults try to involve children in activities that do not fit with that child's interests and needs, youth naturally rebel. Such uniqueness requires an individualized approach to optimize health and well-being.

Conclusion

The scientific study of adolescent development
has burgeoned in the past two decades,
but its findings have not yet influenced juvenile justice policy
nearly as much as they should.
Laurence Steinberg

Child development is an amazingly complex experience for everyone. Knowing what factors promote optimum development, and what factors prevent it, can help maximize attachment by providing a secure base from which children can explore and grow. Caregivers and service providers can see positive results when they treat all children as bright, articulate, and delightful. When children are treated with warmth and genuine concern they grow up to become upstanding community members. Shifting toward a positive outlook for all children, including those at highest risk for youth violence, gives everyone greater opportunities for success.

Understanding the influence of development and life experiences on behavior can help prevent youth violence. Promoting individualized services in order to best meet the developmental needs of each youth enriches lives and contributes to everyone's health and well-being.

Recommendations

- Promote and practice optimum elements of child development.
- Implement environmental protective factors.
- Build strengths.
- Work to minimize vulnerabilities.
- Define clear expectations.
- Practice empathy.
- Express warmth.
- Exercise patience.
- Promote moral reasoning and good decision-making.
- Don't lecture!
- Provide hope and optimism for success.
- Discover a child's interests and dreams.
- Encourage exploration and pursuit of those interests and dreams.
- Do things that children like to do.
- Teach, and model, compassion and caring.
- Develop a positive, non-punitive, age-appropriate plan for managing challenging behaviors.
- Create a plan to ensure respect for everyone's physical and emotional boundaries.
- Have fun!
- Celebrate any success no matter how small or seemingly insignificant!

Resources

Advocates for Youth: www.advocatesforyouth.org

Guttmacher Institute: www.guttmacher.org

Healthy Teen Network: www.healthyteennetwork.org

Institute of Medicine: www.iom.edu

National Child Traumatic Stress Network: www.nctsn.org

National Research Council: www.nationalacademies.org

Planned Parenthood: www.plannedparenthood.org

Rutgers University: www.answer.rutgers.edu

Sex Education Library: www.sexedlibrary.org

Sexuality Information and Education Council of the United States: www.siecus.org

Parkside Family Counseling, LLC: www.parksideforfamilies.com

Chapter 3

The Facts Ma'am, Just the Facts: Research That Informs Services

The truth will set you free,
but first it will make you miserable.

James A. Garfield

Overview

Many communities are succeeding in reducing youth violence. Community policing, coordinated services among juvenile justice, child welfare and mental health, and reduced numbers of unwanted children are all impacting successful efforts to stop youth violence (Piquero, 2008; Finkelhor, 2009; Levitt & Dubner, 2005). A clearinghouse at the University of Colorado's Center for the Study and Prevention of Violence maintains a comprehensive database of research about what works. This chapter summarizes information pertinent to creating a clearly defined and effective approach that can be adapted for all communities.

Objectives

By the end of this chapter we hope you will be able to:
- Define research-based practices for all levels of prevention.
- Describe relevant models.
- Understand the importance of integrating interventions demonstrated to be safe and effective into a community-wide, multi-dimensional approach for youth violence prevention.

Definitions

Empirical means something is verified by observation. In this case it is referring to valid research.

Strategies are plans of action or policies designed to achieve a major or overall aim.

Practices are the actual application of a method identified as a strategy.

Evidence-based practice (EBP) is a term used to identify the highest level of research supported by multiple, controlled, randomized outcomes studies. While there are a range of evidence-based practices for youth violence prevention, there are few that specifically address specific crimes like juvenile sexual offending. Descriptions of all evidence-based practices for violence prevention can be found at the University of Colorado Center for the Study and Prevention of Violence, www.colorado.edu/cspv/blueprints/model-programs.html

Promising practices are those supported by empirical studies but that require more investigation to meet standards for evidence-based practices. Since achieving evidence-based status is relatively new, many practices fall in the mid or low range of effectiveness. This may simply reflect a shortage of outcome studies, or realizations that some practices based on conventional wisdom are not effective (Chaffin & Bonner, 1998).

Best practice is a term used to describe widely recognized and recommended models. This term is potentially fraught with problems as some recommended practices represent methods having

---

little to no empirical evidence supporting their use. Use of the term "best practices" must be used with care and not taken for granted. All best practices should be supported by evidence.

Empirically driven practices are efforts to apply specific research into service delivery. This is a broad term used to identify interventions based on scientific study as opposed to conventional wisdom, which has no foundation in research.

Ineffective strategies are those that according to research do not work and may have potential to do harm. These practices have been identified in at least one study demonstrating harmful effects.

Empirical Evidence for Youth Violence Prevention

It is common to hear terms such as "best practices," "evidence-based practices," "clinically proven," and a range of other terms supporting effectiveness. While these terms are well defined by a variety of sources (Hamilton, 2005; Chorpita, B., Yim, L., Donkervoet, J., Arensdorf, A., Amundsen, M., McGee, C., Serrano, A., Yates, A., Burns, J., & Morelli, P., 2002), they can be challenging to figure out and remember.

Additionally the terms "practice" and "strategy" can be confusing. A strategy is an overall plan while a practice is a specific method. The Centers for Disease Control and Prevention identify four strategies for youth violence prevention while the University of Colorado Center for the Study and Prevention of Violence and the Office of the Surgeon General focus on specific practices.

Mark Chaffin, a researcher at the University of Oklahoma, defines evidence-based practices (EBP) as "the competent and high-fidelity implementation of practices that have been demonstrated safe and effective, usually in randomized controlled trials" (2006, p.661). These are manualized approaches for interventions. *A manualized approach simply means that the model has a specific manual, or guide, to follow in order to standardize services and promote successful outcomes.* This chapter highlights specific evidence-based practices or strategies for youth violence prevention.

University of Colorado Center for the
Study and Prevention of Violence

The Blueprints for Violence Prevention project (University of Colorado, 2011) describes a number of model programs (practices) that have a positive impact. These include the Midwestern Prevention Project, Big Brothers Big Sisters of America, Functional Family Therapy, Life Skills Training, Multisystemic Therapy, Multidimensional Treatment Foster Care, the Project Toward No Drug Abuse, Olweus Bullying Prevention Program, and Promoting Alternate Thinking Strategies (PATHS).

Additionally the Substance Abuse and Mental Health Services Administration (SAMHSA) maintains a National Registry of Evidence-based Programs and Practices (NREPP) that addresses violence through self-harm such as substance abuse and suicide. The American Foundation for Suicide Prevention has a website that provides information on evidence-based practices also. The Office of Juvenile Justice and Delinquency Prevention (OJJDP) is also a resource for exploring evidence about all aspects of youth violence, including gang activity.

It is important to note that these evidence-based practices typically occur in a youth's home, school, or neighborhood with their families and other supportive people. They do not take place in conventional one-hour sessions of talk therapy at traditional mental health clinics, or in residential treatment. There is little evidence that years of individual or group therapy stop youth violence. Unfortunately, many youth are required to participate in activities that are not empirically based and are not effective.

Evidence-based practices do not focus on insight-oriented work to help individuals understand causes of youth violence. They focus on stopping problematic behavior, regardless of understanding and awareness. They are practical and often short-term. They measure specific goals and progress made toward achieving those goals.

Office of the Surgeon General

After a series of tragic school shootings by youth, the Office of the Surgeon General published *Youth Violence: A Report of the Surgeon General* (2001), that identified research-based interventions to stop youth violence..

This turned out to be an extremely important and controversial document that continues to guide both policy development and practice. It is important because it provides clear evidence of what does and doesn't work. It is controversial because it exposed ineffective practices that have been used in the United States for a long time. Not only do ineffective practices not work, but some are found to actually cause harm.

The report of the Office of the Surgeon General (2001) describes effective strategies for all three types of prevention. These include primary prevention (efforts aimed at keeping violence from happening), secondary (efforts aimed toward at-risk groups before violence happens), and tertiary (efforts aimed at preventing violence from happening again).

More specifically, the Surgeon General's report describes effective primary prevention as: skills training, behavior monitoring and reinforcement, behavior techniques for classroom management, building school capacity, continuous progress programs, cooperative learning, and positive youth development programs. It describes effective secondary prevention efforts as: parent training, home visitation, compensatory education, moral reasoning, social problem- solving, and thinking skills. Finally, it describes effective tertiary prevention programs as: social perspective taking, multimodal interventions, behavioral interventions, skills training, marital and family therapy by clinical staff, and wraparound services.

A vital part of this report identifies ineffective practices in all three areas of prevention. Unfortunately this information has not been fully integrated into policy or practice. Even though this information has been available since 2001, in many cases, services for youth and families have not incorporated such important information.

An example of an ineffective practice is group therapy for juvenile delinquents (Henggeler et al., 2009: Dodge, Dishion, & Lansford, 2006). Many programs continue to provide group therapy in both residential and community settings even though research findings consistently warn against it. It is not helpful to bring violent youth together as it puts them at risk of influencing each other in negative ways that may include continued, and more diverse, violent behavior.

Report of the Surgeon General, 2001

Effective Strategies

Primary Prevention:
Skills training
Behavior monitoring and
    reinforcement
Behavior techniques for
    classroom management
Building school capacity
Continuous progress
    programs
Cooperative learning
Positive youth development
    programs

Secondary Prevention:
Parent training
Home visitation
Compensatory education
Moral reasoning
Social problem-solving
Thinking skills

Tertiary Prevention:
Social perspective taking,
    role taking
Multimodal interventions
Behavioral interventions
Skills training
Marital and family therapy
    by clinical staff
Wraparound services

Ineffective Strategies

Primary prevention:
Peer counseling, peer
    mediation, peer leaders
Non-promotion to succeed-
    ing grades

Secondary Prevention:
Gun buyback programs
Firearm training
Mandatory gun ownership
Redirecting youth behavior
Shifting peer group norms

Tertiary Prevention:
Boot camps
Residential programs
Milieu treatment
Behavioral token programs
Waivers to adult court
Social casework
Individual counseling

Centers for Disease Control

The Centers for Disease Control and Prevention (Thornton, et. al., 2002) and the Center for the Study and Prevention of Violence (2006) document a need for a multi-modal approach focusing on parents and family, home visiting, mentoring, and social/cognitive strategies.

Multi-modal simply means using more than one method or modality of treatment, such as a combination of individual and family therapy. Family team meetings are often considered an important modality as well.

Effective Strategies for Youth Violence Prevention
Centers for Disease Control and Prevention, 2010

Focus on Parents and Family   Social-Cognitive Intervention
Home Visiting   Mentoring

Focus on parents and family *is active and consistent involvement of the family as the core of all service delivery.* It is a key to successful outcomes for the whole family. Support for parents honors and establishes their leadership role in the family. It will be addressed at length in the next chapter.

Home visiting *is providing services to youth and families in their own homes.* It is more effective because family members may become comfortable more quickly with the process of treatment when they don't have to meet in unfamiliar settings. Family members are more likely to behave genuinely at home and interactions that typically lead to conflict might unfold in front of the therapist. These opportunities help service providers better understand needs and also provide an opportunity for teachable moments with the family if problems arise.

Mentoring *involves an experienced adult role model, usually not a family member, who is available to a youth, in an informal setting on a regular basis.* The youth and the mentor engage in fun activities and informal conversations that promote opportunities for success in skill building. Mentoring helps youth become responsible and productive community members.

Social-cognitive interventions or strategies *are any activities that promote social skill building and cognitive restructuring.* Social-cognitive strategies combine social skill development with opportunities to help young people change the way they think in order to stop violence. Unfortunately the Centers for Disease Control and Prevention combine two very important issues into one. They are (1) social skill development; and (2) cognitive restructuring—two very different things. **Practically speaking, kids need to have good social skills and believe violence is wrong in order to prevent it.**

Social-cognitive interventions can be as simple as participating in sports, band, 4-H programs, social clubs, volunteer organizations, community theater, school plays, religious youth groups, afterschool clubs, etc. These types of fun learning experiences can involve all youth with the expectation that they will learn useful life skills through enjoyable activities.

Cognitive restructuring simply means changing the way someone thinks. If a person thinks violence is an acceptable way to resolve conflict he or she is at risk of being violent. Children learn that violence is an option when they see trusted adults and respected peers behave in violent ways. Stopping youth violence requires helping youth and their family members to think differently about violence and to acknowledge problems it may be causing in their lives. Teaching and modeling non-violent ways to manage difficult situations in all aspects of life is the essence of prevention. The goal is for all youth to develop values and beliefs that violence is wrong, that it is illegal, and that they should stop it.

Rosie developed a habit of swearing at her older children when she was angry with them, regardless of whether her younger children heard her. She screamed, swore, and threatened to smack the teenagers. Eventually the younger children, even 3-year-old Rhonda, began using the same language when they didn't get their way at home. One day when Rosie was picking Rhonda up from preschool the teacher asked to talk to her. Rosie learned that when Rhonda was frustrated at school, she was using the swear words she heard at home and recently started hitting other children. Rosie's first instinct was to punish Rhonda. Once she thought it through more clearly, her anger turned to embarrassment. She realized that if she and the older children didn't stop their violent communication at home, Rhonda would continue to think that violent communication is okay and a bad habit would soon form.

Competency Development

A competency is a task or activity that a person does well. *Competency development is a youth's ability to increase knowledge and skills in order to become a "productive, connected, and law- abiding members of their community"* (Torbet & Thomas, 2005, p.3.). Everyone develops competencies throughout life, and specific competencies provide a buffer against violence. Competency development is not treatment. "Youth do not become competent just because they complete a treatment program" (Torbet & Thomas, 2005, p.5).

Education does not necessarily equal change. People can learn a lot of things, but if they do not make changes based on new knowledge life does not get better. In order to stop violence, youth must behave differently. Behaving competently shows how youth violence stops when new activities and skills take the place of harm. **Practically speaking, "words are cheap." If youth only give lip service to change without altering their behavior, then treatment, no matter how educational, has not been effective.**

Competency development and treatment are parallel processes to be completed in order to effectively achieve successful long-term change. Monitoring each youth's competency development is a critical aspect of ongoing and comprehensive assessment. Demonstrating competency does not necessarily mean a youth is finished with treatment when he or she is involved in secondary, or tertiary, prevention. Youth may still be required to participate in designated activities as part of holistic treatment or judicial process.

Research indicates five core competency domains. They are: social skills (interaction, cognition, and self-control); moral reasoning; academic skills; workforce development skills; and independent living skills. All youth must be able to integrate knowledge into consistent practice in order to demonstrate measurable progress. A user friendly scale of the following competencies is provided in the Appendix.

The role of the juvenile justice system is to "facilitate efforts that advance youths' competencies so that offenders are less likely to take part in anti-social, delinquent behaviors and better able to become responsible and productive members of their communities" (Torbet & Thomas, 2005, p.12). Whether or not the services that youth are receiving are court mandated, developing pro-social competencies is critical for lifelong success.

Some youth receiving services are involved with the juvenile justice system. According to the Juvenile Justice and Delinquency Prevention Committee of the Pennsylvania Commission on Crime and Delinquency, the purpose of juvenile justice is "to provide for children committing delinquent acts programs of supervision, care and rehabilitation which provide balanced attention to the protection of the community, the imposition of accountability for offenses committed and the development of competencies to enable children to become responsible and productive members of the community" (Torbet & Thomas, 2005, p.1).

Competency development requires effective skill training that has a lasting effect on youth. Research is clear; interventions that do not ultimately build stronger relationships or bonds to pro-social groups and positive role models for youth in the community are unlikely to have long-term impact.

This helps

All youth receiving court services need opportunities to:
- Practice and demonstrate new skills.
- Engage in productive experiential activities.
- Establish positive relationship with law-abiding adults and peers.
- Form ties with pro-social community groups and institutions.
- Receive services and supports that advance competency development.

The tasks of adults are to:
- Present ideas.
- Model desired behavior.
- Guide practice.
- Provide corrective feedback.
- Generalize to other areas of life.
- Coach.
- Reinforce success and consequence failure.

Community Service

Helping others is an essential protective factor for youth violence prevention. Good community service engages youth in productive, hands-on experiences with opportunities to learn and practices skills, strengthens relationships with pro-social adults, and increases bonds to positive groups or institutions. **Practically speaking, successful community service is mean-**

ingful to the community and worthwhile for the youth. Who knows, it might even turn out to be fun!

Responsibility and Accountability

The National Center for Juvenile Justice (Torbet & Thomas, 2005) provides the following information on shared responsibility and accountability for court involved youth. Juvenile justice has an important, but limited, place in developing competencies. Many providers, including parents and guardians, schools, churches, employers, coaches, and mentors, have responsibility for supporting these youth.

Everyone involved is responsible for:
- Developing a good relationship with each youth.
- Creating hope for success.
- Building on identified strengths.
- Encouraging individual responsibility for law-abiding behavior.

Juvenile justice personnel are responsible for:
- Assessing each youth across all five domains.
- Addressing specific competency development needs most closely associated with the youth's offending behavior.
- Delivering or contracting for services likely to achieve competency development goals.
- Ensuring participation in good community service projects.

Performance expectations for juvenile justice personnel:
- Conduct a structured strengths and needs assessment across all five core competency domains.
- Develop a supervision plan based upon assessment results. This should include criteria for success and failure, monitoring progress, and consequences for noncompliance.
- Coach, encourage, and support each client.
- Identify community services and supports.
- Monitor participation and progress and make adjustments to remediate any off-track performance.

Core Competency Domains

National Center for Juvenile Justice, 2005

1. Pro-Social Skills

	Competency
Interaction: Discrete observable social behaviors and assertiveness skills	Initiate greetings or interactions; listen well; resist peer pressure; deal with positive and negative feedback; negotiate; accept criticism; effectively disagree and handle conflict
Cognitive: Thinking skills, particularly problem-solving skills, that are applicable to a variety of situations	Recognize, define, and clarify a problem; connect cause and effect; identify solutions, set realistic goals; predict and evaluate consequences; engage in step-by-step planning; anticipate pitfalls in carrying out solutions
Self-Control: Interaction and cognitive skills that help prevent an individual from displaying aversive or anti-social behavior	Delay gratification; display impulse, anger and aggression-control; engage in emotional self-awareness, self-talk, and self-monitoring

2. Moral Reasoning Skills: Making the right decisions for the right reasons

3. Academic Skills: Advancing in school to the highest possible level of academic achievement

4. Workforce Development Skills   Economic self-sufficiency

5. Independent Living Skills: Self-sufficient living

- Apply incentives and sanctions to reinforce accountability.
- Provide opportunities to practice and demonstrate new skills and pro-social relationships.
- Document intermediate outcomes at case closing.

Qualified mental health clinicians are responsible for:
- Providing competent, empirically driven evaluations and interventions to address all elements of youth violence prevention.
- Intervening in ways that promote skill building and competency development.
- Providing all interventions in the context of each youth's family and community.

Performance expectations for qualified mental health clinicians:
- Hold a master's degree or doctorate from an accredited program in a mental health field.
- Have successfully completed specialized training and demonstrated competency for addressing childhood trauma and youth violence.
- Participate in timely and regular face-to-face supervision, either individual or group, specific to youth violence.
- Have crisis supervision available as needed.
- Maintain continuing education in order to stay abreast of current research findings relating to childhood trauma and youth violence prevention.
- Assess and facilitate development of a treatment plan with each youth based on individual and family strengths and needs.
- Document, and share with youth and family, ongoing treatment progress.
- Collaborate with community members familiar with the youth, such as parents, teachers, therapists, and significant others.

Judges, prosecuting attorneys, and defense attorneys are responsible for:
- Adhering to Key Principles for Permanency Planning For Children (Judicial Education Center, 1999).
- Advocating for good skill training, community service, and positive youth development programs.

Performance expectations for judges, prosecuting attorneys, and defense attorneys:

- Maintain continuing legal education in order to stay abreast of current research findings relating to family violence, childhood trauma, substance abuse, and youth violence prevention.

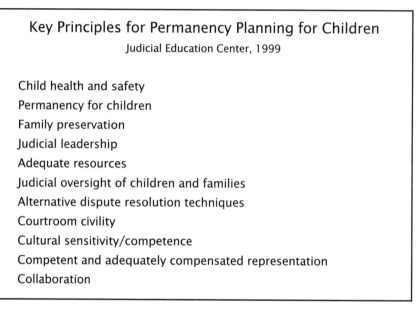

Key Principles for Permanency Planning for Children
Judicial Education Center, 1999

Child health and safety
Permanency for children
Family preservation
Judicial leadership
Adequate resources
Judicial oversight of children and families
Alternative dispute resolution techniques
Courtroom civility
Cultural sensitivity/competence
Competent and adequately compensated representation
Collaboration

Detention personnel are responsible for:

- Providing community safety and consequences for illegal and/or seriously inappropriate behavior displayed by youth.
- Applying a strength-based approach that promotes development of youth into a productive, connected, and law-abiding community member.

Performance expectations for detention personnel:

- Provide training to staff in strength-based communication and intervention.
- Develop ongoing short-term programming that integrates core competency skill building and positive youth development.
- Collaborate with community members familiar with the youth, such as parents, teachers, therapists, and significant others.
- Develop an individualized approach for each youth to maximally uti-

lize his or her time in detention and reduce the chance of returning once released back into the community.
- Integrate youth into short-term programming in a way that best suits their needs.

Residential programs are responsible for:
- Respecting the uniqueness of each youth and his or her family.
- Applying a strength-based approach focusing on positive youth development.
- Providing competent, empirically driven interventions that address childhood trauma and all elements of youth violence prevention.
- Intervening in ways that promote skill building and competency development.
- Providing all interventions in the context of each youth's family and community.
- Promoting self-determination and responsible decision making.
- Being seen as part of a continuum of community services available to youth and families.

Performance expectations of residential programs:
- Provide training to staff in strength-based communication and intervention and develop programming that integrates positive youth development.
- Collaborate with adults familiar with the youth, such as parents, teachers, therapists, and significant others.
- Develop an individualized approach for each youth to maximally utilize his or her time in detention and reduce the chance of returning once released back into the community.
- Integrate residential programming and family therapy to promote long-term use of newly acquired skills when youth return to the community.

Schools are responsible for:
- Providing educational assessment and academic support to maximize achievement.
- Encouraging attendance.
- Removing barriers to re-enrollment.

Performance expectations for schools:
- Teach, support, and encourage learning.
- Assess, when indicated, for learning differences.
- Provide accommodations for students' individual needs.
- Collaborate with professionals in the community familiar with the youth, such as parents, teachers, therapists, and significant others.

Youth are responsible for:
- Actively participating in developing personal competencies.

Performance expectations for youth:
- Participate in pro-social activities.
- Seek out pro-social peers.
- Attend school.
- Take good care of their minds, bodies, and spirit.

Community supports (businesses, churches, and community groups) are responsible for:
- Creating and supporting pro-social activities.
- Providing support for youth and families.
- Promoting holistic development for mind, body, and spirit.

Performance expectations for community supports:
- Mentor youth.
- Make activities available and easily accessible to all youth.
- Provide equal opportunities for individual expression addressing the diverse needs of all youth.

Parents and guardians are responsible for:
- Actively supporting competency development.
- Holding children accountable.
- Being viewed as assets and partners who may need to be motivated to accept their rightful role.
- Learning new parenting techniques when necessary.

Performance expectations for parents and guardians:

- Provide pro-social role modeling for all youth.
- Actively engage in all elements of optimum child development.
- Create a structured and predictable environment through the establishment of rituals and routines.
- Manage behavior and set limits without threats or violence.
- Pay attention to a child's emotions and respond with support and nurturing.
- Guide children in both labeling and coping with difficult emotions in ways that do not cause harm.
- Handle difficult personal situations by labeling feelings and modeling healthy coping skills.
- Praise, reinforce, and focus on positive rather than negative behavior.

When everyone is clear about responsibilities and performance expectations, teams can collaborate and eliminate barriers to successful outcomes. This helps everyone to stay focused on stopping harm. When a community is dedicated to excellence in service provision and any responsibilities are not being met, identified concerns can be addressed through training and shared resources. At an agency level, supervision and administrative actions may be warranted.

All of the information provided so far is what works and doesn't work as far as community collaboration and youth violence prevention in general. Successful outcomes also depend on knowing specifically what effective treatment models look like.

Treatment Services

Treatment is a research-based approach for addressing change. It is a thoughtful plan of care created with a youth and his or her family to prevent violence (secondary and tertiary prevention). Historically treatment was based on *conventional wisdom, which is service delivery not founded in scientific evidence.* Many well-meaning service providers simply believed without question and did what was generally done. Before empirical evidence was available services were developed from best guesses and economic convenience.

Treatment for youth misbehaving violently used to focus on what is wrong rather than what is right about a youth and family. Identifying deficits rather than strengths created a dysfunctional view of a child and his or her family. It focused on problems rather than solutions. Scientific studies now provide solutions that promote long-term successful outcomes. A trauma-informed approach for positive youth development is replacing old pathology-based or problem-focused methods taken from conventional wisdom about delinquency (Ford, Chapman et al.,2007). Treatment recommendations presented throughout this book are based on this data and focus on positive youth development.

Successful treatment to stop youth violence is not limited to behavioral change. It requires a holistic, individualized approach based upon empirically driven best practices for youth violence prevention (Chaffin, 2008 Schladale et al., 2007; Torbet & Thomas, 2005). *Holistic means all parts of a person's life and includes all physical, social, psychological, and spiritual aspects.* It includes strengths and successes as well as risk factors and problem behaviors. Recognizing complexity provides a foundation for exploring individual strengths and needs that contribute to a youth's overall long-term success. A youth's support by, and connection to, the community are critical for successful treatment outcomes. Family sensitive services that embrace strength, competency, and resilience provide the most direct and effective route to therapeutic solutions. **Practically speaking, youth are most likely to stop violence when they receive services in their home and community, with family and other people important to them who are most likely to be an ongoing part of their life. When a youth and family participate in creating treatment goals they are more likely to be successful.**

Current evidence indicates that most effective treatment is based on a foundation of nonjudgmental attitude, empathy, genuineness, and warmth (Duncan, B. et al., 2010; Miller & Rollnick, 2002). Additionally, recent studies indicate that successful outcomes in therapy are based upon four factors (Duncan, B. et al., 2010). They are: therapeutic technique (15%); creation of hope and expectation for change (15%); the therapeutic relationship between service providers and clients (30%); and client characteristics (40%), including strengths, resources, social support, and living environment.

Treatment begins with a thorough family systems and ecological evaluation in order to best meet a youth's goals for change (Ford et al., 2007.).

Family systems refers to a youth's family and ecological is all parts of the community in which a youth lives. This topic is addressed in Chapter 5. Ongoing assessment of individual and environmental protective factors and core competencies create a foundation for positive youth development vital to harm reduction. This information guides safety and treatment planning throughout the therapeutic process.

Once an evaluation is complete everyone can collaborate to intervene effectively. This is done through a treatment process outlined in Chapter 6. Treatment involves the following research-based factors:

- **Affect regulation** (Schore, 2003; Groves, 2002; Stien & Kendall, 2004; Torbet & Thomas, 2005; Van der Kolk, 2004)
- **Social skills development** (Office of the Surgeon General, 2001; Thornton et al., 2002; Torbet & Thomas, 2005)
- **Social problem-solving, including resolving interpersonal disputes** (Office of the Surgeon General, 2001; Thornton et al., 2002; Henderson, 1996; Torbet & Thomas, 2005)
- **Social perspective taking to enhance empathy for and sensitivity to the impact of harm on victims, families, and communities** (Office of the Surgeon General, 2001)
- **Mentoring** (Ferber et al., 2002; Thornton et al., 2002; Center for the Study and Prevention of Violence, 2006)
- **Promoting positive self-worth and self-confidence** (Henderson et al., 1996; Ferber & Pittman, with Marshall, 2002)
- **Appreciation for and connection to one's culture** (Centers for Disease Control and Prevention, 2011; SAMHSA, 2011; Piquero, 2008)
- **Pro-social values and behavior relating to respect for self and others** (Henderson et al., 1996; Torbet & Thomas, 2005)
- **Moral reasoning** (Torbet & Thomas, 2005)
- **Sexual health** (World Health Organization, 2010; SIECUS, 2010; Schladale, 2010)
- **Healing trauma** (Cook et. al., 2003; Ford et.al., 2007; Kauffman Best Practices Report, 2004; McMackin et al., 2002; Schladale, 2002, 2006, 2010; Schore, 2003)
- **Academic skills and workforce development** (Torbet & Thomas, 2005)

Interventions for youth violence prevention are continually evolving. Empirically based studies continue to emerge and guide practice. Advances in research will influence ongoing change in best practices for stopping harm. Staying up to date about such important research requires responsive and flexible collaboration, as current best practices become outdated.

Research-based workbooks that address core components of treatment include: *Real Life Heroes* (Kagan, 2004); *The T.O.P.* Workbook for Taming Violence and Sexual Aggression* (Schladale, 2002); and *The T.O.P.* Workbook for Sexual Health* (Schladale, 2010).

Affect Regulation
THE MOST IMPORTANT PART OF THIS BOOK!

Affect regulation is at the core of all violence prevention. It *is a person's ability to manage emotions without causing harm* (Schore, 2003). When young people have not been taught pro-social ways to manage upsetting emotions, they are at risk of behaving in harmful ways. *Dysregulation occurs when emotions, or feelings, are managed in ways that cause harm to self or others.*

"Affect regulation" and "dysregulation" are not user-friendly terms. It can be hard to remember both the terms and what they mean. Affect regulation is fully explained in this chapter as the foundation for prevention. Information for practical application and flow charts are provided in Chapter 6.

Disturbance of Arousal, or
Getting Upset and Feeling Out of Control

Disturbance of arousal is another term that is not user-friendly. Here's what it means. *When people get upset they have thoughts, feelings, and physiological reactions that influence their behavior. Behavior then influences outcomes.* Disturbance of arousal is an experience that tests a person's ability to manage his or her feelings, or affect. Affect regulation promotes positive outcomes and dysregulation is likely to result in negative outcomes. **Practically speaking, when people get upset they have thoughts, feelings, and bodily reactions that influence behavior.** When they understand what's going on, youth may feel more in control and able to use healthy coping strategies.

> If Pete arrives at school in a bad mood because Mom was yelling at him before school he has to work to stay calm, and he needs skills to do this. If he dysregulates and misbehaves violently the outcome may be suspension. If he uses healthy coping skills, regardless of the morning's events, the outcome may be behaving well, completing classroom work, and having a good day.

When asked what comes to mind when hearing the word "arousal" most Americans say "sex." *Arousal means to evoke or awaken a feeling, emotion, or response.* Humans experience many forms of arousal. A range of stimuli, including, but not limited to, pain, hunger, thirst, temperature, love, sex, loneliness, fear, and/or terror, can all influence arousal. **Practically speaking, everyone is challenged to manage or regulate arousal in pro-social ways. This is affect regulation.**

Disturbances of arousal can occur when a stimulus brings up uncomfortable, unsettling, and unwanted reactions. Managing such arousal in ways that cause harm to self or others are examples of dysregulation. Understanding how a disturbance of arousal can lead to dysregulation provides a foundation for intervention. **Practically speaking, when people see or hear something upsetting, they may yell or become physically violent, or they might shut down or freeze up. These are examples of dysregulation.**

A range of life experiences can influence dysregulation. They include violence, sickness or injury, family problems and break-ups, natural disasters, poverty, discrimination, school problems, social problems, child abuse, substance abuse, terrorism, and death. In addition a number of mental health disorders can be significant factors in dysregulation. Research about trauma provides very important information about affect regulation and how it can be used to stop violence.

Promoting Affect Regulation

Everyone requires a safe and stable environment in which to stop violence. Sound familiar? This is the same as the first element of optimum child development, physical and psychological safety, introduced in Chapter 2. If people are not physically and emotionally safe they cannot focus

> The most effective therapy is based on a foundation of nonjudgmental attitude, empathy, genuineness, and warmth (Duncan, et al., 2010).

on stopping violence because so much energy is used for protection and harm reduction. When humans are in a physically safe place and feel safe emotionally they can gain support and begin planning how to stop violence. A stable environment provides predictability and a sense of security. These are important factors that help people regulate their emotions.

As mentioned in Chapter 2, when people learn to think differently, change their brain processing, and improve memory, symptoms of violence can be reduced (Groves, 2002). This is possible through exercise and body movement, healing touch, personal expression through art, drama, dance, and music (Stien & Kendall, 2004). A part of trauma-focused cognitive behavior therapy (TF-CBT) also uses something called narrative trauma scripting, which helps people write about the trauma in order to better manage it.

Developmental skill building, another term for competency development, helps heal pain from violence and abuse. The more skills children learn the more likely they are to successfully practice affect regulation and avoid violence. Using these resources can go a long way to stop youth violence.

Key Factors for Affect Regulation
Stien & Kendall, 2004

1. Safety and stabilization
2. Multi-sensory activities that reduce dysregulation:
   - Exercise and body movement
   - Healing touch
   - Expression through art, drama, dance, and music
   - Narrative trauma scripting (Trauma-Focused Cognitive Behavioral Therapy)
3. Developmental skill building (competency development)

Starting to see a trend? Research from multiple sources is consistently showing similar findings relating to overlapping issues such as optimum child development, affect regulation, and youth violence prevention. Important stuff!

Tasks for Harm Reduction
Van der Kolk, 2004

- Mindfully observe internal experience
- Stay organized in the threat of psychological upheaval
- Change body activity when addressing pain
- Learn to state success
- Remember survival techniques
- Celebrate survival resources
- Honor life!

When children have experienced violence, treatment involves tasks for harm reduction (Van der Kolk, 2004). These tasks involve teaching youth and family members to pay attention to what is going on in their bodies when they experience a disturbance of arousal. They are taught to pay attention to thoughts, feelings, and physiological reactions that influence both behavior and outcomes. Van der Kolk refers to this as, "mindfully observing internal experience," another term that is not user-friendly but is a very important part of affect regulation. When people learn to track thoughts, feelings, and physiological reactions they can change behavior accordingly, and prevent negative outcomes by behaving respectfully.

When youth learn to mindfully observe their internal experiences the next task is to learn how to stay organized in the threat of psychological upheaval, another term for disturbance of arousal. **Practically speaking, mindful observation involves stopping to think in order to make good decisions.** This is the critical turning point at which a person chooses affect regulation versus dysregulation. People stay organized through disturbances of arousal in a variety of ways. Deep breathing can help as well as positive internal self-talk like saying "get a grip," "slow down," "stay calm," "take it easy," etc.

Tommy experienced multiple traumas and abuse during his early childhood. He was tied to a bed at night by one of his mother's boyfriends. When the man untied him in the morning Tommy recalled being given bananas for breakfast. While he was in residential treatment because of his own criminal behavior, Tommy was physically restrained by staff after "going off" when he saw bananas in the cafeteria and sent them and the bowl they were in flying across the room. Tommy later told staff he felt like it was happening again. The resulting dysregulation (out of control behavior) alerted staff and the outcome was a physical restraint, loss of privileges, and restricted movement around the facility due to unsafe behavior. Unfortunately nobody handled the situation in a good way, and it wasn't until staff were trained and Tommy learned about affect regulation that the situation improved.

Slowing down brain processing helps youth learn how to change their body state when addressing their deepest pain (Van der Kolk, 2004). They can learn how to handle disturbances of arousal without behaving violently. Helping youth explore ways to substitute harm with healthy activity does this. This can take a lot of practice and, in fact, requires lifelong commitment. Youth and adults do this through multi-sensory self-soothing. *Multisensory self-soothing is a way of using any of the five senses (sight, sound, smell, taste, and touch) to remain calm in difficult situations.* **Practically speaking, when youth get upset and feel out of control, instead of misbehaving, they can quickly do something like listen to soothing music, go for a run or bike ride, or call someone they trust.**

While youth continue to practice these tasks they learn to talk about personal success by acknowledging their improved behavior. Youth who behave violently have often been disrespected and demeaned in a lot of ways. They have often been made to feel badly about themselves. Focusing on success is a vital part of positive youth development and helps clarify competency and mastery. Many young people feel uncomfortable with this at first, but most learn to enjoy legitimate praise and support for a job well done.

The next task is to remember how they survived. Some youth have literally been in life-threatening situations and may never have been asked to recall such important information. Like the previous task of learning to state success, remembering how they survived through trauma can greatly influence a youth's sense of competency and self-confidence.

> When John was asked to describe how he survived being stabbed multiple times, he reflexively put his hands to the wounds and said, "I remembered that you're supposed to put pressure on wounds to get them to stop bleeding, so I just kept pushing my hands against any blood I saw spurting out." He clearly remembered what he did to survive.

Youth violence prevention requires both competency and confidence. People can be competent to handle a difficult situation, but if they do not have confidence in their ability to do so, it may prove too difficult an undertaking. On the other hand, they may have confidence to manage something and find out they are unable to do so. Successful task completion requires a realistic balance between competency and confidence. Positive youth development and mentoring aid in mastering competency and confidence when children have not had opportunities to do so.

Once youth learn to talk about their success and remember how they survived, they are encouraged to celebrate their survival skills. While some of those skills may not serve them well now, or may be illegal, it is very important to acknowledge how important those survival skills were at the time. For example, stealing food to help feed a family is illegal, but it helped prevent starvation. Some youth from financially impoverished homes recall stealing food, not only for themselves, but for family members as well. Acknowledging that stealing is a crime and honoring their efforts on behalf of their family provide a responsible way of honoring their life, which is the final task for harm reduction (Van der Kolk, 2004).

Youth violence prevention requires an understanding that these youth have often weathered tremendous difficulties in their young lives. They may have experienced demoralizing and dehumanizing ordeals involving disgrace and dishonor. They are often met with high levels of criticism and little warmth or consideration. To honor their life provides an avenue for creating a new story about overcoming adversity. When young people experience adults as warm, nonjudgmental, empathic, and genuine, they learn how to develop these attributes themselves. While it is important to experience the kindness and compassion of others, stopping youth violence requires an ability to nurture and honor one's self. When youth honor their own life they create a path to health and well-being.

There is always one moment in childhood
when the door opens and lets the future in.

Graham Green

Evidence-Based Practices for Addressing Child Abuse

Evidence-based practices for addressing child physical and sexual abuse provide a type of secondary prevention. When children are engaged in these interventions as soon as their abuse comes to the attention of authorities, there is great potential to stop the children from causing harm to themselves or others.

The National Crime Victims Research and Treatment Center (Saunders, Berliner, & Hanson, 2004) identifies the following core components for all evidence-based models addressing treatment for child physical and sexual abuse. While these guidelines are for victim services, current evidence suggests they are also relevant for youth violence prevention (Ford et. al., 2007; Thornton et al., 20102 Office of the Surgeon General, 2001).

In 2004, the Kauffman Foundation identified the following research-based best practices for child abuse treatment: Trauma-Focused Cognitive Behavioral Therapy (TF-CBT), Abuse-Focused Cognitive Behavioral Therapy, and Parent-Child Interaction Therapy. The research on TF-CBT has been so successful that the federal government has supported a free, web-based, self-paced certification process for service providers. This information is available at: tfcbt.musc.edu. Parents and referring professionals can promote successful outcomes by requiring service providers to have such important specialized training and refer to licensed mental health therapists who do this work.

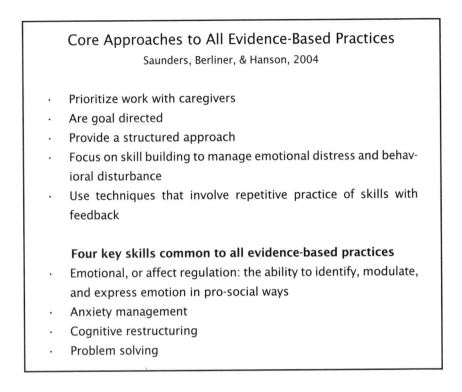

Core Approaches to All Evidence-Based Practices
Saunders, Berliner, & Hanson, 2004

- Prioritize work with caregivers
- Are goal directed
- Provide a structured approach
- Focus on skill building to manage emotional distress and behavioral disturbance
- Use techniques that involve repetitive practice of skills with feedback

Four key skills common to all evidence-based practices
- Emotional, or affect regulation: the ability to identify, modulate, and express emotion in pro-social ways
- Anxiety management
- Cognitive restructuring
- Problem solving

Research-Based Philosophies

In addition to the evidence-based practices previously mentioned, there are empirically driven approaches that reflect values and beliefs about change. While philosophies provide a value-based foundation for interventions, evidence-based practices have specific protocols that require fidelity to a model. Empirically based practices, or models, are very specific interventions while empirically based philosophies are value-based approaches that guide practice. **Practically speaking, believing all youth have strengths they can use to stop violence is a value (Positive Youth Development). Believing that service providers influence whether or not youth are resistant to treatment is a value (Motivational Interviewing). The values just mentioned are part of empirically based philosophies. MST (Multisystemic Therapy) can be used to stop violence and is an evidence-based model for youth violence prevention.**

Positive Youth Development

Positive youth development is an approach that recognizes and encourages "the good in young people, focusing on each and every child's unique talents, strengths, interests, and future potential" (Damon, 2004, quoted in *Commission on Positive Youth Development*, 2005, p.500). It builds on strengths and attributes of resilience, or protective factors, that each youth and his or her family have. **Practically speaking, the more talents and skills that young people can focus on and develop, the more confidence they can build in their ability to be successful in overall life goals and dreams.**

Positive youth development enhances potential for successful outcomes (Butts, Mayer, & Ruth, 2005; Henderson & Sharp-Light, 1996). An inventory for addressing positive youth development through attributes of resilience and protective factors is included in the Appendix. **Practically speaking, the busier young people are with healthy activities, the less time and inclination they have to get in trouble. The less youth get in trouble, the more likely they are to believe in a successful future.**

"Positive youth development programs offer a coordinated, progressive series of activities and experiences such as mentoring, community service, leadership development, peer-centered activities, and long-term follow-up and supports, intended to help young people become socially, morally, emotionally, physically, and cognitively competent" (Torbet & Thomas, 2005, p.2.).

James was a young teen when he began committing petty crimes and physically abusing a younger brother after he was prevented from seeing his father due to allegations that his father sexually abused James's older sister. James and his mother and sister all have developmental disabilities. His mother was overwhelmed and struggled to see the good in her children. All her energy focused on the logistics of taking care of her children's physical needs and emotionally managing the impact of the sexual abuse. She did not know the importance of affection and encouragement. James suffered from nine of the fourteen vulnerabilities in families at high risk of youth violence identified in Chapter 2 (Thornton et. al, 2002.

Through home-based services James's mother learned to identify strengths in her children and practiced complimenting and supporting them. She learned how to communicate with child welfare and juvenile justice personnel in order to advocate for her family. She was also able to help the children explore personal interests and develop pro-social coping strategies and get them involved in free community services to develop social skills and multi-sensory coping strategies, and to have some fun. James had community service requirements for probation and received very positive support from his community service supervisor. He and his sister participated in sexual health education provided by their mother and family therapist. Two years later James's mother reports that everything continues to go well even though family members still struggle with the pain caused by James's father.

Motivational Interviewing

Motivational Interviewing is a research-based therapeutic philosophy for motivating people to change. It focuses on a person's unique struggle to stop harmful behavior through understanding that the power to change comes from within. Another approach closely related to this philosophy is Alan Jenkins's *Invitation to Responsibility: The Therapeutic Engagement of Men Who Are Violent and Abusive* (1990).

Well-meaning service providers may resort to telling youth what to do through statements like "you need to...," which seldom promote the desired response. Most people do not respond well to being told what to do, particularly by someone who may not know them. Both positive youth development and Motivational Interviewing assume that participants have strengths and competencies to successfully explore their own unique solutions to life's problems. While these youth can greatly benefit from mentoring and pro-social relationships with a variety of adults, it is important for adults to ask youth questions about the youths' desires and needs, rather than telling them what to do. Asking youth and family members if they are interested in stopping violence often results in fascinating answers. Further asking about their level of confidence in being able to successfully stop violence provides critical information about needs, and a focus for interventions. Questions such as, "What do you think it is important for us to be thinking about?" and "What do you do to help yourself when the going gets rough?" (Groves, 2002) can help youth learn to manage difficult situations without causing harm.

In this approach all family members are asked if they want violence to stop. If they say "yes," they are asked to report on a one to ten scale their level of confidence in the family's ability to stop the violence. They are further asked to think of ways the family might get started on this quest. They are then supported in exploring their family's readiness, willingness, and abilities to successfully stop it. Interventions involve bolstering these three critical components of change and helping each family member to realize his or her goals. When family members do not say yes, they are invited to explore the pros and cons of stopping violence in their lives.

The 10 Worse Things to Say, Other Than #!@* %#*!
No matter how nicely you say it!

1. You need to…
2. Calm down.
3. Suck it up.
4. Get a grip.
5. Man up.
6. That's inappropriate.
7. Here's what we're going to do.
8. How many times have I told you?
9. I'm not putting up with…
10. You will not disrespect me!

> Mark was beginning to address his own violent behavior in treatment. He told his therapist he was willing to stop the violence "as long as it doesn't take me away from home." The therapist expressed concern that his violence was leading exactly in that direction, and reflected that the young man appeared to be training for a life in the state penitentiary. Mark was then asked if he was interested in changing his training to focus on activities that would keep him out of prison. He was able to explore a range of options for managing pain without resorting to violence.

Conclusion

We can't solve problems by using the same kind of thinking
we used when we created them.
Albert Einstein

Facts should guide practice. The fact is there is a lot of pretty amazing research being done to stop youth violence. However, there are different levels of research-based practices based on the type and amount of studies about a designated topic. Knowing the differences between research categories can help communities make informed decisions for planning and implementation. Knowing where and how to obtain information on research-based practices and establishing familiarity with relevant models can make a big difference in outcomes.

Successful outcomes depend on solid evidence, and current evidence tells us that youth are best served in their home communities, preferably in their own homes, in the context of their own family. Helping them develop core competencies through social and cognitive skill-building promotes self-confidence that leads to mastery and autonomy. Mentoring helps youth become more connected, responsible, and productive community members.

Youth and families can be supported in learning to manage pain in ways that no longer cause harm to self or others. They can learn to tame violence that has sometimes plagued their family and neighborhood for generations.

They can do this through affect regulation, which involves responding to disturbances of arousal in pro-social ways. Promoting positive youth development through Motivational Interviewing creates a foundation from which youth and families can effectively stop violence. Integrating interventions demonstrated to be safe and effective into a community-wide, multi-dimensional approach for youth violence prevention helps stop it.

Recommendations

- Stay abreast of evidence-based and empirically driven research through websites, staff development and training, conferences and workshops, and community initiatives.
- Advocate for the use of evidence-based practices in your community.
- Promote home and family-based services.
- Mentor youth.
- Learn all you can about affect regulation and positive youth development.
- Practice affect regulation!
- Make sure there are a range of community activities promoting body movement and expression through art, drama, dance, and music.
- Have fun with teenagers!

Resources

Centers for Disease Control and Prevention: www.cdc.gov/violenceprevention

Cornell Research Program on Self-Injurious Behavior: www.crpsib.com

The Future of Children: www.futureofchildren.org

Models for Change: www.modelsforchange.net

National Council on Mental Health and Juvenile Justice: www.ncmhjj.com

Office of the Surgeon General: www.surgeongeneral.gov/library/youthviolence

Portland State University Research and Training Center on Family Support and Children's Mental Health: www.rtc.pdx.edu

Trauma Focused Cognitive Behavioral Therapy: www.tfcbt.musc.edu

Safe Youth: www.safeyouth.gov

Self Injury: www.selfinjury.com

Positive Youth Development: http://www.findyouthinfo.gov/topic_pyd.shtml

Section Two

_____

How to Stop It

Chapter Four

Connecting with Kids and Families

Kindness knows no shame.

Stevie Wonder

Overview

Research consistently shows that engaging youth and families in services promotes successful outcomes. Even when court orders mandate treatment, how services are provided can make a huge difference in outcomes. All youth have family. Sometimes a closer look is required to find that people important to a youth may not be blood relatives.

This chapter clarifies how important connecting with kids and families is to all parts of youth violence prevention. It also further promotes what works in practical ways for easy implementation.

Objectives

By the end of this chapter we hope you will be able to:
- Understand why connection or engagement is so important.
- Communicate with everyone in ways that maximize successful outcomes.
- Motivate violence prevention among youth and in families.

Meeting the Needs of Families

Youth and families receive services from a variety of organizations with an interest in the youth's success. A collaborative, multidisciplinary approach is necessary to meet the many complex elements of youth violence prevention. Helping a youth feel supported by, and connected to, his or her community is vital for success. This approach requires access to and communication with each youth, family members, and service providers.

Family Life

Family is central to all human experience. Most current information about youth violence prevention addresses the importance of supporting youth where they live, in the context of their biological and extended family and social support network.

Change occurs in the context of relationships. Family members can often provide support and influence new behavior in a way that professionals or other outsiders cannot. Decisions about change can be greatly influenced by a youth's desire to please family members and make them proud, or by wanting to rebel against family members for any number of reasons. Family always influences youth, regardless of where everyone lives.

Parents have important information about their children that is not available to service providers from any other source. When parents are not available it is important to obtain family information from extended family or others close to the youth. Family history and details about relationships provide knowledge and understanding of a youth's strengths and needs. In secondary and tertiary prevention, outcomes are influenced by family members' participation in the healing process relating to trauma and violence. Engaging families in designing and working toward their vision of success holds the most promise for healing and harm reduction.

> **Family:** "Two or more persons who share resources, share responsibility for decisions, share values and goals, and have commitments to one another over time. The family is that climate that one 'comes home to,' and it is this network of sharing and commitments that most accurately describes the family unit, regardless of blood, legal ties, adoption, or marriage" (American Home Economics Association, as cited in Friedan, 1981, p. 78).

Connecting with kids and families requires a holistic approach to service provision, one that addresses a youth's full ecological context relating to physical, social, psychological, and spiritual life domains. Additionally, focusing on both strengths and needs maximizes potential for change in all areas of the youth's life and the family's life. Doing so creates a solid foundation for pro-social behavior in all areas of a youth's life. Strategies for youth violence prevention involve parents and families, mentoring, home visiting, parent training, and marital and family therapy by clinically trained service providers (Office of the Surgeon General, 2001; Thornton et al., 2002).

Challenges in Systems of Care

It is hard to change established services. While many professionals are committed to the idea of engaging families in service provision, traditional systems of care have not been conducive to family involvement. Historically insurance companies have not been willing to pay for family therapy and home-based services. Funding sources usually identify only an individual client rather than a client family, yet numerous family members often need an array of services. Barriers to success are created when funding sources do not approve and service providers do not coordinate services for the whole family. Such policies create barriers to effective service delivery. Chapter 5 addresses the importance of basing treatment decisions on a thorough evaluation of the identified youth and family members' strengths and needs.

Many families face significant challenges to participating in prevention efforts. Practical barriers such as distance from services, reliable transportation, and childcare can reduce family involvement. Even when families have time and financial recourses, distance can be a great barrier when services are provided far from home. Feelings of shame, guilt, and inadequacy, as well as being blamed, can also keep parents from trying to find services for their child.

> Many rural communities are working diligently to provide holistic services for all families. Medical family practice clinics in rural areas are joining with mental health professionals to better serve both individuals and families. Doctors in such settings can much more easily refer and influence service delivery for families when a mental health professional is across the hall rather than miles away.

When children are served in their home communities, treatment is typically office-based and mental health agencies have historically focused on individual therapy. Transportation and complicated lives and schedules account for missed appointments and unavailable family members who could be important to the process of working toward change. Multiple service providers may be involved with the same family and have little or no communication with each other, and they may not be working toward the same goals.

Some youth are placed in residential treatment facilities significant distances from their homes, sometimes in other states. Financial limitations impose transportation barriers and time constraints to meaningful participation in treatment. Tightly packed schedules also limit both visitation and time for family meetings.

Treatment settings for youth who have behaved violently can be an intimidating and even scary places for families. Communication can be intimidating and disrespectful when language used by service providers requires a glossary to understand it. Subtle elements of disregard and disdain may come across in staff attitudes toward parents. Settings in which space limitations threaten confidentiality can restrict development of the safety and trust necessary to build collaborative relationships.

Historical emphasis on residential care has only recently begun to give way to community-based services. Even community-based programs can focus on individual and group therapy and not involve families. Putting youth with behavioral problems together in juvenile justice settings, schools, and community programs often reinforces unwanted behaviors (Dodge et al., 2006). Yet youth who behave violently are brought together in group therapy, due to time constraints and financial reasons, regardless of evidence indicating that group therapy with delinquent youth is ineffective (Dishion, McCord, & Poulin, 1999; Henggeler et al., 2009). Logistical concerns about getting family members to attend office-based sessions abound. Many services are still provided through traditional office visits scheduled for "talk" therapy.

Marissa, a 15-year-old girl participating in a family systems evaluation, responded to a question about her older brother Ron's violence by stating, "I don't want him in the house at this moment. I don't want him here because I'm sick and tired of my little brothers hiding because they are afraid. Every time he says he'll work on things he doesn't. I don't want to be there [for family meetings]. I just don't want Ronnie home.

"He walked up to me and said I'm sorry for this, this, and this, and the program thinks it went fine but it didn't. In the reports they only listen to his side of the story but they never ask me. I feel nobody listens to me when I tell people I feel unsafe. And they don't ask me, and they make me really angry.

"Most people come here and assume everything is peachy. Ronnie comes here with a bad attitude and acts like nothing happened. I'm very, very sick of him. He targets mom and me more than anyone else when he's around. He said he's afraid of women and that's why he targets them. That's ridiculous. I just don't want him home because I'm afraid that might happen again."

When asked if the bad things that happened come up when Ron is around she said, "Yes, it happens a lot of the time."

A program's failure to provide basic introductory information and expectations for family involvement can further hinder already hesitant parents from initiating and maintaining contact. Lack of a defined treatment structure and goals for family involvement can cause confusion, discouragement, and disconnection among family members and can disrupt the process of change.

While many agency staff members provide tremendous support, care, and concern for these youth and their families, some have difficulty doing so. It is not unusual to hear well-meaning service providers refer to families in derogatory terms, engage in parent blaming, and make excuses for not involving parents in services. Behind closed doors, in clinical supervision, some staff share fears about families. Some struggle with perceptions of aggression or hostility attributed to parents and extended family members. Unprepared service providers may cower in response to strong emotions displayed by family members instead of expecting them and providing a practiced and measured response. Conversely, service providers may respond defensively or punitively when not adequately trained to provide an optimal response. Periodically family members do threaten or behave abusively towards service providers and immediate action should be taken. Most often family members are overwhelmed by emotions about the violence and are in desperate need of compassionate action.

Service providers seldom receive adequate specialized training for responding therapeutically to both youth and families. Staff may characterize a lack of family involvement as "sabotage" by clients and parents, when agencies have made little effort to engage family members in warm, genuine, empathic, and nonjudgmental ways. When service providers do not directly ask for family members' opinions, false assumptions may wreck havoc on treatment. The following example illustrates how a youth's sister complained about staff's incorrect assumption that things were okay with her.

Service Provider Challenges

A range of personal issues can also impact interactions among service providers and families and greatly influence outcomes. While they are also addressed in Chapter 10, definitions and some information is provided here.

Parallel process is the simultaneous experience of similar feelings, attitudes, and behavior in two or more situations. Parallel processes occur when two experiences appear related to each other in some way. When service providers have a history of violence in their own life they may struggle to address situations similar to their own experience. When service providers do not maintain awareness of such challenges they are at risk of responding in ways that are not helpful to the youth and family.

Transference is a reproduction of emotions in which a client substitutes a service provider for another person in the youth's life, or a family member's life. Sometimes a youngster knows this is happening and tells a worker who the service provider reminds them of. Sometimes a youth or family member is not conscious of behaving in such a way. When service providers begin to wonder why a youth or family member is behaving towards the service provider in an odd or confusing way it is important to ask if the service provider reminds them of someone else, and if so, who. Such discussions can clarify transference and help everyone understand what is going on and how to effectively manage the situation.

> For no apparent reason Lucas began getting gruff with a service provider and told the service provider she reminded Lucas of one of his teacher's. The service provider asked, "how so?" and Lucas said she talked and sounded like the teacher. He went on to express displeasure about the teacher's perceived harshness towards him. The service provider asked about differences between her and the teacher and explored how Lucas might keep the two separate in his mind. Lucas agreed to bring it up whenever he thought about it and was willing to have the service provider bring it up when she experienced it so he was clear that the service provider was not the teacher and did not want to judge him in any way.

Transference is not a bad thing; it's just something for everyone to be aware of so service providers can support youth and family members in making sense of the experience. Everyone can learn how to pay attention to what's going on so they can become clear about the impact of transference. They can learn how to figure out how other people impact them and the part such relationships may play in stopping violence.

When it comes to youth violence prevention, gender may influence certain types of transference. Statistics show that men are most often involved in violence, so it follows that male service providers, simply because they are men, may remind youth or family members of someone who behaved violently in the client's past. Female service providers may be more likely to remind a youth of a female adult they may blame for not protecting them when they were little. Either way, clients may behave toward these service providers in ways that indicate unexplained fear, anger, or pain. On the other hand, service providers can also remind clients of other adults who were particularly kind to them in the past, and the clients may behave with unexplained familiarity. Talking about transference helps youth understand how it can impact relationships.

Transference can be burdensome for service providers and weigh heavy on relationships with the youth and families they serve. Being viewed as a bad guy often goes against the very core of a service provider's desire to do good. Even when not seen as a bad guy, interacting with false familiarity can make service providers feel uncomfortable.

Counter-transference occurs when a service provider reproduces emotions and substitutes a client for another person in the worker's life. If a youth or family member reminds a service provider of someone they know personally and the service provider interacts with the youth or family member as though they were that person, all kinds of problems can occur.

Acknowledging counter-transference is easy to do. A service provider can simply say to himself or herself, "Wow, this person reminds me of (whoever the person is)." With such acknowledgment comes an ability to state the challenge and address it as need be.

Parallel processes, transference, and counter-transference are a normal part of service delivery. Openly addressing each one whenever it comes up can strengthen connections with youth and families and help reduce confusion that might lead to problems in the helping relationship.

Genuine Connection

To engage means to establish a meaningful contact or connection with someone. Therapeutic engagement refers to a shared commitment between service providers and family members to actively support a child's effort to stop harm.

In order to stop violence, the first priority is to connect, or engage, with all participants in such a way that they are motivated to make positive changes in their lives. This task requires the involvement of all service providers who touch the lives of children. School personnel, community leaders, mental health clinicians, medical staff, youth care workers, and agency administrators are challenged to provide a congruent approach for all children and family members in order to provide a comprehensive therapeutic message that reflects a research-based philosophy of care.

The point of such collaboration is to affirm a clear message that loving and caring adults can work together in a youth's best interest. Providing a range of services for families and maintaining a commitment to a genuine connection can occur in a variety of creative and cost-effective ways. Genuinely connecting with youth and families is the most important step to ensure successful outcomes. Engagement involves introducing and modeling interaction based upon respect, care, and concern for others. As previously mentioned, a nonjudgmental attitude, warmth, empathy, and genuineness are factors that influence successful therapeutic relationships (Duncan et al., 2009).

> Early in treatment, 13-year-old Anthony could not settle down to talk with his father and new therapist. Knowing that Anthony was diagnosed with ADHD, had anxiety about treatment, and had just came home from school, the therapist allowed him to wander in and out of the living room. Anthony was clearly listening to the discussion as he interjected relevant information into the conversation. While he was coming and going from the room, he was stopping at the dining-room table where some craft materials were laid out. Before too long Anthony came into the living room with a homemade gift for the therapist. Using a stack of twist ties, he created a bendable figure of a man and presented it to the therapist. Anthony was very good at creating things out of just about anything and his pride in his finished product was clear. The information he wanted to offer the therapist was not always something he could put into words. Throughout treatment Anthony offered homemade projects as signs of engagement and as a means of helping the therapist and his father to see his strengths when discussions about changing problematic behaviors seemed too difficult.

Engaging families in treatment is not simply a superficial conversation to introduce treatment. Nor is it a marketing ploy, or cheerleading effort, to convince wary family members that their child's treatment program has all the answers to their family's problems. Therapeutic engagement is not compliance. Engagement occurs when participants genuinely join together to stop all violence. It is challenging, rewarding, and can make work much more fun while influencing successful outcomes.

Successful connection embraces the distrust and resistance that often occur in the early stages of treatment with youth and their families. Open recognition of ambivalence or resistance to addressing violence creates a context of respect, care, and concern for building trust in working relationships. Children and parents offer subtle cues that they are beginning to engage with a therapist. Service providers learn to identify subtle behavior indicating engagement. These subtle behaviors can be powerful indicators of potential for change. Addressing ambivalence and resistance are core components of Motivational Interviewing (Miller & Rollnick, 2002). Individualized treatment begins when service providers connect with a child, even when the child is running in circles around the house.

Family members can be prepared for a range of positive and negative feelings brought about through violence. Providing an environment that invites people to address pain in emotionally and physically safe ways may prevent them from acting out in harmful ways. Service providers and families have the ability to collaborate in the best interest of family cohesion and community safety. Courage and honesty help to address and heal the pain. **Practically speaking, when service providers embrace a family's struggle to take a stand against violence and join with them as supportive advocates, they all become a powerful force for good.**

Collaborating with Families in Treatment

Therapeutic engagement and genuine connection are the foundation for collaboration with youth and families. A collaborative approach is founded on the premise that youth often face the task of harm reduction in the very environment that influenced their initial decisions to behave violently. Historically, youth have been alone in their efforts to stop violence. Involving family members has greatly influenced successful efforts to prevent youth violence.

The strengths, resources, social support, living environment, and experiences of both the youth and his or her family members all contribute to change (Duncan et al., 2009). Service providers obtain such important information while actively listening to everything family members say. This occurs while promoting new understanding of behavior, embracing difficult emotions, and working to stop violence.

Collaboration can be enhanced through a respectful and courteous process of introducing clearly defined information and structure, such as program descriptions, handbooks, policies, and procedures. Service providers who model open, direct communication and desired behavior for youth and family members have greater success engaging families in treatment.

Jonah told new service providers that he wanted his imprisoned father to be an active part of his treatment and social support network. Upon investigation, corrections personnel revealed that Jonah's father was incarcerated for sexually abusing his daughter, the youth's sister. Of equal concern was information in the court reports indicating that Jonah may have been involved in the molestation. The young man expressed a high level of anger when the treatment team did not support his father's involvement with his son until the father was actively taking responsibility for his own criminal behavior and participating in the prison sexual offender treatment program. Jonah's therapist and other service providers worked diligently with Jonah to identify and involve other family members who could act as role models and mentors to provide clear messages opposing sexual aggression.

Engaging Jonah and his family involved assessing dangerousness, acknowledging child sexual abuse, addressing anger brought about by destructive family ties and loyalty, supporting the youth's ambivalence about criminal behavior, and helping him explore other avenues for support and encouragement. If it weren't for exploring this connection with the incarcerated father, Jonah's abuse of his sister may not have been uncovered during treatment.

One critical element of collaboration involves identifying and assessing potential social support network members who will help a youth throughout treatment. Engagement, connection, and collaboration take place between service providers and families, and among family members themselves. Sometimes results can be surprising when exploration reveals unexpected support, or unanticipated problems as indicated by Jonah's story.

Fully exploring family relationships addresses the important balance between restricting and encouraging family involvement so that success-ful outcomes are promoted rather than threatened. Just because a parent or family member struggles with substance abuse or mental illness or is incarcerated does not mean that that family member cannot make impor-tant contributions to stopping violence. The process of thoroughly exam-ining important relationships shows how vital assessment is for treatment planning.

Systems theory is central to a collaborative approach. Maintaining a belief that the whole is greater than the sum of its parts illustrates the impor-tance of engaging an entire family in a commitment to stop harm. This philosophy embraces an assumption that many people working together have a greater opportunity for success than a few working in isolation. It also shows how parents actively influence similar emotional states in their children (Stien & Kendall, 2004). For instance, when parents consistently express high levels of anger children are vulnerable to doing the same. While fear may influence a parent's rage, a child may be debilitated by the same emotion and appear numb and withdrawn. Sharing similar emotional states does not necessarily mean sharing similar symptoms. While negative parent-child experiences hinder development and brain functioning, posi-tive interactions can promote healing, stress reduction, memory retention, maturation, well-being, and healing. Such interaction has a ripple effect in which all family members can embrace and support a commitment to stop all harm within the entire family system. This approach has potential to influence intergenerational healing from an array of painful experiences that may enhance long-term successful outcomes. **Practically speaking, when parents model positive communication and problem-solving, chil-dren are more apt to do the same. This is violence prevention.**

By slowing down we get there faster. Understaffed programs and over-loaded schedules place extreme limitations on meaningful time spent with parents and caregivers. Many families have weathered painful experiences that have stirred up difficult feelings within their family. By taking time to explore parental concerns and listening to fears, worries, ambivalence, and resistance, service providers can help treatment begin more smoothly. While time is a premium in all programs, thoughtful management of time with youth and their families can actually streamline improvement. While everyone slows down to grapple with delicate issues, maintaining focus on clearly defined goals for change prevents unnecessary diversions that can delay progress.

Asking family members about their experiences and perceptions, rather than attempting to tell them what they should be doing, can help them feel valued throughout the healing process. Well-meaning service providers can confuse responsibility to support families with the myth that they are supposed to "fix" each youth and his or her, family. It is important to remember that education does not equal therapeutic change. Telling people what is in their best interest does not guarantee they will heed such advice. As a reminder to practice this change, one treatment team created a sign for the staff lounge that simply said "Ask, don't tell."

While treatment challenges youth to stop harm, families receive support to make sense of how violence has impacted their lives. These youth and their families learn to destroy powerful secrets about violence that may have influenced the family for generations. Treatment can addresses struggles with abusive use of power, control, connection, and secrecy that have often dominated the lives of these youth and their families.

Collaborating with family members in the creation of treatment goals, and monitoring progress toward those goals, solidifies a working relationship based on constructive interdependence. Such an approach can reduce resistance and create a context for reciprocity and mutual affirmation. As youth progress, families are encouraged to focus on reconciliation through atonement and forgiveness. When service providers work together to provide such collaboration, everyone benefits. Youth and family members get their needs met and experience satisfaction in a job well done.

Models for Optimal Engagement

As introduced in Chapter 3, Motivational Interviewing is a therapeutic philosophy designed to promote success and maintain change over time (Miller & Rollnick, 2002). Practical application of Motivational Interviewing is addressed in Chapter 6. The language of change comes from the youth's own words as he or she voices desires for things to be different. The first priority is to engage all participants in such a way that they are motivated to consider change. Change often begins with ambivalence or contradictory feelings. Youth may hold on to negative values and beliefs about violence while beginning to see value in an opposite viewpoint. Service providers can engage youth around the pros and cons of the decision "to change or not to change." The *T.O.P.* * *Workbook for Taming Violence and Sexual Aggression* refers to this as "getting into trouble versus staying out of trouble" (Schladale, 2002). Helping youth and family members to think about what life might look like if they stop violence allows service providers to guide youth through a process of change created in the youth's own words.

Alan Jenkins's *Invitations to Responsibility* (1990) uses respectful language and "irresistible invitations" to convince youth that taking responsibility for harmful behavior promotes honor, integrity, and pro-social behavior. This model engages youth by helping them look at respectful and disrespectful characteristics of significant others in their life. Through this process youth are motivated to consider becoming more like the respectful people they know. Youth are supported in taming violence and/or sexual aggression through a quest to become upstanding and honorable community members.

Service providers are responsible for communicating hope and a vision for success to families who may be overwhelmed and demoralized by violence. In addition to the violence, families are often challenged by a community's response to it. When youth violence becomes public knowledge families are often unprepared for the experience. They may be humbled by unexpected support, horrified by condemnation or surprised by a range of responses they receive from a variety of people. Genuine connection begins with a welcoming ritual that introduces treatment and provides hope and expectations for change. Initial conversations focus on strengths, particularly those that may have been overlooked by the family and other service providers.

> While facilitating an evaluation with a large blended family, the therapist met with the parents to assess each family member's motivation for change. The three adults worked together to create a chart identifying each child's interest in stopping harm, and the parent's confidence level of each child's readiness, willingness, and ability to stop it. Seeing the completed chart helped the parents identify the range of motivation in the family and prepare accordingly. It also helped them develop realistic expectations for change. They reported that they had never looked at it this way and created several ideas about how they might best support each child. After the evaluation family members were invited to draw a picture of what the family would look like when all the violence stopped. This was done to create a vision for success. The therapist worked with all family members individually and collectively as they revealed a wide range of motivation, ambivalence, and resistance to change. Each family member was consistently invited to take responsibility for his or her role in any violence and make amends for the pain it caused to others. This was done through a process described in Chapter 6.

Families are then invited to create a vision for their lives based on health and well-being. Service providers work with families to create a service and safety plan using family members' words so the plan is clearly their own. Youth and family members are additionally asked to identify anyone they might trust to provide support as they receive services. They then explore the role that these other individuals might take, and contact them to participate.

Conclusion

Compassion is the radicalism of our time.
His Holiness the Dalai Lama

Genuine connection with all youth, families, and social support network members is so important because it provides an opportunity to establish meaningful relationships. Change occurs within the context of these relationships. Development of a therapeutic alliance allows individuals to find courage and the capacity to make successful changes in their lives. Positive engagement with families is the basis for creating and maintaining a vision, plan, and avenue for lifelong violence prevention.

Communicating with everyone in warm, nonjudgmental, empathic, and genuine ways is the quickest and easiest route to successful outcomes. Research-based treatment philosophies provide a way of motivating people to change and are most likely to impact lifelong health and well-being.

Recommendations

- Involve families, teachers, coaches, religious leaders, and anyone else willing to help youth stop violence.
- Show respect, care, and concern to develop trust.
- Engage everyone so they are motivated to integrate positive change into their lives.
- Assume a desire to change even though it is seldom evident during initial contact.
- Ask permission to talk about sensitive issues.
- Allow the family to lead the process.
- Embrace distrust and resistance that is normal in the early stages of treatment.
- Recognize barriers to addressing pain.
- Advocate for and support all family members in using untapped strengths and competencies to prevent further violence.
- Expect disclosures of severe trauma that may include family disruption, child abuse, neglect, poverty, violence, substance abuse, racism, accidents, and illness.

- Ensure that each family member is emotionally prepared to address the violence,
- Invite all family members to attend to their pain in emotionally and physically safe ways (affect regulation) so they no longer need to act it out harmfully (dysregualtion),
- Honor histories of trauma in treatment so youth and family members can make sense of how the trauma influenced harm and, most importantly, how such information can help heal pain.
- Help family members define the type of people and family they want to become,

Resources

Motivational Interview: www.motivationalinterview.org

Motivational Interviewing: www.motivationalinterviewing.org

Narrative Practice: www.narrativepractice.com

* This chapter is adapted in part from: Schladale, J. (2006). Family matters: The importance of engaging families in treatment with youth who have caused sexual harm. In R. Longo & D. Prescott (Eds.), *Current perspectives: Working with sexually aggressive youth and youth with sexual behavior problems.* Holyoke, MA: NEARI Press.

Chapter 5

Assessing Family Strengths and Needs

It's no trick loving somebody at their best.
Love is loving them at their worst.

Tom Stoppard

Overview

Whenever and wherever youth violence occurs, a quick response with a clearly defined and coordinated plan for short-, medium-, and long-term assessment is important. Police, juvenile justice personnel, social service providers, designated school personnel, and qualified mental health professionals quickly assess for short-term safety. Once an initial safety plan is in place, mid-range planning involves decisions about potential evaluation needs for the youth, his or her family, and others impacted by the violence. This document becomes the basis for all service delivery.

Additionally, ongoing assessment involves measuring the progress made by the youth and his or her family toward service goals. Finally, transition assessments document completion of tasks when services change, are suspended, or are terminated. This chapter addresses all types of assessment for youth violence prevention with practical templates for obtaining and documenting pertinent information.

Screening, assessment, and evaluations predominantly involve secondary and tertiary prevention.

Objectives

By the end of this chapter we hope you will:
- Know what factors may indicate a need for violence prevention.
- Have a working definition of and understand differences in evaluation and assessment.
- Use family systems and ecological evaluations to guide all service provision.
- Influence your community in using effective evaluation and assessment for youth violence prevention.

What's the point?

What does it really mean to assess family strengths and needs, and what does it have to do with youth violence prevention? We know that focusing on strengths and positive youth development is the best way of getting kids to stop harm. Everyone responds better to praise than to criticism. The object of assessing strengths and needs is to focus on what individuals and families are already doing well and to build on those strengths in order to stop harm.

Why evaluate a family when a child is the one at risk of being violent? All children have a family. Sometimes children are disconnected from family through divorce, death, termination of parental rights, substance abuse, or abandonment. Strengths and vulnerabilities can be passed from parents to their children. Parents are sometimes blamed for their children's harmful behavior. Assessment is intended to identify what works and what does not work so a plan for success can be made.

Definitions

Screening: A systematic way of looking at an identified population in order to consider needs for intervention. This is primary prevention.

Evaluation: A process of documenting a comprehensive review and accumulation of information regarding a specific youth's status at a given time. The process involves face-to-face interviews with youth, family members, and designated others such as pertinent extended family and service providers. The purpose is to collect information for initial or transitional service planning. Objective measures, when available, should be used. Holistic evaluation includes all areas of a youth's life.

Assessment: An ongoing process of face-to-face interactions and observations of youth and family members in order to collect information for ongoing service delivery. Assessment is the continuous process of monitoring a youth's status in order to thoughtfully plan and intervene in the most effective manner across all service delivery. Objective measures, when available, should be used.

Both evaluation and assessment are secondary and tertiary prevention.

Assessment scales: Scientific tools used for identifying specific information to help understand strengths and needs. Assessment scales must be valid and reliable (as proven through research) in order to accurately show what they claim to measure. Examples include topics such as intelligence levels, depression, assertiveness, etc.

Protocol: A specific procedure and/or process required by research findings, organizations, and legal entities.

There is a big difference between identifying risk factors and judging families. Lack of ability does not necessarily indicate lack of motivation. An inability to prevent youth violence may simply show a lack of support and resources due to difficult circumstances. Assessment provides a clearer picture of how a youth and his or her family might stop violence and enjoy health and well-being.

When people are good at something they are more likely to enjoy doing it, potentially more easily motivated to practice, and, in turn, more apt to get better at it. Like doing well in sports, in school, or in art, drama, dance, or music, when people build on a natural talent they just keep getting better and better.

Exploring strengths is the bedrock for building more strengths. Asking, "what do you think has worked well so far?" and "what do you think might help?" supports families in identifying both their unique strengths and the ways they may build on them. **Practically speaking, the more strengths a youth and family can identify the more they can focus on the positive. This has potential to result in better attitudes, improved skills, and less negative behavior.**

Identifying strengths can make it easier to develop more strengths from those originally identified. For example, if family members have a sense of humor they can build on that strength through practice. They can learn to use respectful humor to deal with a range of situations. When they become skilled in the use of well-placed humor, they can explore using it to deflect tension as a way of de-escalating potential violence. Shakespeare wrote that, "Many a truth is said in jest." When family members learn to speak their truth through heartfelt concern with a bit of loving humor, violence can decrease. Such an approach enhances competency, confidence, health, and well-being.

Clarifying needs is a way individuals and families, as a whole, direct service delivery. Asking questions like, "what do you think is important for us to be thinking about?" and "what do you think needs to change?" tells service providers what a youth and family thinks is needed to best help stop harm. When families work together to address identified needs, youth may feel less blamed and more supported. A family becomes stronger when responsibility for stopping violence is shared by everyone.

Strengths are a solid foundation on which health and wellbeing are built. Needs are a blueprint that shows where extra support is required to construct a solid family structure lasting many generations.

It's a Bit Complicated ...

Clarifying definitions may help with prevention.

Screening is primary prevention that systematically identifies potential vulnerabilities for youth violence in the general population in order to consider needs for intervention. It can occur in a variety of ways in a wide array of settings. Early identification is the first step toward effective youth violence prevention. Programs serving youth and families can screen youth with questions designed to identify vulnerabilities toward violence.

Parents are primary screeners for their children. When they suspect harm parents can talk to people, such as school teachers or doctors, who may be able to confirm their suspicions or have suggestions about where to get help. What signs should everyone look for that indicate potential for harm? Some signs are: interaction with deviant peers (Henggeler, et al., 2009); anti-social behavior (Stien & Kendall, 2004); lashing out toward others or withdrawing and shutting down emotionally; marital conflict and poor communication; harsh or inconsistent discipline; poor parental supervision; witnessing violence; bullying, or being the target of bullying; and being arrested before age 14 (Thornton, et al, 2002).

Child-serving agencies may screen kids and families through informal questioning or formal protocols. Childcare programs such as Head Start, schools, pediatricians, boys and girls clubs, and health clinics may all have ways of looking out for those youth who might benefit from extra support to prevent violence from occurring. Evidence-based practices such as Nurse-Family Partnerships and The Incredible Years are well-established primary violence prevention efforts (Olds, Hill, Milhalic, & O'Brien, 2006).

Evaluation is a process of documenting a comprehensive review and accumulation of information regarding a specific youth's status at a given time. Prior to intervention, a thorough evaluation should be initiated in order to best meet a youth's needs for services. In addition to individual factors, a family systems and ecological evaluation explores elements of optimum development and individual and environmental protective factors that can influence outcomes.

Assessment is an ongoing process of face-to-face interaction and observation of youth and family members, in order to effectively plan ongoing services. Assessment can be done when adults are concerned about potential for violence or when a child is causing harm. Further assessment takes place at established intervals to assess treatment progress and address any new needs that may arise. Children and families are constantly changing. Ongoing assessment can track changes so service delivery can be altered to best meet current needs.

Once services begin, ongoing assessment of competency development provides an avenue for monitoring change and is vital to harm reduction. This information guides service and safety planning and delivery.

Assessment scales are scientific tools used for identifying specific information to help understand strengths and needs. Assessment scales are used in both evaluations and assessment. Variables, such as involvement with deviant peers, impulsive and anti-social behaviors, and family disruption, are used to assess risk. There are a lot of scales used to measure a range of variables in order to gain greater understanding of a youth's potential for violence.

While everyone wants to know if and when youth pose a risk to themselves or to the community there are limited ways of determining this (Mulvey & Iselin, 2008). Many scales can influence service delivery and interventions but cannot guarantee future behavior. There is no scientific evidence to define what constitutes low, medium or high risk, yet those terms are generally accepted conventional wisdom. Since we cannot definitively categorize risk levels, there is no point in perpetuating the myth that we can. Holding onto conventional wisdom about risk prevents people from facing facts.

> Charles was suspended from school after being involved in a fight in the cafeteria. It was not his first fight on school grounds. The school referred him for services at a local mental health agency. As part of a holistic evaluation, the mental health clinician completed a CAFAS and requested records from the school including an IQ assessment and academic functioning scale. These tools helped the clinician determine how to best provide services for Charles based on his strengths and needs.

One such myth concerns out of home placement, which is addressed at length in Chapter 9. Since evidence indicates that most violent youth can successfully be managed in the community, acknowledging that youth, victims, families, and communities are not necessarily being served in the most effective ways is very important (Henggeler et al., 2009; Scott & Steinberg, 2008).

While researchers continue to study validity and reliability of assessment scales for these youth and their families, service providers are challenged to ethically conduct evaluations and ongoing assessment based on current scientific evidence.

While current scales are unable to predict future violence, there are many assessment scales that contribute vital information for service delivery. One example is called CAFAS, the Child and Adolescent Functioning Assessment Scale (Hodges & Kim, 2000) which helps determine the level of services needed. School psychologists have a host of scales they use for things like IQ and learning disabilities. The Beck Depression Inventory (Beck, Steer, & Brown, 1996) can help service providers who are concerned about a youth's or family member's potential harm to self.

Assessing strengths and needs in all aspects of a youth's life establishes a foundation for lifelong health and well-being. An *evaluation* brings all elements of assessment into a cohesive document at a designated point in time. Current evidence shows that a holistic, ecological evaluation addressing all parts of a youth's life can inform disposition, service planning, and supervision in least restrictive settings and influence successful outcomes (Henggeler et. al., 2009; Schladale, 2008). Gathering information from a wide variety of perspectives is important to create a realistic picture of what is currently working and not working in the lives of youth and families. As change occurs, new information is gathered and plans are revised.

What Do We Want to Know?

Primary and Secondary Prevention

It is important to have clear questions we want answered when assessing strengths and needs. Primarily we want to know what prevents youth violence from ever happening. The short answer is optimal child development, which was addressed in Chapter 2.

Federally funded programs offered through the public school systems in the United States screen and assess children from birth to 3 years old.

This is done so that children identified with any developmental delay can get services to help them catch up with their age cohorts. The programs also help identify educational services that can best meet children's needs. Screening tools such as the DECA, the Devereux Early Childhood Assessment for Infants and Toddlers (LeBuffe & Naglieri, 1999), and IDA, the Infant-Toddler Developmental Assessment (Provence et al., 1999), are used to determine if any developmental problems exist and, if so, how to best address them. The screening and assessment protocol looks at cognitive abilities, social and emotional development, speech, language, gross motor skills, fine motor skills, vision, and hearing.

Additionally, secondary prevention screening addresses these questions: are any kids and/or families more likely than the general population to experience youth violence? If so, what do we do to prevent it? These questions were discussed in Chapter 3, and in the previous section. More information about effective screening can be obtained at: colorado. edu/cspv/blueprints/modelprograms.

Secondary and Tertiary Prevention

When there is a threat of violence (secondary prevention), but it is not actually occurring, the question is, "How can it be prevented right now?" Depending on the setting, this may or may not involve specially trained professionals. Regardless of who is witnessing the escalation, bystanders are immediately assessing danger and acting in response to their thoughts, feelings, and physiological reactions, all of which influence behavior and outcomes. Assessing a potentially violent situation greatly impacts whether or not harm is prevented. When violence is prevented participants have a responsibility to review the situation and create a plan to prevent future escalation.

When youth violence does occur the first priority is to immediately stop it (tertiary prevention). The question is, "How can it be stopped right now?" Hopefully the answer is to follow an established protocol or safety plan for doing so. As in escalation, immediate assessment is primarily an internal process in each witness's body, and greatly determines outcome.

Safety. Safety must be established before trying to understand a particular act of violence, or plan for long-term change. Assessing safety is immediate and ongoing. When aggression is escalating, or violence occurs, the primary focus must be on reestablishing safety as quickly as possible. Once this is done, considerations of longer-term safety needs can be addressed.

Crisis Assessment. Assessment in response to escalation and violence predominantly involves immediate safety planning for both the youth and the environment in which the escalation or violence occurred, such as a school, playground, or home. The goal is to reestablish physical and emotional safety as quickly as possible for everyone involved. This is a short-term assessment that may be very informal and communicated with an immediate written or spoken statement, or that may require formal documentation through incident reports or specific protocols. A short-term assessment brings up the question of whether, or not, an evaluation is called for.

A truly balanced approach that values restorative justice involves consideration of victim needs for treatment and safety. Such information is critical when community-based services are a consideration, and/or a victim resides in close proximity. Assessing safety is vital in such situations. Decisions about treatment setting and residence in relation to victims are vital to maintaining the safety of both the youth and any victims (Chaffin, Bonner & Pierce, 2003; Schladale, 2006, 2008).

The Evaluation Process

Evaluations attempt to answer a variety of questions depending on who wants the evaluation. Social services and juvenile justice professionals often want to know what factors contributed to the youths' violence and where they can best be served in order to stop it as soon as possible, and for the rest of the youth's life. Parents often want to know how they can most effectively help stop it. School personnel want to know the same things. When asked why she was requesting an evaluation one case manager stated, "This evaluation is to see where Chris and his family are at this point and to find out what services can best help Chris eliminate harm."

Once a need for services is determined a family systems and ecological evaluation may be indicated. *Family systems simply refers to everyone a youth considers family. Human ecology is the study of individuals in relationship to others and the environment.* In this case an evaluation is attempting to understand youth in the context of their families, schools, and other community activities such as churches, sports. and leisure activities. A child's ecology includes biological and extended family, relevant neighbors, and church, school, and community members. It takes into consideration issues of gender, race, socio-economic status, religion, and culture. An evaluation including such information provides information about safety from many perspectives that can inform successful service delivery.

A crisis assessment began when Carissa frantically called her minister when she found out her older son, David, had sexually abused her younger son, Marco. Carissa was devastated and angry so she arranged for David to stay at his grandfather's. This ensured Marco's safety and gave Carissa time to think about what happened and calm down. The minister encouraged Carissa to call the state child abuse hotline and she spoke with a protective services worker. They created a plan to begin an investigation. Carissa knew the sexual abuse happened at night in the boys' bedroom while she was sleeping. The next morning Carissa borrowed a rollaway bed from a neighbor and set it up in her bedroom, installed an alarm on David's bedroom door, and contacted the police. When the protective services worker came to the house, a safety plan was already being put into place. Neither child was taken away from home and the protective service worker made a referral for home-based therapy. This ensured that services would take place right at the source of the problem. Ongoing communication among the home-based therapist, the protective services worker, and Carissa was scheduled. When any safety concerns surfaced, more frequent collaboration took place.

A need for evaluation is indicated when minimal, inadequate, or no documentation is available, such as the first time a youth is referred for services, or when available information is outdated. When service providers know a youth and family, previous evaluations and assessments may be adequate to begin service delivery. Based on the fluid nature of childhood development it is recommended that evaluations be considered valid for a maximum of one year. A lot can change in a year's time, and it is important to have up-to-date information about everyone receiving services. Trained professionals knowledgeable about current research regarding trauma, youth violence, and family systems theory, and who can obtain a good understanding of the child's life and the violence that occurred, should facilitate evaluations.

Historically youth behaving violently were evaluated and treated individually, without their family. Such evaluations and services neglected critically important components of the family and community experiences that may have played a role in violence beginning and/or continuing in their lives. Research described in earlier chapters influenced and made significant improvements to evaluations.

Evaluation is not an objective and neutral experience unrelated to a therapeutic process. Youth and family members make decisions about open and honest participation throughout an evaluation based on their interactions with the evaluator. Obtaining the truth about violence requires skill in therapeutic engagement (remember Motivational Interviewing) and thoughtful use of that knowledge. Creating a calm and soothing setting for truth-telling can help people share information important for prevention.

Optimistic and enthusiastic service providers who instill hope and expectation for change, while expressing genuine warmth and empathy in a nonjudgmental way, are more likely to influence successful outcomes (Henderson et al., 1996; Duncan et al., 2009; Miller & Rollnick, 2002). Engagement skills can greatly impact the assessment process, the content, and, ultimately, the outcome.

Juvenile courts may request pre- or post-sentence evaluations for the purpose of disposition and/or referral. *Disposition is a term legal systems use to describe what is going to be done legally.* Child welfare organizations also request evaluations that include recommended services for youth and families. These evaluations are very specific in nature. Important topics and source of information are:

Establishing a standardized format for evaluation can make this work a lot easier. Everyone should be able to easily read, understand, and use the evaluation for prevention as quickly as possible in the least restrictive setting. In addition to government entities such as state, county, or judicial jurisdictions, private organizations such as managed care or child-serving organizations may require standardized evaluation formats.

Topics for Evaluation

- Review and documentation of background information and history
- Optimum elements of child development
- Individual and environmental strengths and resources
- Internal and environmental protective factors
- Developmental history and milestones
- Sexual knowledge and history
- History of trauma, abuse, and/or victimization of youth and family members
- History of harmful behavior
- Current harmful situation
- Youth's version of harm
- Victim's version of harm
- Witness's version of harm
- Dynamics of harmful behavior
- Psychological functioning
- Educational and intellectual functioning
- Ecological context (factors that address a youth's relationships and experiences with family, social support network members, peers, school, community activities, etc.)
- Identification of any non-related persons who are seen as important to the youth (social support network)
- Factors indicating potential for further harm
- Conclusions/recommendations

Sources of Information for Evaluation

- Youth being evaluated
- Youth's family members
- Victim (when indicated)
- Victim's family (when indicated)
- Social support network
- Court records
- Police report
- School records
- Medical records
- Mental health records
- Previous treatment and evaluation records

Context

Family systems and ecological evaluations emphasize inclusion of biological and extended family, as well as relevant neighbors, and church, school, and community members. In all ecological contexts youth should be assessed for: strengths; the ability to perceive and access social support; resilience; social learning; values and beliefs; and vulnerabilities.

Effective family systems and ecological evaluations provide an understanding of:
- How a youth came to behave violently
- Family strengths and vulnerabilities that can influence outcomes
- Protective factors that can reduce risk
- Vulnerabilities for continued harm

Family systems and ecological evaluations provide important information about risk factors for harm. Many studies show that histories of childhood abuse, most often experienced within the family, and witnessing family violence can be connected with harm to self and others. Problems with social interactions, peer relationships. and isolation have been identified as significant risk factors for youth violence. Additionally, anti-social behaviorsand unstable home lives are predictors of further harm. (Henggeler et al., 2009; Mulvey & Iselin, 2008)

Evaluation Template

A template is a preset format for a document. A generic evaluation template is available at www.resourcesforresolvingviolence.com. Questionnaires based on several items listed below are provided in the Appendix. Documenting a family systems and ecological evaluation includes the following information. Several of the topics are addressed at length in other chapters, and others are highlighted below.

- Elements of optimum child development
- Strengths and protective factors
- Core competency domains

- Vulnerabilities in families at high risk for youth violence
- Affect regulation
- Static and dynamic risk factors
- Best practices for youth violence prevention
- Motivation for change
- Social support

Static and Dynamic Risk Factors

Static indicates something that cannot change; dynamic indicates something that can change.

Static risk factors are experiences in a child's life that cannot be changed, such as the death or disappearance of a parent. Research refers to this as "family dissolution," and it is a significant risk factor for youth violence.

It is frightening how many young people at risk of youth violence are disconnected from their biological fathers. This phenomenon is so widespread that it appears to be taken for granted and is seldom part of the conversation about youth violence prevention. Whether acknowledged or not, children grieve the loss of family members and are often confused and have unanswered questions about that person. When assessing loss of family members it is vital to explore how the experience has impacted the lives of youth and other family members.

Dynamic risk factors are things like substance abuse and intimate partner violence that can be stopped. Both static and dynamic risk factors cause problems with connection or attachment. Problems with attachment feed violence and aggression.

According to Stien and Kendall in their book *Psychological Trauma and the Developing Brain,* "children who do not experience an intense, loving relationship with at least one person may never feel a shared sense of humanity and are at risk for developing anti-social behaviors" (2004, p. 49). We know that anti-social behavior is one of the most significant predictors of youth violence.

When parents fail to bond with children through adequate sustenance and nurturing, youth establish patterns of self-reliance based on an inability to trust that adults will take care of them. Children growing up in violent places learn that pleasure and pain are closely associated and that safety is an illusion. Such early deficits influence isolation and ineffective ways to manage feelings (affect regulation).

The diagnostic category of Anti-Social Personality Disorder indicates dynamic risk for continued violence. Regardless of specific diagnoses all behaviors indicating disorders of conduct provide cause for concern.

"Association with deviant peers is a powerful predictor of anti-social behavior in adolescents." (Henggeler et al., 2009 p. 153). Exploring a youth's activities with peers is a pertinent dynamic risk factor for ongoing assessment. These risk factors should always be included in both evaluations and assessment.

Best Practices for Youth Violence Prevention

Even though this topic is addressed at length in Chapter 3, information about how to include it in evaluation and assessment is provided here. The Centers for Disease Control and Prevention's four strategies for youth violence prevention are: parent-family based; home visiting; social-cognitive; and mentoring. The majority of children behaving violently remain connected with their families, thus making strategies one and two very significant.

Parents are vital to stopping harm. If children are learning violence at home, home is therefore the best place for them to learn how to stop it. Healing from trauma that influenced decisions to commit acts of violence is best done with family. The Centers for Disease Control and Prevention identify a need to involve parents and address the context in which parenting takes place. Making home visits part of the evaluation process can provide invaluable information about this context.

The third strategy, social-cognitive, involves social learning such as values, attitudes, and interpersonal skills. This strategy involves cognitive restructuring for all family members in order to eliminate values and attitudes that promote harm to self and others. It is the primary foundation for intervention within the family context.

The fourth strategy is mentoring. Children mimic adult behavior. If communities want pro-social children who are learning how to express themselves without causing harm, evaluations need to identify potential mentors and recommend such important connections for vulnerable youth. When assessing role models and mentors it is important to know what research-based resources are available. Big Brothers and Big Sisters is consistently identified as an evidence-based secondary prevention program and others can be found at colorado.edu/blueprints.

Motivation for Change

Assessing motivation for change requires knowledge of both Motivational Interviewing (Miller & Rollnick, 2002) and stages of change (Prochaska, DiClemente, & Norcross, 1992). Evaluating a youth's resistance, ambivalence or motivation can help service providers determine where to begin helping a youth to stop violence.

Social Support

Social support is identified as a primary protective factor for all levels of prevention, and is perhaps the most vital element. Informal community support describes a youth's informal relationships and involvement in leisure activities. Formal community support involves professional services to enhance optimal family functioning. Identifying social support in both individual and family life can provide information about natural supports that can help the family see its way through tough times.

Evaluation Recommendations

In order to maximize effectiveness, evaluation reports should include very specific research-based recommendations, preferably bulleted to promote clarity. The more detailed the recommendations the easier it is for team members to understand the role each can play in prevention. Details also help identify optimal services and service providers. Here is an example of a list of actual recommendations from an evaluation. While these are highly detailed, not all evaluations include such specifics.

An Example of Recommendations from a Family Systems and Ecological Evaluation*

The evaluation was requested to assess a family's ability to maintain safety after youth violence occurred. These recommendations were made in response to a history of family violence that was tearing a young family apart. A high level of detail is provided for clarity and streamlined decision making.

1. Maintain a multidisciplinary, multi-agency team with a designated leader to communicate, coordinate, and organize all interventions. This team should include, but not be limited to, the following people:
   - Mother and stepfather
   - Case Manager
   - Representative, State of Department of Social Services
   - Primary service providers from residential and community services
   - In-home family therapist

2. Assess, establish, and maintain safety and stability in all interactions between all family members.

3. Implement in-home family therapy in order to determine realistic potential for reconciliation, reconnection, and reunification:
   - Require any team members providing family therapy to demonstrate competency in facilitating specialized interventions for addressing the history of family violence, child abuse, and current youth violence.
   - Focus interventions on healing the relational trauma of family violence, affect regulation, youth violence prevention, competency development, and support for pro-social development of both children.
   - Support mother and son in making sense of, and in reconciling, the abuse he experienced at the hands of his father.

- Support family and individual participation in clearly defined psycho education about affect regulation that provides evaluative information on integration of concepts. This should include patterns of harm to self and others.
- Support family and individual participation in clearly defined and structured psycho education about the trauma outcome process that provides evaluative information on integration of concepts. This should include an understanding of the impact of violence and family dissolution; trauma cues; harmful coping strategies; plans for self-regulation; and clearly defined goals for self-care.

4. Maintain individual therapy for son with a therapist specially trained in family violence and able to provide Trauma-Focused Cognitive Behavioral Therapy if indicated. The in-home family therapist, or a community-based therapist, may provide this.

Address the following therapeutic tasks:
- Empathy development acknowledging that son most likely never received empathy from his father prior to termination of paternal visits.
- Support for son as he makes amends to everyone impacted by his harmful behavior.
- Affect regulation.
- Competency development.

5. Facilitate development and maintenance of a social support network to provide practical and emotional help for everyone in the family.

6. Involve son in an evidence-based mentorship program if available.

7. Invite mother to participate in individual therapy to address the impact intimate partner and youth violence has on her life and reduce problematic symptoms.

8. Prepare for family reconciliation, reconnection, and reunification through a structured timeline with ongoing assessment of progress toward such goals. Distinguish among the three elements, as indicated below:

    Reconciliation means to make friendly again, to settle or bring into harmony. It is a process of supporting families in this effort when any family members have behaved harmfully. The goal is healing emotional wounds caused by family violence and abuse. This can occur without reunification.

    Reconnection is the ability of family members to visit in a way that ensures physical and emotional safety for everyone involved. Home visits should be consistently monitored and/or supervised in order to assess for safety and potential for reunification.

    Reunification means to unify again after being divided. Family reunification represents the physical rejoining of family members with a youth who has been removed from the home. It is a complex process that requires reconciliation in order to be successful.

9. Create specific goals for reconciliation and reconnection.
10. Determine if the family qualifies for High Fidelity Wraparound Services or Virtual Residential Programming (VRP) services to enhance potential for reunification. If so, begin these services as indicated.
11. If reunification is indicated, transition son home with specific treatment goals and objectives to promote elimination of all harm.
12. Consider alternative living arrangements for permanency planning if son is not able to return home.
13. Monitor progress toward those goals weekly (informally) and monthly (formally) through treatment team activity and meetings.

When an evaluation is completed and distributed, everyone involved should read it and meet to determine how to best proceed with service delivery. Protocols for such a meeting can include: clarifying everyone's understanding of the findings; answering any questions about the findings; exploring ways to obtain recommended services; creating a plan for so doing; and assigning tasks to all participants. A follow-up meeting may be necessary to establish a formal initial service plan and clearly defined treatment team for the family. This process establishes a foundation for continuous assessment.

When people express disagreements about an evaluation it is important to address such concerns. Some evaluators are willing to make changes and some are not. Even those who are generally open to this may not be willing to do so under certain circumstances. When evaluations reveal something potentially embarrassing or a criminal activity within a family, for example, family members may express a desire to have such information removed. Other times service providers may disagree on information and/or recommendations. The best way to deal with this is to have key service providers sit down and determine how to move forward.

Optimal evaluations are a road map for services that provide clarity and lead to consistent delivery of research-based services.

Assessing Progress

When an evaluation meets the goal of providing a foundation for service delivery, ongoing assessment naturally begins. All team members are encouraged to track progress, or the lack thereof, by monitoring the extent to which each of the evaluation's recommendations are being followed, and, if so, how successfully. This can be done both informally (usually weekly) and formally through treatment team meetings (usually monthly, or as indicated). Wraparound services recommend weekly or biweekly formal team meetings while Multisystemic Therapy (MST) protocol is less formal and more fluid. Part of the ongoing assessment of progress toward goals involves checking in with all core team members to obtain everyone's perspectives.

Ongoing assessment involves monitoring safety, treatment progress, team communication, and relationship building. It provides a foundation for family reconciliation. Transitional evaluations and/or continuous assessment address changes that may include: safety; out of home placement; family reconciliation, reconnection and reunification; step-down from more restrictive to less restrictive services; and treatment completion and/or termination.

Multisystemic therapy, or MST is an evidence-based approach for youth violence prevention. This therapeutic model has nine guiding principles, two of which are relevant here.

Two Principles of MST that can help guide this process:

Principle 1. The primary purpose of assessment is to understand the fit between the identified problems and their broader system context; and

Principle 8. Intervention effectiveness is evaluated continuously from multiple perspectives with providers, assuming accountability for overcoming barriers to successful outcomes (Henggeler et al., 2009, pp 15-16).

Assessing progress involves monitoring affect regulation in all family members. Children learn how to manage feelings in their families. Youth who witness parents acquiring new skills to resolve differences and channel anger into constructive problem-solving learn that all feelings are safe. They learn to regulate those feelings without causing harm. Intervention supports experiencing intense feelings with someone helping to regulate frightening affect in a manageable way. An ecological approach helps caregivers learn to soothe a hurt child both physically and emotionally. It also focuses on teaching youth to do these things for themselves when others are not around.

Youth violence prevention involves promoting more effective emotional attachment within a family as a foundation for more effective connection to the world. This attachment further allows a youth to develop affect regulation based on empathy and compassion and improve communication and relationship skills.

Conclusion

Good process creates good outcomes.

Ron Suskind

Assessing family strengths and needs is a foundation for youth violence prevention. Knowing what factors may indicate a need for violence prevention aids in effective screening, which is primary prevention.

Most youth do not need services to prevent violence in their lives. Prevention starts with good parenting, support, and resources that promote healthy development. General screening can occur for all children through pediatric and educational services. Individual screening begins when parents or service providers suspect something is out of order in a child's life. Screening may simply confirm that everything is okay, or successfully prevent youth violence.

Have a working definition of, and understanding differences in, evaluation and assessment helps clarify what is needed to provide the most effective services for youth violence prevention. When indicated, organizing a complex web of information into a cohesive evaluation with specific recommendations for service delivery requires specialized knowledge and thoughtful preparation. Evaluations then become the road map for service delivery and ongoing assessment as youth and families participate in services to stop violence.

Using family systems and ecological evaluations to guide all service delivery helps everyone to best understand family strengths and needs. Influencing communities to use effective evaluations and ongoing assessment of potential for violence promotes safety and security for everyone.

Recommendations

- Stay on top of research about screening, evaluation, and assessment.
- Use evidence-based screening for youth violence prevention.
- Create protocols for de-escalating youth at risk of behaving violently.
- Create protocols for debriefing immediately after acts of violence in order to create safety plans for preventing it from happening again.

- Develop a uniform template for documenting family systems and ecological evaluations.
- Follow evaluation recommendations when they reflect research-based practices for youth violence prevention.

Resources

Devereux: www.devereux.org

Child and Adolescent Functional Assessment Scale (CAFAS): www.fasoutcomes.com

IDA Institute: www.ida-institute.org

National Center for Juvenile Justice: www.ncjj.org

National Research Council and Institute of Medicine: www.nationalacademies.org

Resiliency in Action: www.resiliency.com

Resources For Resolving Violence, Inc.: www.resourcesforresolvingviolence.com

Chapter 6

Working for Success

When I dare to be powerful,
to use my strength in the service of my vision,
it becomes less and less important whether I am afraid.
Audre Lorde

Overview

It's an exciting time to be involved in youth violence prevention. As mentioned previously, current statistics indicate a decrease in youth violence and research offers effective ways to stop it. The entire goal of youth violence prevention is just that: preventing it from happening in the first place, or stopping it as fast as possible once it has occurred.

Chapter 2 provided a primary prevention perspective, using optimal child development as a foundation for preventing violence from ever taking place. This chapter addresses secondary and tertiary prevention; situations that occur when there is a risk of violence or when violence has already occurred. It draws from the main ideas of the first five chapters in this book and offers a structured research-based approach for stopping violence.

Objectives

By the end of this chapter we hope you will be able to:
- Have a clear picture of how services work.
- Identify what services to look for, or how to create these services in your community.
- Know what youth need from therapeutic intervention so they will decide to stop it.

Getting Started

In the last chapter we described the process and content of screening, evaluation, and assessment, which are the bedrock for all service delivery. Once everyone is clear about the strengths and needs of the youth and his or her family, it's time to turn that information into a working model for action.

Safety and service plans guide this activity. Everyone involved has a part in creating them and each youth and family lead the way to success. Templates for these documents, along with some simple examples, are provided in the Appendix.

Engaging Youth and Families

This issue of how to engage youth and families was covered extensively in Chapter 4. Establishing and maintaining relationships with each youth and his or her pertinent family members is critical for prevention. Getting someone to change requires offering them compelling reasons to do so. They are more likely to consider change when the person trying to persuade them behaves respectfully and without judgment.

Developing a therapeutic alliance, or collaboration, helps individuals find courage and strength to consider change. Using predictive questions from Motivational Interviewing has potential to influence successful outcomes.

Asking a range of questions, such as the following, may introduce new ways of thinking about violence, and may help youth assess their own motivation to stop harm. All questions are taken from Motivational Interviewing (Miller & Rollnick, 2002).

- Are you interested in stopping harmful behavior?
- If so, how important is it for you to stop causing harm?
- On a scale from 1 to 10, where 1 is not at all important and 10 is extremely important, where would you say you are right now?
- How confident are you that if you decide to stop causing harm you can do it?

> **Definitions**
> **Services:** Any research-based activities that influence youth violence prevention. This may include therapy, community service, mentoring, physical fitness activities, and expression through art drama, dance, or music.
> **Treatment/Therapy:** Specific, research-based, therapeutic models, or practices, that influence youth violence prevention. This may involve evidence-based practices such as Multisystemic Therapy (MST), or Trauma-Focused Cognitive Behavioral Therapy (TF-CBT).

The authors suggest promoting "change talk" by asking questions such as:
- Why are you at a ___ and not a lower number? or
- What would it take for you to go from ___ to a [a higher number]?

Questions to enhance confidence can include:
- How might you go about making this change?
- What would be a good first step?
- What obstacles do you foresee, and how might you deal with them?
- What gives you some confidence that you can do this?

Other good books with specific questions for engaging youth and family members in treatment are: *Invitations to Responsibility: The Therapeutic Engagement of Men Who are Violent and Abusive* (Jenkins, 1990), and *Children Who See Too Much; Findings From the Child Witness to Violence Project* (Groves, 2002).

A goal for every meeting with youth and families is to engage them in service delivery. *Engagement is a continuous process of respectful communica-*

tion *that addresses the identified concerns and goals of the youth and his or family.* A simple welcoming ritual such as making sure each person attending is addressed by name, offered refreshment, and included in conversation establishes respectful interaction by service providers.

> During an initial meeting with a family about the oldest son's sexual abuse toward two of his younger brothers, the therapist was using some of the questions listed above. One of the young victims was so taken with the conversation that he revealed having abused the family dog. It was the first time the youngster had participated in such a session and he later reported that he had wanted to talk about it for a long time, but nobody ever spoke about the sexual abuse in front of him. He appeared very motivated to address his harmful behavior and stressed his desire to stop it.

Facing Up to Harm

Acknowledging harm that brought a youth into treatment provides an opportunity for youth to begin taking responsibility for their behavior. It does not require details of the behavior or admitting responsibility all at once or right away. This part of the process can be scary for a variety of reasons.

Why shouldn't we expect youth to admit to the details of the harm they caused all at once? Youth may feel ashamed for behaving violently. They may be afraid of consequences, such as being arrested or being rejected by their family. A thoughtful and sensitive response by all service providers can help youth and families face up to pain caused by violence in their lives. When youth are able to talk at all about any harm they caused, thoughtful encouragement by a service provider can help them continue to address the problem.

Slowing down may actually have a paradoxical effect and may help youth address the problem sooner. When service providers listen carefully and offer empathy and consideration, youth are more likely to feel safe and talk about the violence. They are more likely to feel disrespected when they are hurried, coerced, or don't feel like people are really listening to what they have to say. When that happens they are not likely to speak truthfully.

Engaging youth and family members involves:

- Welcoming rituals that promote positive youth development
- Assisting families in identifying strengths and successes in their daily lives
- Clearly defining expectations for participation and change
- Instilling hope and expectation for positive outcomes
- Identifying people who can potentially be trusted to make up a social support network and participate in treatment
- Deciding how each social support network member can help
- Initiating contact with social support network members
- Clarifying the role each social support network member will play
- Participating in service activities
- Teaching self-soothing activities to enhance stress reduction and affect regulation (these were introduced in Chapter 3)
- Demonstrating respectful behavior
- Actively giving and receiving feedback
- Participating in psycho-education that includes but is not limited to: social skills, affect regulation, sexual health, and substance abuse (if indicated)
- Monitoring competency development

All adults involved in secondary and tertiary prevention can learn about the process of facing up to harm. People tell lies when they are afraid to tell the truth. Admission of guilt is less likely to happen when youth behaving violently don't know what to expect if they tell the truth. Providing a clear explanation of what might occur, and exploring pros and cons of coming clean about harm, helps youth to make informed decisions. When adults offer patient guidance and model truth-telling, youth can see that taking responsibility is the best way to proceed.

Facing up to harm is a type of cognitive restructuring. **Practically speaking, when youth don't face up to harm they have caused, they are thinking one way (it's not okay to talk about it; I shouldn't tell anyone; etc). When they do face up to it, they are considering change (maybe talking about it** can help; if I talk about it, maybe things will change; etc.).

When Joe was first caught assaulting his sister, he only admitted to what his stepdad witnessed. His sister said assaults had happened before but he would not admit to them. Joe was willing to create a safety plan with his family, probation officer, and therapist. He participated actively in therapy, started being more cooperative at home, and got involved in sports at school. When he was ready to apologize, he was able to admit to more harmful behavior. Joe was embarrassed and ashamed but took the apology process seriously and stopped denying behavior for which he was responsible.

Facing up to harm involves:
- Identifying behavior that brought about a need for services.
- Acknowledging harmful behavior in therapy.
- Continuing to participate in psycho-education that includes but is not limited to: social skills, affect regulation, sexual health, and substance abuse (if indicated).
- Demonstrating harm reduction.
- Behaving in pro-social ways according to safety and service plans and therapeutic goals.
- Adjusting safety and service plans, if needed.
- Monitoring competency development.

Cognitive restructuring influences affect regulation and competency development. **Practically speaking, when people successfully change their thinking about violence they stop doing it (affect regulation) and behave in pro-social ways (competency development).**

Exploring the Impact of Trauma on Current Behavior

Trauma is a deeply distressing or disturbing experience that has lasting effects. Everyone experiences it uniquely. When anyone experiences any type of trauma, healing occurs through the body's ability to manage the impact both physically and emotionally in ways that promote health and well-being.

Taking good care of one's self is the most important thing anyone can do. Developing personal responsibility and accountability for optimum physical and mental health provides a foundation for competency development, self-sufficiency, and personal satisfaction.

Healing trauma involves learning how to address painful life experiences that played a part in violence. Youth and family members may be extremely fearful of facing trauma. Children who have witnessed violence may struggle to learn healthy coping strategies for managing the pain. They may desperately try to put it out of their mind, or misbehave in an effort to keep bad memories at bay (Groves, 2002). Intense fear is a normal defense against addressing trauma. People often try to cover up pain in an effort to hide vulnerabilities. Such behavior can be especially challenging.

> The United States government supports state initiatives to provide evidence-based practices for children receiving services through child welfare, mental health, and/or juvenile justice. In Maine this initiative is called Thrive. It is the statewide clearinghouse for trauma-informed service delivery. All licensed mental health agencies must be certified in a trauma-informed approach in order to receive state contracts and funding for services. Everyone involved in youth violence prevention should obtain knowledge about government-supported efforts that make everyone's job easier and produce more successful outcomes.

Services for youth and family should always use evidence-based practices for healing trauma. These include trauma-focused cognitive behavioral therapy, abuse-focused cognitive behavioral therapy, and parent-child interaction therapy.

Trauma that takes place within a family can be successfully addressed through evidence-based practices. All family members involved in the trauma should participate in trauma-informed therapy. Parents' abilities to acknowledge children's feelings and take responsibility for their own actions (whether intended or not) that played a part in the trauma help youth take responsibility for the harm they caused. **Practically speaking, when the act** of taking responsibility for causing trauma can be demonstrated by an authority figure in the family, youth are more apt to take responsibility for the harm they have caused.

Healing trauma involves:

- Learning about, and showing understanding of, disturbances of arousal, affect regulation, and the trauma outcome process.
- Practicing self-soothing activities that promote affect regulation.
- Figuring out how previous trauma influences current behavior.
- Acknowledging grief and loss, and practicing pro-social self-expression.
- Participating in evidence-based therapies when indicated.
- Continuing to participate in psycho-education curricula as indicated.
- Demonstrating improved social skills, moral reasoning, and behavior.
- Monitoring competency development.

Talking about trauma in a safe setting is crucial. Real or perceived mistreatment or rejection by loved ones greatly affects behavior and relationships. Communication and new understanding produce cognitive restructuring of past events and can stop violence.

Healing trauma is important for everyone to begin to see a need to take responsibility for harm. This process may need to include individual sessions with the youth and parents separately. Individual therapy gives each family member a chance to sort through feelings and various perspectives in a safe way while gaining a better understanding of other people's experiences. Family sessions can then focus on reconciliation and restoring loving connection.

In Tenisha's example, individual sessions allowed her mother time to process the pain her behavior had caused and to understand complications of misunderstood intentions. It is important to assist parents in looking at a situation from the child's point of view and considering what it might be like to lose such important parental support, particularly after witnessing violence, substance abuse, and parental divorce.

When Tenisha was four years old her mother divorced her father because of his alcoholism and violence. Her mother decided to go back to college so she could better support her family as a single parent. Tenisha then lived with her grandparents most of the time until she was eight years old while her mother worked part-time and went to school.

During that time Tenisha was unable to communicate how she longed for more of her mother's attention. Her mother also missed Tenisha but was focused on building a better life for the family and was relieved that Tenisha could spend time with her grandmother. Tenisha adored her grandmother and when she wasn't thinking about missing her mother, she was having fun with her grandmother.

When Tenisha reached adolescence, after years of living with her mother again, her resentment toward her mother began to show in indirect ways. She ignored her mother's curfew rules and had friends at home when she wasn't supposed to. Tenisha stopped letting her mother know where she was going after school and began getting into trouble with friends her mother didn't know. Tenisha had police contact because of fights she was getting into after school. One time, when the police picked her up, Tenisha had marijuana in her purse. She had a hard time taking any responsibility for her behavior.

In family therapy, Tenisha revealed deep resentment toward her mother for what she thought was abandonment. Her mother listened to Tenisha's views on the past, including her feelings of abandonment. She was able to share her intentions about that time and accept responsibility for what unintentionally caused her daughter trauma. Tenisha then began to take more responsibility for her own behavior as her resentment toward her mother diminished and their relationship began to heal.

Another important step is helping parents to see that a youth's harmful behavior may be a reaction to unaddressed pain that was caused years ago. Assisting parents and children in listening to each other, and explaining the past, can create greater understanding and more respectful behavior in the future.

Even though the following information was introduced in Chapter 3, it's important to reiterate it here. The National Crime Victims Research and Treatment Center (Saunders, Berliner, & Hanson, 2004) identifies core approaches to all evidence-based practices for child physical and sexual abuse. They are:

- Prioritizing work with caregivers
- Being goal directed
- Providing a structured approach
- Focusing on skill building to manage emotional distress and behavioral disturbances
- Using techniques that involved repetitive practice of skills with feedback

They also identify the following four key skills common to all evidence-based practices:

- Emotional, or affect regulation (the ability to identify, modulate, and express emotions in pro-social ways)
- Anxiety management
- Cognitive restructuring
- Problem-solving

Affect Regulation (Here it is again!)

Research on affect regulation was introduced and described in Chapter 3. The focus here is on practical application for healing trauma to stop youth violence. So *affect regulation, or the ability to manage emotions without causing harm to self or others,* is the foundation for both healing trauma and preventing violence. *Dysregulation is the inability to manage feelings in pro-social ways.* Dysregulation occurs when emotions, or feelings, are managed in ways that cause harm to self or others. Violence is a type of dysregulation.

Disturbance of Arousal

Disturbances of arousal can cause dysregulation. Trauma research provides important information about disturbances of arousal and dysregulation. The following flowcharts provide an illustration for intervention. The first one shows how research identifies a range of responses that influence different behaviors.

These charts (one shows the research and the other one is a more user-friendly version) illustrate affect regulation in response to trauma by describing it in terms of immobilization leading to dysregulation. Different paths are identified as fight, flight, freezing, or multi-sensory self-soothing. Self-soothing can lead to mobilization, elimination of pathological patterns, and future orientation. The flowchart helps youth identify how problematic coping strategies prevent healing, and provides a visual map to begin learning how to take good care of one's self.

Disturbance of Arousal

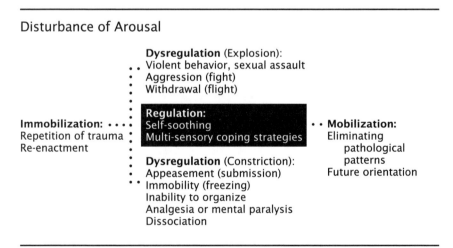

Getting Upset and Feeling Out of Control

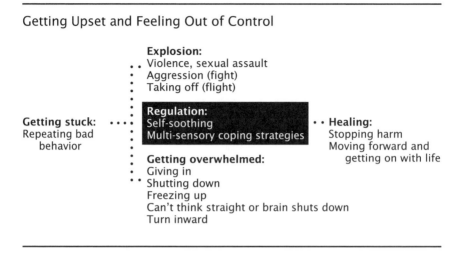

Explosion:
Violence, sexual assault
Aggression (fight)
Taking off (flight)

Regulation:
Self-soothing
Multi-sensory coping strategies

Getting stuck:
Repeating bad
    behavior

Healing:
Stopping harm
Moving forward and
    getting on with life

Getting overwhelmed:
Giving in
Shutting down
Freezing up
Can't think straight or brain shuts down
Turn inward

This second one is a user-friendly version to help youth and family members explore ways of handling difficult situations.

These flowcharts can help youth and family members make sense of trauma in their lives and explore how to develop healthy coping strategies to prevent violence. Successful affect regulation involves maintaining a personal sense of safety and stability; using exercise and body movement, healthy touch, and expression through art, drama, dance, and music for self-soothing and relaxation; and skill building to manage pain without causing harm (Stien & Kendall, 2004).

Building Skills to Stop Violence

Van der Kolk, (2004) talks about learning how to "mindfully observe internal experience" as an important task for harm reduction after experiencing trauma. You may be wondering what the heck this is. Mindfully observing internal experience simply means learning how to pay attention to thoughts, feelings, bodily reactions, behavior, and outcomes while being upset and feeling out of control. **Practically speaking, the task is to slow the brain down and pay attention to what's going on inside.** Mindful observation helps the brain to stay organized while being upset by trauma memories or flashbacks. It helps people to stay in control of their bodies when thinking about, or talking about, highly emotional pain. One way to do this is through writing or drawing pictures about thoughts and feelings of past experiences as they surface. Youth and family members can learn to talk about personal successes, remember how they survived the trauma, celebrate survival resources, and honor their lives.

Multi-sensory activities

Multi-sensory activities are coping strategies involving any of the five senses to address difficult feelings as a way to manage pain and calm down. These activities are a means of self-regulation useful in all areas of trauma recovery. **Practically speaking, anyone can handle difficult emotions better by using any of their five senses to help them calm down.**

Affect: Memories can stir up distressing feelings about trauma. Service providers can prepare youth and family members for emotional discomfort by teaching them how to use multi-sensory self-soothing activities. These are behaviors designed to help manage discomfort and reduce anxiety. Some examples are deep breathing, guided imagery, doodling, playing with something like Play Doh, listening to soothing music, and most any exercise or body movement. Using such activities promotes healthy coping strategies for managing difficult situations and symptoms related to unresolved trauma and post-traumatic stress. They can also decrease potential for dysregulation, or violence.

Cognition: Facing up to harm will likely affect thinking about traumatic experiences. Training youth to use multi-sensory self-soothing activities can stimulate cognition, boost memory, and help to organize brain processing (Stien & Kendall, 2004). Helping youth learn to mindfully observe internal experience, stay organized in the threat of psychological upheaval, change their body state when addressing their deepest pain, learn to state success, remember how they survived, celebrate survival resources, and honor their life promotes cognitive restructuring that may influence harm reduction (Van der Kolk, 2004).

Physiology: *Physiology is the way in which body parts function. Arousal is a response to a stimulus. Physiological arousal is the way in which the human body responds to a stimulus.* One example is the body's response to the feeling of surprise. When people are surprised their heart rate changes and their body is alerted to potentially strong feelings, such as joy, or to a real or perceived threat, such as danger. Physiological arousal influences behavior. When people are surprised they may be startled and their body may jerk in response. This is a reflex. Traumatic experiences influence physiological arousal and reflex reactions (Kagan, 2004; Schore, 2003; Van der Kolk, 1994). Educating youth and family members about arousal can help them learn to identify it and use multi-sensory self-soothing to enhance healing (Stien & Kendall, 2004).

Behavior: Youth can learn to manage trauma in ways that do not cause harm to self or others. Exploring and practicing multi-sensory coping strategies unique to the youth's interests, skills, and abilities can help the individual to develop lifelong patterns that promote health and well-being. Such developmental skill-building promotes safety, stabilization, and symptom reduction (Stien & Kendall, 2004).

Eliminating harm involves:
- Maintaining a personal commitment to stop all harm.
- Practicing affect regulation in all areas of life (home, school, and community).
- Monitoring competency development.

The Trauma Outcome Process

The trauma outcome process is a conceptual framework designed to simplify how painful life experiences impact thoughts (cognition), feelings (affect), physiological reactions, and behavior. The trauma outcome process is used to create a better understanding of traumatic life events and use that understanding to stop harm through competency development. **Practically speaking, the goal is to help young people make sense of past trauma in order to prevent future problems.** It provides a way of tracking behavior, planning for success, and behaving respectfully.

Illustrating a conceptual framework naturally creates limitations and exceptions. The trauma outcome process (Rasmussen, Burton, & Christopherson, 1992) doesn't necessarily occur in a stepwise fashion even though the flowchart looks that way. In reality, making sense of trauma does not always fit into categories. The trauma outcome process is simply a way to help youth understand and organize experience in order to promote affect regulation and healing. In order to stop harm, each youth and his or her social support network members can look at events, thoughts, feelings, physiological reactions, and behaviors that created and maintained a need for services. The trauma outcome process can be used as a map to stop harm.

The Trauma Outcome Process

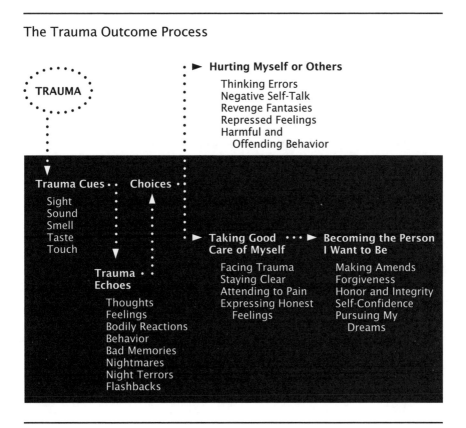

TRAUMA

► **Hurting Myself or Others**

Thinking Errors
Negative Self-Talk
Revenge Fantasies
Repressed Feelings
Harmful and
    Offending Behavior

Trauma Cues · · **Choices**

Sight
Sound
Smell
Taste
Touch

Trauma Echoes

Thoughts
Feelings
Bodily Reactions
Behavior
Bad Memories
Nightmares
Night Terrors
Flashbacks

► **Taking Good** · · · ► **Becoming the Person**
Care of Myself   **I Want to Be**

Facing Trauma   Making Amends
Staying Clear   Forgiveness
Attending to Pain   Honor and Integrity
Expressing Honest   Self-Confidence
    Feelings   Pursuing My
                           Dreams

The trauma outcome process is used to help people understand the ongoing effects of trauma and promote self-regulation. Youth learn to regulate or manage their own reactions to trauma through partnership (attachment and connection) with nurturing adults. The model is designed for collaboration among youth, trusted others, and/or staff trained in a therapeutic response to trauma. It provides a way to generalize skills across all aspects of life and helps youth to connect with others in meaningful and benevolent ways.

While doing this work, service providers report hearing youth say things like, "Wow, I'm not crazy after all!" They begin to understand the effect trauma has had on how they treat themselves and others. With this important insight, healing starts to takes place. Individuals come to accept the good and bad things they have done in life and begin pursuing their dreams in order to create a brighter future without violence.

Creating a Plan for Success

Each youth develops a detailed plan for what he or she will do to decrease the likelihood of future harm. The process takes place with the guidance of trusted adults. This plan becomes the framework for lifelong prevention.

Restorative Justice

Zehr, 2002

Restorative justice is a process to involve, to the extent possible, those who have a stake in a specific offense and to collectively identify and address harms, needs, and obligations in order to heal and put things as right as possible.

Planning for success involves taking full responsibility for violence and making amends to those hurt by a youth's harmful behavior. *Making amends is a process by which people take responsibility for harm they have caused and commit to never doing it again.* When youth not only take responsibility and apologize to everyone impacted by the violence, but actually, or symbolically, give back anything that was taken away through the violence, restorative justice occurs. *Restorative justice is just that: real or symbolic efforts to restore a sense of fairness or justice to crime victims.* It is important to note that people other than victims may be deeply traumatized by the harm to self or others youth cause through violence. Acknowledging the impact on everyone helps individuals, families, and communities heal from violence.

Creating a Plan for Success involves:

- Creating a plan for restitution and participating in restorative justice victim-offender dialogues.
  - Identify everyone who was hurt by the youth's harmful behavior.
  - Decide how the youth will make amends to each of those people.
  - Participate in community service as restitution (when indicated).
  - Apologize to everyone who was in any way hurt by his or her harm.
- Demonstrating affect regulation.
- Conducting social support network meetings to plan for transition out of services.
- Presenting a plan for success to the social support network.
- Demonstrating empathy, compassion, and moral reasoning.
- Consistently displaying pro-social behavior.
- Exploring specific options for aftercare when placed out of home.
- Monitoring competency development.

Practicing the Plan

Leading a life free of violence requires dedication and commitment. All involved adults can encourage a youth to stick to his or her plan for success. This involves consistently responding to difficult situations in pro-social ways.

Planning for Continued Success

Successful outcomes are dependent upon a youth's commitment to live respectfully. This commitment can be honored and witnessed by people who have supported the youth throughout treatment. For youth involved in community-based services, transitioning from service providers toward informal supports can be frightening. Through support and practicing new skills, youth and family members build confidence for a successful future. For youth in residential care, discharge is a time of high risk when they may be returning to the environment where the violence began (this is addressed in Chapter 10). This is why transitional services are so important and are also addressed in the next chapter.

Practicing the Plan involves:

· Transitioning out of services.

· Planning specific termination activities with primary service providers and social support network members. This usually involves celebrating success and expressing appreciation for ongoing support.

· For those in residential treatment, having graduated lengths of stay in the community.

· For those in residential treatment, meeting with primary and clinical staff after each community visit in order to assess the experience and plan for continued success.

· For those in residential treatment, participating in family meetings to assess each member's preparation for reunification.

· Clarifying and implementing the transition plan.

· Monitoring competency development.

Transitional Services

Transitional services focus on successful practice of newly acquired skills and abilities for lifelong pro-social behavior. Maintaining ethical connections with service providers and developing new relationships can help youth settle into new competencies for violence prevention.

Planning for Continued Success involves:

- Creating a ritual or celebration for completing services.
- Facilitating the ritual with social support network members.
- Participating in a celebration of success.
- Discharging from residential treatment (when applicable) or other formal services.
- Offering connections for youth and families when youth are in transition between services.
- Monitoring competency development.

Practically speaking, if a service provider is only focused on a youth's needs during the time he or she is receiving services, chances for long-term success are reduced. Programs that envision their responsibility ending when youth simply master only those tasks required for successful program completion do not promote lifelong success. Lifelong success requires all services, beginning immediately when a youth is referred for services, to provide a holistic approach throughout a full continuum of care. Treating youth away from home and possibly a distance from family can have negative effects and creates barriers to reunification. Potential for out of home placement should be considered and discussed right from the beginning of service delivery.

When treatment team members think a youth is ready to end services, the team can meet to assess and measure progress. The National Center for Juvenile Justice provides the following guidelines for so doing.

Measuring Competency Development

Torbet & Thomas, 2005, p.17.

Intermediate Outcomes are those measured at termination or case closing.

Long-Term Outcomes are those measured at some point after case closing, and indicate whether the ultimate goals have been achieved.

Transitional Services involve:

- Maintaining telephone contact with service providers on a scheduled basis after service completion.
- Monitoring progress toward goals for continued success.
- Notifying designated service providers immediately when success is threatened.
- Facilitating connections with new service providers and other supportive community members.
- Returning for treatment if necessary.
- Documenting outcomes:
    - Intermediate Outcomes are those measured at termination or case closing.
    - Long-Term Outcomes are those measured at some point after case closing, and indicate whether ultimate goals have been achieved.

Competency Development Composite

National Center for Juvenile Justice, 2005

Intermediate Outcomes	Indicators
Productive	Attending school and passing, or attending GED prep, alternative ed, or participating in vocational training, or actively seeking employment, or employed
Connected	Engaged with a mentor, or engaged with positive peer groups, or engaged in club or other organized school, community group, or activity
Law-abiding	No new adjudication, adult convictions or pending court cases

Conclusion

Things do not change; we change.
                                        Henry David Thoreau

Having a clear picture of how services work makes everyone's job a lot easier and more successful. Planning for success with families involves a clearly defined structured approach for both treatment and a broad array of additional services. Using a research-based approach helps youth and families heal pain that created a need for services.

Knowing what to look for or how to create effectives services is vital to a successful community-wide approach for prevention. A collaborative, family focused and trauma-informed approach for cognitive restructuring, affect regulation, and competency development streamlines efforts and is cost-effective. When everyone involved knows what youth need from treatment violence will stop. Investing in the future of all children in this way is rewarding for everyone!

Recommendations

- Provide a clearly defined, state-wide trauma-informed approach for youth violence prevention.
- Work collaboratively every step of the way.
- Create user-friendly documents and procedures for everyone involved in order to help families navigate services.
- Use cognitive restructuring, affect regulation, and competency development as the foundation for all services.
- Require all child-serving agencies to provide staff development, training, and supervision focusing on research-based practices.
- Celebrate success wherever you see it!

Resources

International Institute for Restorative Practices: www.realjustice.org

National Council of Juvenile and Family Court Judges: www.ncjfcj.org

National Center for Juvenile Justice: www.ncjj.org

National Child Traumatic Stress Network: www.nctsn.org

Office of Juvenile Justice and Delinquency Prevention: www.ojjdp.gov

Restorative Justice Online: www.restorativejustice.org

Chapter 7

Stopping Violence for Good

Blue skies smiling at me, nothing but blue skies do I see.
Irving Berlin

Overview

When goals for lifelong success are always kept in mind, all efforts toward health and well-being are building blocks for a non-violent future. This chapter focuses on community efforts to prevent youth violence in ways that promote lifelong change. It addresses factors in a youth's life that cause risk for violence to remain, and describes specific things that families and service providers can do once violence is under control, to stop it for good.

At a personal level, adults can do a range of things to prevent youth violence from ever happening. Envisioning a successful future rather than dwelling on past problems promotes resilience, motivation for health, and well-being.

Even with good news about reduction in youth violence, communities are challenged to remain vigilant in efforts to stop it. While no single effort makes all the difference, it's important to know how communities can best decide where to focus resources to maximize outcomes in the most cost-effective ways. Maintaining the philosophy that violence is never the answer requires continuous knowledge about what really works to prevent it.

Transition to adulthood is a crucial time to stop violence for good. Successful efforts address family cohesion, school success, career exploration, leisure interests, health and wellness, dating and sexual health, and teen pregnancy prevention.

Objectives

By the end of this chapter we hope you will be able to:
- Focus on long-term success by recognizing how today's efforts have a lasting effect on the entire community's future.
- Provide optimal services for all youth transitioning into adulthood.
- Identify personal ways to participate in prevention.
- Remember specific community factors that successfully prevent and reduce youth violence.
- Explore ways to use these resources in your community.

Promoting Long-Term Success

Most communities in America are doing a tremendous amount to prevent youth violence, often without even knowing it. Communities are made up of a tremendously wide array of individuals and groups making significant contributions to community safety, sometimes without knowing what others are doing. While these are all wonderful efforts, uniting people and organizations to establish a comprehensive response can reap even greater rewards. No community is likely to accomplish all of the tasks required to totally eliminate youth violence, but each community is still better off when dedicated citizens do whatever they can to stop it for good.

This effort begins with a commitment to long-term outcomes and means looking far ahead to future generations. One, often overlooked, aspect of this important work is youth transitioning into adulthood, especially those who need secondary and tertiary prevention. Young people requiring support between the ages of 17 and 23 often struggle during this time because so many services arbitrarily stop at differing points along this continuum. Some automatically terminate at 17, 18, 21, or other ages during this developmental time. It is vital to include these young adults in community efforts to stop violence for good. They are future parents, or teen parents whose children will either experience optimal development and thrive, or represent yet another generation of youth at risk of behaving violently.

Supporting Youth Transitioning into Adulthood

Teenagers often resist help and want to make their own decisions. Sometimes well-meaning adults let them even when the adults know the youth may not be quite ready to do so. The human brain is not fully developed until about age 25, which indicates that young adults continue to need strong support with decision making. Some parents are simply worn out from years of trying to help their child stay safe and others consider their legal responsibility done. Still others believe they have taught their children everything they can and efforts are now useless and result in continued conflict.

Transitioning into adulthood can be a challenging and sometimes scary experience for all youth. For those who have been violent it can be particularly tough to maintain successful change as they become adults. Having supportive relationships and direction from professionals with access to resources can be an important part of a successful transition. According to Child Trends (www.childtrends.org), mentoring and case management are associated with positive outcomes in education and career development. Case managers and mentors offer individualized support and aid along with stable, caring, and positive relationships, which youth may not have access to otherwise.

In addition to optimum elements of child development, core competencies for court-involved youth (Torbet & Thomas, 2005) addressed throughout this book provide an easy way to support youth transitioning into adulthood. Social skill building, moral reasoning, academic development, workforce development, and independent living skills are all key parts of young adult development. Community organizations intent on prevention can make sure that all of these factors are consistently addressed throughout service delivery.

Primary Prevention

Primary prevention for youth transitioning to adulthood is unique for each individual. Young adults are often graduating from high school, looking for jobs or applying to college, dating, and leaving home. Assistance in moving forward should be offered based on each youth's level of independence and maturity. They may ask for help or wait for a parent or other supportive adult to offer support. Some youth struggle to effectively communicate their needs. Adults do well to pay attention to mood and behavior changes and compassionately offer support and guidance.

Primary, Secondary, and Tertiary Prevention Recommendations:
- Remember that teenagers only look fully grown!
- Keep your emotions in check when dealing with them.
- Teach young people to take both physical and emotional care of themselves.
- Listen.
- Offer suggestions respectfully.
- Listen some more.
- Have fun with teens.
- Involve other trustworthy adults in their lives.
- Stay positive.

Secondary Prevention

Some youth make mistakes when they haven't considered possible consequences. Prevention involves focusing on legal ramifications of decisions young people make as they gain greater independence. Having a car or apartment involves both freedom and responsibility. Both can easily create problems. **Practically speaking, if a young person drives when he or she is angry, has an accident, and hurts someone, the consequences may be devastating.**

Kyle saved money and on his 18th birthday moved out of his home. He rented an apartment with friends and expected to graduate from high school in a few months. His mom wasn't happy with his decision but she couldn't stop him, and his younger brother was glad to finally have his own room. Kyle learned that moving into an apartment is a mix of freedom and responsibility. His friends were excited to have somewhere to go after school and often played loud music in the apartment or the parking lot. Neighbors called the landlord and police a few times with complaints about the noise. Kyle risked losing his apartment when the landlord was fed up. His friends began taunting him, saying he should get revenge on the landlord if he got evicted. Kyle began having trouble concentrating in school and his grades got worse. He didn't want to tell his mom and go home feeling like a failure.

Secondary and Tertiary Prevention Recommendations:
- Keep in mind that individuals mature at different rates.
- Remember that childhood trauma impacts development and maturity.
- Respond to maturity level rather than chronological age.
- Find or create easily accessible services that support youth transitioning into adulthood.
- Create special services for youth transitioning out of foster care or residential treatment.
- Integrate school and community services for academic, career, and life skills development.
- Continue to assess strengths and needs.
- Address new needs as they arise.
- Offer time and assistance when providing transitional youth services.
- Assist young people in developing positive adult relationships in the community.

Tertiary Prevention

Most young people gradually transition into adulthood without having to overcome violence. Others may be the first person in their family attempting to stop violence for good. Additionally, they face the same tasks as other young adults such as school, work, housing, and relationships. Youth with a history of violence may struggle to finish high school and find a job after making money in illegal ways. They may be on their own, looking forward to an intimate relationship and attempting to settle conflicts for the first time without violence. They may struggle to find coping strategies other than drugs and alcohol.

Young adults who were violent in the past often work hard to practice new coping skills. They are less practiced than peers who had supportive guidance in ongoing competency development. It can be easy to lose motivation and become demoralized when maintaining positive change seems too hard, especially when youth feel they are competing with peers who have been supported in developing pro-social skills their whole lives. **Practically speaking, if a young person focuses on positive youth development by learning to play music, paint, sculpt, act, participate in sports, or volunteer, and if he or she finds support for these new pursuits, the individual is more likely to achieve success and continue on a positive path.**

When significant people in a youth's life have not made positive changes, youth may be tempted to go back to old ways. One example is trying to quit smoking cigarettes. It often takes a lot of effort, support, and willpower to quit smoking. If other people around them are still smoking it may be too difficult to quit, even when they try very hard.

Transitioning into adulthood after completing treatment for violence is like translating language, skills, and new perspectives into a different culture. Long-term change may require different friends, a new perspective on education, or being with supportive family members rather than hanging out with friends most of the time.

For these young people, the process of moving forward into adulthood has to be addressed in slightly different ways. **Practically speaking, it's like learning a foreign language in school, then going to a country where the language is spoken and figuring out how to understand and be understood in a new language that does not come easily. Even when communication is frustrating, youth may be invested in working hard at conversing in the new language, and slowly may make progress. If the task is too hard, or if people are not very willing to help with communication, youth may find it easier to fall back on the language they know best and may quit trying**

to communicate to fit into the new culture.

Tertiary Prevention Recommendations:
- Remember how hard it may be for youth to consistently practice non-violent behavior.
- Help them use a variety of healthy coping strategies.
- Exercise patience.
- Mentor them.
- Treat them respectfully as a young adult even when they do not act like one.

Personal Efforts for Prevention

Primary Prevention

Health and well-being are remedies for violence. The more people practice optimal health the greater their sense of well-being, and the less likely they are to be involved in violence. Whenever adults interact with children there are many easy ways to influence youth violence prevention. It can easily be done in families, neighborhoods, and on the job, particularly when work involves kids of any age. Some of the following strategies come from the four basic principles for strengthening attachment (Cook et. al., 2003) addressed in Chapter 2.

General Recommendations for Primary, Secondary, and Tertiary Prevention

- Take good care of yourself!
- Set good examples.
- Support kids wherever you interact with them.
- Model affect regulation by managing your feelings without causing harm to yourself or others, especially when you're upset.
- Create and maintain a soothing home or business environment that promotes health, well-being, and affect regulation.
- If you are a parent, raise children according to optimum elements of child development.

- Support all parents and caregivers you interact with in doing the same.
- Create a structured and predictable environment for children through rituals and routines.
- Teach children how to label feelings so they are clear about them.
- Relate to children by putting yourself in their situation.
- When a child misbehaves, tune in to the feelings he or she might be having (affect) rather than focusing on the problematic behavior.
- Manage problem behavior with respect, limit setting, and clear goals for non-violence.
- Praise, reinforce, and focus on children doing something positive.
- Have fun with children and youth!
- Speak up for policies and practices that promote health and well-being in your community.
- If you have time and energy, volunteer to serve in your community on behalf of child health and well-being.
- Mentor children and youth whenever and wherever you can.
- Throw out your television! (just kidding).
- Throw out your kid's video games! (partially kidding).
- Limit children's television viewing and video game playing! (not kidding at all!).
- Restrict children's exposure to any violent media images and sounds.
- Use parental locks and screen television and the Internet.
- Promote collaborative problem solving in all communication.

Secondary Prevention

In her book, *Children Who See Too Much*, Betsy McAlister Groves (2002) addresses vulnerabilities in systems of care serving youngsters who have witnessed violence. While these concerns could have been included in the previous section on community prevention, it is important to address them from an individual perspective. These vulnerabilities include: adult assumptions about the way children think and how they view the world; tendencies to deny or discount children's awareness of violence; inaccurate appraisal of children who witness violence, or behave violently; and a lack of willingness to talk about frightening events with children.

When individuals realize a youth may be at risk of behaving violently many feel at a loss about what to do. Many professionals have not received adequate training to provide secondary prevention and have a lot of questions about optimal intervention. Parents and family members are seldom prepared for challenges they face. Hopefully the following recommendations will help you feel more confident about preventing violence when a youth is vulnerable. Many of the recommendations for service providers are taken directly from *Children Who See Too Much* (Groves, 2002).

Secondary Prevention Recommendations for Parents or Guardians

In addition to recommendations for all levels of prevention, individuals can also:

- Create and maintain a soothing home environment that promotes health, well-being, and affect regulation.
- Ask all of your family members and friends to support you in raising your children according to optimal elements of child development.
- Talk with your children about frightening events and offer solutions for dealing with them.

Secondary Prevention Recommendations for Parents, Guardians, and Service Providers
Adapted in part from Groves, 2002

- Face any reluctance you have about bringing up issues of violence.
- Develop and practice healthy coping strategies to deal with it.
- Do not keep silent about any violence or abuse.
- Create a plan for responding to children's questions and fears.
- Reassure everyone that violence can be talked about and facilitate open discussions about it.
- Slow down!
- Support a child's pace and tolerance for talking about difficult subjects.
- Never push!
- Have play things around when you're talking.
- Do not deny or minimize a child's awareness of violence, even if it

happened a long time ago and they were very little.
- Assume they think about things differently than you do.
- Do not think they are bad or don't care (they are usually confused and afraid).
- Ask about their understanding of what's happening.
- Ask what they think is important for us to be thinking about.
- Ask what they are most afraid of.
- Ask what the worst part was.
- Ask what they think might be helpful.
- Ask how they cope when they are frightened.
- Listen carefully to everything they say

Secondary Prevention Recommendations for Service Providers

- Meet with parents or legal guardians and children together first.
- In order to assess, when meeting with the family, refrain from intervening unless the situation is dangerous.
- Interview family members separately.
- Explore ways to help them get relief from intrusive thoughts, flashbacks, memories, etc.
- Determine whom they can talk to.
- Share information across all involved service (with signed consent).
- Help families find stable and safe housing.
- Help adults learn how to be an emotional buffer for children.
- Educate yourself about research-based practices for community response and consider participation in these efforts.

Tertiary Prevention

Individuals providing tertiary prevention can use all of the previous recommendations for primary and secondary prevention while adding those listed below.

Tertiary Prevention Recommendations for Parents or Guardians

- Resolve to take a stand against violence in your life and the lives of your children.
- Hold yourself accountable for all harmful behavior.
- Hold your child accountable for all harmful behavior .
- Actively participate in all service provision.
- Actively support competency development.
- Partner with service providers in accepting your rightful role as a parent.
- Learn and practice optimum parenting skills.

Tertiary Prevention Recommendations for Parents, Guardians, and Service Providers

- Develop a good relationship with each youth who has misbehaved violently and his or her parents or guardians.
- Build on each person's identified strengths.
- Ensure a youth's participation in meaningful community service projects.
- Encourage individual responsibility for law-abiding behavior.

Tertiary Prevention Recommendations for Service Providers
Adapted in part from Torbet & Thomas, 2005

- Prioritize work with parents, guardians, and any other caregivers.
- Facilitate or obtain a family systems and ecological evaluation for youth behaving violently.
- Assess each youth across all five competency domains.
- Address specific competency development needs most closely associated with the juvenile's offending behavior.
- Deliver or contract for services likely to achieve competency development goals.
- Develop a supervision plan based upon evaluation results (this should

include criteria for success or failure, monitoring progress, and consequences for noncompliance).
- Coach, encourage, and support each client.
- Identify community services and supports.
- Encourage and expect full collaboration among all involved family members and service providers.
- Use clearly defined, goal-directed, research-based interventions.
- Monitor participation and progress and make adjustments to help youth get back on track when problems arise.
- Apply incentives and sanctions to reinforce accountability.
- Provide opportunities to practice and demonstrate new skills and pro-social relationships.
- Document intermediate outcomes at case closing.
- Provide a structured approach.
- Focus on skill building to manage emotional distress and behavioral disturbance.
- Use techniques that involve repetitive practice of skills with feedback.

Tertiary Prevention Recommendations
for Specific Service Providers
Torbet & Thomas, 2005

- **Prosecuting and defense attorneys:** advocate for good skill training, community service and positive youth development programs.
- **Therapists:** teach affect regulation skills, anxiety management, cognitive restructuring, and problem solving.
- **Detention:** apply a strength-based approach that promotes development into a productive, connected, and law-abiding community member.
- **Residential programs:** apply a strength-based approach that promotes development into a productive, connected, and law-abiding community member.
- **Schools:** provide educational assessment and academic support to maximize achievement; encourage attendance; remove barriers to re-enrollment.
- **Community supports (businesses, churches, and community**

groups): create and support pro-social activities and provide support for youth and families.

Exploring Ways to Integrate Resources into Your Community

Whew, what a lot of recommendations! If they seem overwhelming, take a deep breath and know they are geared toward a whole lot of people. No one is alone in this effort, and if it feels that way, it's time to locate some kindred spirits! *Kindred spirits are other people who think like you do.* There are a lot of people dedicating their careers to stopping youth violence. It is important for kindred spirits to support each other in all of these important efforts.

What wants and needs do I have regarding youth violence prevention?

Primary: _____

Secondary: _____

Tertiary: _____

Think about where it will be easiest to begin. First, think about what type of support or involvement you want and need. If you are a parent or guardian, what type of prevention support are you interested in? Where do you see your needs for prevention? Do they fit into a single area, or do they cross over more than one type of prevention? If you need secondary or tertiary prevention you may want to seek professional support right away. If you are a service provider what type of support or involvement do you want or need? Is it for personal and/or professional reasons? Sometimes we service providers are parents with the same needs as parents who don't work in this field. Either way, think about and try to define your interest in youth violence prevention. You might want to write some thoughts down so you don't forget them.

How do I want to be involved in youth violence prevention?

Primary: _____

Secondary: _____

Tertiary: _____

The next step in exploring how to integrate these recommendations into your community is to locate other like-minded people. If you are a parent or guardian, think of anyone you know who is supportive of you and who is a potential ally. *An ally is simply a person or organization that cooperates with or helps another in a particular activity.* If you are a service provider, find out what organizations are doing this work and find ways to collaborate. Make a list of these people and organizations.

Who are potential kindred spirits, or allies with whom I might find support?

Family Members: _____

Friends: _____

Colleagues: _____

Service Providers: _____

Once you have a list, think about what you hope to accomplish in contacting potential kindred spirits. You might want to visit some of the websites listed in this book to help you clarify thoughts and ideas. If it feels helpful, write down some of these ideas. Noticing a trend here? The more you note information the easier it will be for you to remember and access information. The more you organize your thinking the less effort all of this takes. You are also less likely to feel like you are trying to reinvent the wheel when you see what others are doing and realize there is a great deal of excellent material available. This makes the effort a whole lot easier!

Websites I want to visit: _____

Website: _____

Useful Information: _____

Website: _____

Useful Information: _____

Website: _____

Useful Information: _____

Once you have organized this information it's time to make a few goals for your involvement. They can be very simple ones, such as "I just want to see if this book is telling the truth!" They might be very personal, such as "I want to be a better parent," or "I want help to stop violence for myself and my family." They might also be bigger goals, like "I want to create an official youth violence prevention coalition in my community." Whatever they are, write them down if you feel like it.

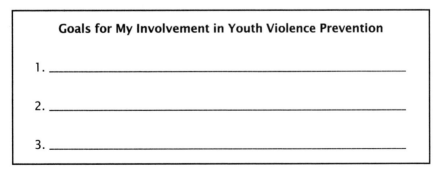

Goals for My Involvement in Youth Violence Prevention

1. _____

2. _____

3. _____

Community Efforts for Prevention

... if your neighbor is screwed, you've got to help him.

Sean Penn

Community efforts for youth violence prevention involve numerous activities that provide physical and emotional health for all children, beginning at birth. Successful approaches bring a variety of organizations together to create a vision and strategic plan for implementing long-term evidence-based practices. This section focuses on both public and private initiatives throughout the community. Individual efforts are addressed in the following section.

The Centers for Disease Control and Prevention (CDC) provide a tremendous amount of easily accessible, user-friendly information on youth violence prevention. The CDC website also identifies academic centers of excellence conducting research on the topic. One of these sites, the University of Colorado's Center for the Study and Prevention of Violence, is a clearinghouse for all evidence-based violence prevention projects in the United States. Several examples are highlighted throughout this chapter. You don't need to search hard for excellent resources. Here are some ideas for exploring solutions in your community.

The following institutions are responsible for promoting optimal child development to prevent youth violence: families; schools; churches; recreation and leisure organizations; medical health providers; childcare centers; and mentoring organizations. When they are successful youth violence does not occur. The first section of this book, *What Works?*, highlights this effort.

Many communities such as Minneapolis and many community organizations such as the Harlem Children's Zone are actively involved in all parts of prevention. Minneapolis has achieved national recognition for youth violence prevention through stellar efforts involving Urban Networks to Increase Thriving Youth (UNITY) through Violence Prevention (www.preventioninstitute.org/unity). Their Blueprint for Action includes four objectives: 1. Connect youth to trusted adults; 2. Intervene at the first sign of risk; 3. restore youth who have been in the juvenile justice system by reintegrating them back into the community; and 4. Unlearn the culture of violence (City Voices and Perspectives, 2011).

The Harlem Children's Zone (www.hcz.org) is an example of an organization involved in primary, secondary,and tertiary prevention. They are a very large and influential part of the Harlem community with a mission to do whatever it takes to help children succeed. While the focus is strength-based for all community members (primary prevention), it works primarily with vulnerable children and families (secondary prevention) and actively serves, supports, and mentors those youth who have behaved violently (tertiary prevention) in an effort to stop both poverty and violence. Poverty and violence are a lethal combination. Helping individuals and young families with education and community support beginning in early childhood reduces vulnerabilities to both.

Other organizations involved in primary prevention may actually be a part of secondary and tertiary prevention but may not know it. Programs that provide sports and recreation may or may not have knowledge that some of the kids they serve are at risk for youth violence. Regardless of whether agencies know if certain youth are vulnerable, or have actually been violent in the past, they may play a vital role in all parts of prevention. **Practically speaking, a basketball coach or youth theater director may be as valuable in preventing violence with a particular youth as any member of a designated treatment team. They may act as a mentor, or be viewed as one, regardless of whether the term "mentor" is used to describe their role.**

Primary Prevention for All Children

Helping all children grow up to become healthy, productive, and law-abiding citizens should be a primary and overarching concern for all communities. Promoting optimum elements of child development from a community standpoint ensures that all child-serving organizations provide a uniform approach for health and well-being. This begins with a foundation of physical and psychological safety and stability created through appropriate structure; supportive relationships; opportunities to belong; positive social norms; support for efficacy and mattering; opportunities for skill building; and integration of family, school, and community efforts. These elements always take into consideration the unique developmental needs of each child. See Chapter 2 for more details about optimal elements of child development, and Chapter 8 for addressing unique needs.

Safety and stability begin with shared core values that everyone in a community deserves to be safe. Regardless of whether or not people have experienced violence, been victimized, or perpetrated acts of violence, they have a right to live safely. When community leaders and elected officials dedicate their services to provide equal opportunities for all citizens a fair distribution of vital resources is possible. Youth violence prevention begins with a community-wide commitment to keeping all citizens safe.

Adequate funding for public safety is vital. When children feel safe and secure, they are more likely to thrive academically and socially. Thriving children are not violent, and they adequately transition into adulthood. When communities are safe, children learn to explore the world around them with interest and curiosity. Safety allows exploration and experimentation, which promote creativity and optimal development. This sets the stage for problem solving, goal setting, skill building, and career exploration.

When community members are overwhelmed by daily demands that require parents to work more than one job because their primary employment does not provide a living wage, or parents feel social pressure to over-schedule their children in multiple extracurricular activities, children are not provided **appropriate structure.** Appropriate structure is a daily experience in which children sleep well (eight to ten hours a night) and have daily routines that allow for energy expenditure, such as playing, and energy renewal, such as napping and quiet time. Schedules that pack in too much activity do not allow for adequate rest and relaxation. Schedules that have too little structure do not allow for adequate productivity. **Practically speaking, too little structure occurs when children are left to entertain themselves on the computer, through electronic games or watching television for long periods of time. It also happens when they are allowed to play in the neighborhood with little supervision. Children suffer from too much structure when they become depleted from too much activity and do not get adequate rest.**

Either extreme is a problem. Children can be overwhelmed by too much to do and become anxious, or they can have too little to do and be at risk of becoming lethargic. The two extremes place youth at risk of acting out in harmful ways.

Communities can provide a broad range of **supportive relationships** for all children. When adults treat children in warm and respectful ways, youth develop a core sense of inherent value that promotes healthy self-esteem and self-confidence. Knowing that school personnel and people they interact with in the community have their best interests in mind helps children learn to trust adults and receive important messages about their own value as a human being.

When children experience law enforcement as a positive force in the community, rather than as an entity to be feared, they learn about supportive collaboration and cooperation. Trust and respect become vital elements of such relationships. These messages greatly influence competency development. **Practically speaking, having police as school resource officers or part of a Wraparound team can have a long-term effect on a youth's respect for authority and the law in general.**

During lean economic times when budgets are being slashed year after year, communities can appeal to citizens for support in bridging gaps in services. Volunteering has a strong foundation in American culture and many people fill a void in services when money is not available for salaried positions. Consistent efforts to recruit and maintain volunteers for children's services in every capacity—including but not limited to volunteers involved with Parent-Teacher Associations (PTA), coaching, mentoring, recreational activities, religious leadership, school boards, and community services—provide an interwoven web of adult supervision and support throughout all areas of a child's life. Maintaining policies for criminal and substance abuse background checks on all volunteers further enhances safety, stability, and violence prevention.

Everyone, especially children, need **opportunities to belong**. This book has consistently addressed the importance of attachment, engagement, and connection. Communities can create a wide range of venues for youth involvement. Once again, a stellar example of such an approach is the Harlem Children's Zone. Through the visionary leadership of Geofffrey Canada, the Harlem Children's Zone is leading the way in understanding not only how to eliminate poverty, but in understanding exactly what communities can do to maximize investment in the health and well-being of all citizens. This initiative is constantly being monitored and studied in order to best understand what works to promote optimal development specifically for children in low-income communities.

On a smaller scale, the concept of giving a child the opportunity to belong and to promote attachment, engagement, and connection may be as simple as promoting family values of helping neighbors, especially those in need, like the elderly. **Practically speaking, when parents take a child along as they do favors for neighbors, such as bringing in a garbage can, or sharing garden vegetables or flowers, the child learns to do these things too. By doing so, community relationships are formed and children develop a sense of relatedness and connection.**

Most adults believe they promote **positive social norms.** *Positive social norms are behaviors that reflect pro-social values based on respect for all living things and the environment.* Interacting with other adults in a pro-social manner promotes cooperation, collaboration, and successful communication. Communicating pro-socially in front of and with children is just as important. **Practically speaking, passing on positive social norms means paying close attention to what you do and say in front of children. Even when it seems that children are not paying attention, they take in most everything from their surroundings and often mimic it, regardless of whether it is good or bad.**

This is no easy task! Everyone gets frustrated, irritated, and downright angry about a variety of things that others do. It is easy to vent such feelings in ways that put others down or cause harm. Maintaining a community commitment to positive social norms in all types of communication is very challenging work! Such communication involves verbal communication, written documents, media advertising, reporting, and commentary.

Individuals influence business practices. When industry leaders document core values and follow business practices that reflect positive social norms, employees have a mandate to do so also. Some positive social norms are laws that all citizens are expected to obey, others are agency policies, and still others simply reflect personal values and beliefs. All of these types of social norms can create a comprehensive approach for consistently sending messages to children and youth about pro-social law-abiding behavior.

Communities show **support for efficacy and mattering** (*the opportunity for a child to feel valued and learn that he or she can make important things happen in life*) through child-friendly policies and consideration of the unique developmental needs of everyone. Even though some children have documented special needs such as developmental disabilities, all children require support and knowledge of their inherent value as a human being in order to thrive.

Providing unconditional care helps youngsters to master skills of everyday living and pursue personal interests. This support shows children they are valued and have the resources to direct their own life. **Practically speaking, when a parent or other valued adult takes time regularly to take a child fishing or practice throwing a ball or works with a child who is learning to paint, this builds self-esteem and helps the child see that he or she is important. When children make mistakes and adults support them in correcting them, rather than demeaning or humiliating them, children get a clear message of being valued.**

> One mother who made a commitment to never use bad language in front of her children made it about eight years before she swore in front of her child in response to frustration about the child being bullied by other neighborhood children. Her child was stunned when he heard her say "shit." She quickly collected herself, apologized, and spoke with him about the use of bad language. She was happy that he did not appear to pick up use of the word (at least around her!).

Speaking of mastering skills for everyday living ... **opportunities for skill building** are just that. Communities have a responsibility to provide all sorts of opportunities for youth to explore all types of skill building. Preschool programs prepare children for the social and academic requirements they will face not only when they begin elementary school, but throughout their lives. Libraries are a resource to enhance intellectual curiosity and exploration. Sports and recreational activities involving any type of body movement develop athletic skills. The arts provide all types of skill building that enhances creative expression. All of these skills promote multi-sensory self-soothing that influences affect regulation, health, and well-being.

Communities that routinely **integrate family, school, and community efforts** are more likely to have a unified collaborative approach for primary prevention. The Substance Abuse and Mental Health Services Administration (SAMHSA), a division of the U.S. Department of Health and Human Services, works diligently to promote communication and collaboration across all elements of service provision. They use the term "silo" to describe situations in which agencies do not integrate services across systems of care. Silos are towers used to store grain on farms. In this case the term silo illustrates situations in which organizations work alone, instead of collaborating with others. All of SAMHSA's conferences require the active involvement of all stakeholders (everyone who has a stake in preventing substance abuse and mental health problems). This means that family members are as important as educators, researchers, and substance abuse and mental health counselors in all SAMHSA efforts. Integration of family, school, and community efforts is vital for youth violence prevention. Engaging everyone involved in the care of children ensures primary prevention through unified provision of research-based services.

Examples of evidence-based primary prevention include the Incredible Years Series (IYS), Promoting Alternative Thinking Strategies (PATHS), and Olweus Bullying Prevention Program (BPP), focusing on elementary school--aged children and preschoolers. The Midwestern Prevention Project (MPP) and Life Skills Training (LST) programs are situated in schools to target teen drug use. Promoting youth leadership and positive peer interaction with children and youth of all ages creates a domino effect of social skill development that influences academic skill building, which then influences employability. All of these factors are key elements of primary youth violence prevention.

Sexual health may be seen as a surprising component of primary prevention. Some people wonder how sexual health is related to youth violence prevention. There is mythology in this country that teaching youth about sexual health promotes premature sexual activity. That is not the case. When young people are sexually confused because adults have not educated children of all ages about their developing bodies, young people are at risk of behaving in sexually harmful ways. When children are educated in developmentally congruent ways about sexuality, confusion is reduced and they are supported in creating personal values about sexual behavior that can protect them from potential harm.

Boys between the ages of 13 and 15 are more likely to commit acts of sexual harm than any other age group. This may be due in part to confusion about both physiological and social changes occurring throughout puberty. Children who have experienced any type of abuse are at risk of being involved in ongoing violence either as victims or as perpetrators of violence. Sexual health not only teaches children self-protection relating specifically to sexual behavior, but it also teaches them a great deal about healthy relationships in general, dating relationships more specifically, and protection from all harm, including violence that may or may not be sexual in nature. Developmentally congruent sexual health education promotes competency development in a whole host of ways.

Primary prevention is based on active promotion of strength building for all children. It is holistic in nature and focuses on community and family resources for all citizens.

General Recommendations for Primary, Secondary, and Tertiary Prevention

- Elect community leaders who commit to funding research-based best practices for health and well-being and youth violence prevention.
- Include consideration of health and well-being for all citizens in all strategic community planning.
- Adequately fund evidence-based public safety and violence prevention initiatives.
- Apply for grants and participate in government-funded initiatives to enhance health and well-being for all citizens.
- Provide parenting classes that include education about child development, including sexual health, for all new parents.
- Provide sexual health education for all children.
- Promote optimal elements of child development throughout all service delivery.
- Give preferential treatment to all child-serving agencies that use evidence-based practices for youth violence prevention.
- Support agencies involved in evidence-based research.
- Provide professional education that includes research-based information about optimal health and well-being.
- Mandate colleges and graduate schools to offer required courses in violence prevention.
- Teach evidence-based best practices in graduate schools for all child-serving professions.

- Influence all professional societies and government agencies to endorse and actively promote research-based initiatives.
- Designate committed advocates and key messengers for youth violence prevention throughout all community child-serving entities.
- Provide outreach in all neighborhoods, particularly those isolated in any way (culturally, economically, or geographically).
- Create a community entity or use an existing one to monitor all efforts for primary prevention.

Secondary Prevention for Youth Potentially Vulnerable to Behave Violently

As mentioned before, the Centers for Disease Control and Prevention maintain data about vulnerabilities in families at risk of youth violence. These risk factors, which were addressed in Chapters 2 and 6, are targeted through secondary prevention.

A variety of people and organizations are involved in secondary prevention, including families, schools, medical personnel such as family physicians, pediatricians, and psychiatrists, childcare agencies, child welfare personnel, substance abuse programs, community organizers, criminal justice agencies, and mentoring programs.. Most of these people and organizations should have documented screening and intake policies and procedures that sensitively address these vulnerabilities. Additionally, they should make concerted efforts to monitor vulnerabilities on an ongoing basis for all youth and families they serve. **Practically speaking, when risk factors are present, professionals involved with these youth should address the need for violence prevention and offer ideas to parents and children depending upon age and situation.**

Poverty and child abuse make children vulnerable to youth violence. Since statistics show that African American and Hispanic youth, and all children growing up in poverty, are disproportionately represented in juvenile justice it is important to provide thoughtful and considerate services to these youth and families, especially if they have experienced discrimination and structural violence in this way. As a reminder, structural violence is the experience of vulnerability or harm created by systemic practices of discrimination and oppression that prevent people from meeting basic needs.

About 500,000 American children live in foster care. Most of them were removed from impoverished families, and about a quarter of them live in foster families whose incomes fall below the federal poverty level. These youth are more likely to have run away, been arrested, and experienced sexual harm, and are more likely to exhibit higher levels of sexual risk-taking (Thiessen-Love, L., McIntosh, J., Rosst, M., & Tertzakian, K., 2009).

In 2004 the Kauffman Foundation published an important document entitled *Closing the Quality Chasm in Child Abuse Treatment: Identifying and Disseminating Best Practices*. This document provides important information about secondary and tertiary prevention. Recommendations from their findings are included in this chapter. Children who witness violence, which includes personally experiencing it, are vulnerable to developing a broad range of symptoms including violent behavior (these are identified Chapter 2). Reducing child abuse is directly related to stopping youth violence.

The Nurse-Family Partnership (NFP), in which nurses make home visits to improve parent-child outcomes, is an example of evidence-based secondary prevention. Big Brothers and Big Sisters is another example.

Recommendations for Secondary Prevention

In addition to recommendations for all levels of prevention, communities can also:

- Provide outreach in vulnerable neighborhoods and those potentially isolated in cultural, economic, or geographic ways.
- Facilitate parenting classes that include education about child development, including sexual health, for new parents who may be vulnerable (teen parents, those living in poverty and/or unsafe areas of the community, and whose children may be at greater risk of experiencing violence).
- Promote efforts to involve vulnerable families in youth violence prevention.
- Reduce funding if parents or caregivers are not included.
- When violence is occurring in a family, mandate specific violence prevention services and provide additional support to non-offending family members.

Tertiary Prevention for
Those Involved in Youth Violence

Research on interventions for youth violence prevention provides very optimistic information for everyone involved in tertiary prevention. Just because a youth behaves violently does not mean that he or she is heading toward a life of crime. A number of evidence-based practices are contributing to the reduction in juvenile crime rates. As mentioned in Chapter 3, the University of Colorado's Center for the Study and Prevention of Violence is a clearinghouse for all evidence relating to youth violence prevention. It is also worth mentioning again that the Centers for Disease Control and Prevention and the Office of Juvenile Justice and Delinquency Prevention (OJJDP) have a lot of very important information on this topic. These are excellent sources for finding out what stops violence for good after it has occurred.

Juvenile justice, child welfare, mental health services, schools, and mentoring programs are the principle providers of tertiary prevention. Examples of evidence-based tertiary prevention include Multisystemic Therapy (MST), Functional Family Therapy (FFT), and Multidimensional Treatment Foster Care (MDTFC). Maintaining a commitment to providing evidence-based practices is one of the most important components of tertiary prevention.

Sexual health is only recently being recognized as an important factor in tertiary prevention. For those youth who have committed sexual offenses sexual health is the foundation for stopping sexual harm, a topic addressed at length in Chapter 2. It is particularly vital for youth adjudicated for sexual crimes, as sexual health is both the means and end to sexual harm. Creating a vision for sexual health introduces an approach to sexuality that addresses prevention of both harm to self and others. This foundation is equally important for teen parents, as it can prevent both harm and reduce potential for additional pregnancies.

Recommendations for Tertiary Prevention

In addition to recommendations for all levels of prevention, communities can also:
• Require all agencies providing tertiary services for youth violence

prevention to publicly document purpose, mission and vision statements, core values, philosophies of care, and research-based treatment processes.

- Provide evaluation and assessment-driven treatment planning and implementation specific to research on the specific type of violence being addressed.
- Train clinical supervisors and consultants in current empirically based best practices for youth violence prevention.
- Hire professionals specifically trained to intervene in youth violence and integrate documentation of continuing education in annual performance evaluations.
- Provide ongoing training and clinical education that reflects current empirically based best practices for youth violence prevention.
- Create and maintain peer support networks for professionals specializing in youth violence prevention.
- Promote self-care and trauma stewardship for all juvenile justice, child welfare, and mental health professionals dealing with youth violence prevention.

Conclusion

Stopping violence for good doesn't have to be hard work. It does take commitment, knowing what works, support, and collaboration with kindred spirits. It's much harder when people don't know what to do. It can be frustrating trying to find out what works when people don't know about important resources, or where to turn for evidence-based information.

Youth may get stuck in transition to adulthood when using new competencies for the first time. Collaboration is crucial when planning for success. Creating a uniform approach for both community-based and individual efforts can make stopping violence for good a whole lot easier than it used to be. We hope this book takes the guesswork out of efforts to stop harm.

Recommendations

- Take a stand against violence by sharing your intent with others.
- Stay focused on the successful future youth can have without violence in their lives.
- Share your ideas for youth violence prevention.
- Organize your thinking by answering questions in this chapter.
- Formulate a plan for how you want to proceed.
- Connect with kindred spirits and allies so you can streamline efforts, collaborate, and have some fun along the way.
- Do whatever feels manageable to stop youth violence for good.
- Pat yourself on the back every day for a job well done!

Resources

American Academy of Pediatrics: www.aap.org

American Association for Marriage and Family Therapy: www.aamft.org

American Psychological Association: www.apa.org

Centers for Disease Control and Prevention: www.cdc.gov

Center for the Study and Prevention of Violence, University of Colorado: www.colorado.edu/cspv

Child Trends: www.Childtrends.org

Great Start: www.greatstart.org

Harlem Children's Zone: www.hcz.org

Healthy Network iNGO: www.healthynetwork.org

Healthy Teen Network: www.healthyteennetwork.org

Kauffman Foundation: www.Kauffman.org

National Association of Social Workers: www.socialworkers.org

National Campaign to Prevent Teen and Unplanned Pregnancy: www.thenationalcampaign.org

National Center for Juvenile Justice: www.ncjj.org

Office of Juvenile Justice and Delinquency Prevention: www.ojjdp.gov

Substance Abuse and Mental Health Services Administration: www.samhsa.gov

Teenage Suicide Prevention: www.teensuicide.us

Youth Suicide Prevention: www.yspp.org

University of Colorado Blueprints for Violence Prevention: www.colorado.edu/cspv/blueprints/

Foster Care Alumni of America: www.fostercarealumni.org

Section Three

Other Important Things

Chapter 8

Everyone's Not the Same:
Addressing Uniqueness in Families

We can do anything we want to do
if we stick to it long enough.

Helen Keller

Overview

As with any effort in life, taking a stand against violence is unique for each person. What works for one individual may not work for other family members. What works for one family may not work for other families. Providing individualized services requires attention to the unique strengths and needs of everyone.

When services are truly individualized there is no need for a chapter like this. But many folks who work diligently to stop youth violence have not had specialized training addressing challenges such as developmental or physical disabilities. Gender, cultural differences, and sexual identity greatly influence uniqueness. Sensitively addressing values and beliefs about violence requires education and thoughtful exploration about how best to intervene. This chapter highlights a variety of things that contribute to the uniqueness of both individuals and families.

Objectives

By the end of this chapter we hope you will be able to:

- Identify unique differences in individuals and families that require attention for youth violence prevention.
- Understand how to effectively address uniqueness in all youth and family members.
- Serve people with developmental disabilities or any designated special needs according to federally established best practices.
- Respond respectfully to differences in youth and family members including, but not limited to, gender, race, ethnicity, sexual orientation, socio-economic status, and level of education.

Not all disabilities are developmental. Some disabilities result from accidents or illnesses later in life. They may affect a variety of life domains such as mobility, attention, understanding, and memory. Youth behaving violently, as well as their parents or other family members, may experience disabilities that can affect youth violence prevention.

Physical Disabilities

> **Definition**
>
> The Americans with Disabilities Act (1990) defines an individual with a disability as a person who has a physical or mental impairment that substantially limits one or more major life activities; has a record of such impairment; or is regarded as having such an impairment.

Physical limitations refer to any challenges a person faces in mobility or sensory functioning. People who are paralyzed in any way may experience unique challenges in mobility and transportation. People who are blind or deaf present challenges for service providers that may be addressed through skills in sign language or Braille communication. While laws specify requirements for physically addressing such uniqueness, it is important that all service providers be sensitive to both the physical and emotional needs of these individuals and families. Respectfully asking youth and family members what help they want is the best way to support their attempts to stop harm.

Disabilities

The Developmental Disabilities Act (Public Law 106-402, Section 102-8, 2000) of the United States defines developmental disabilities as "a severe, chronic disability of an individual 5 years of age or older that:

1. Is attributable to a mental or physical impairment or combination of mental and physical impairments;
2. Is manifested before the individual attains age 22;
3. Is likely to continue indefinitely;
4. Results in substantial functional limitations in three or more of the following areas of major life activity: self care; receptive and expressive language; learning; mobility; self-direction; capacity for independent living; and economic self-sufficiency.
5. Reflects the individual's need for a combination and sequence of special, interdisciplinary, or generic services, supports, or other assistance that is of lifelong or extended duration and is individually planned and coordinated, except that such term, when applied to infants and young children means individuals from birth to age 5, inclusive, who have substantial developmental delay or specific congenital or acquired conditions with a high probability of resulting in developmental disabilities if services are not provided."

Addressing the uniqueness of each disability is the most direct route to optimum service delivery. Considering where and how services should be provided is a critical first step. Deciding where it is easiest for individuals and the family as a whole to meet and focus on the tasks at hand can make a big difference in outcomes. Service providers who use American Sign Language for those who are hearing impaired, and who have Braille documents for the blind, make the work a lot easier. Patiently listening and effectively responding to a speech impediment sends a clear message that everyone's voice matters.

> A young man who was hit by a car at age seven struggled greatly with verbal communication. His intellectual functioning was fine but he spoke very slowly as a result of brain damage. Most people appeared impatient to hear him out and he became violent toward a dating partner. Therapy involved a tremendously slow process in which he was often only able to speak a few complete sentences in the span of an hour. Slowing down allowed him to feel respected and heard. He was able to communicate how the frustration played a major role in his violent actions and to explore creative options for change.

Intellectual or Cognitive Impairment

Limited intelligence quotient, or IQ, makes learning and understanding more difficult. When youth and/or family members have intellectual disabilities there are some key things to consider when helping them to stop youth violence.

First, these youth are vulnerable in two ways. First, they are more susceptible to being victimized and are vulnerable to committing acts of violence when they do not receive adequate information about moral reasoning and decision making in ways they can understand and practice.

Second, services may take longer and require greater direction from service providers. Therefore, it is important to begin by adjusting expectations based on limitations and assessing reading, writing, and comprehension skills. Slowing down and providing easy to understand resources can actually streamline service delivery.

Functional assessments, which are evaluations focusing specifically on assessing the impact of disabilities, provide critical information for developing service recommendations. Requirements for reading and writing should be based on the youth's ability and may need to be limited. Involving professionals who specialize in disabilities allows everyone to feel more secure about the potential for successful outcomes.

Mental Health Diagnoses

Disabilities relating to mental health involve clearly defined diagnostic categories such as anxiety, depression, post-traumatic stress, and/or attention deficits. These diagnoses are based on the *Diagnostic and Statistical Manual of Mental Disorders* (DSM), which is in the fourth and thoroughly revised edition and is referred to as the DSM-IV-TR. The federal government requires licensed mental health professionals to determine individual diagnoses for all federally funded mental health services.

Disabilities relating to autism spectrum disorders are also included in the DSM. *Autism is a mental condition that comes about in childhood and causes great difficulty in communication and connection with others.* For more information about mental health disorders please check the resource list at the end of this chapter.

Learning Disabilities

Learning disabilities are brain processes that interfere with learning. They do not necessarily affect general intelligence. Learning disabilities indicate that a person's brain takes in information differently. Dyslexia is an example of how some people read or experience letters or symbols differently than most others.

Many young people who behave violently struggle with learning disabilities. The Centers for Disease Control and Prevention (Thornton, et.al., 2002) identify learning problems and school absenteeism as vulnerabilities in youth at high risk for violence. Secondary and tertiary prevention efforts must take learning disabilities into consideration when planning for success with these youth. Intervening with youngsters prior to and throughout elementary and middle school may go a long way toward impacting healthy families and safer communities.

Comprehensive testing in early childhood is extremely important. Using results from such testing can greatly enhance a child's educational experience, self-esteem, confidence, and competency development. Educating and supporting parents helps them to further advocate for their children, which enhances attachment and optimum development.

Prevention Strategies

Primary prevention strategies for addressing challenges resulting from disabilities involve teaching all children respect for all living things. Optimally parents, caregivers, and all service providers share information about diversity that includes these challenges. When young children see blind people with canes or seeing-eye dogs, or people in wheelchairs, adults may thoughtfully and sensitively explain how these people are unique. Everyone can teach children to accept and respect differences, to understand that differences make everyone unique. This includes teaching children with physical, intellectual, and mental health challenges the same life lessons.

Trying to teach such important lessons may be frustrating. When limitations keep children from being able to communicate their needs, frustration might lead to violence. Helen Keller is a famous example of how frustration with physical challenges turned into violence and was overcome with patience and finding new ways to communicate.

Secondary prevention involves open communication about the impact of these challenges on individuals and families. It is important to identify how physical, intellectual, and mental health challenges place someone at risk of victimization, and also place them at greater risk of harm to self or others.

A person with limited physical mobility may not be able to protect himself or herself and get away from an attacker. Someone with speech limitations may not feel competent to communicate assertively when feeling disrespected, demeaned, harassed, bullied, or assaulted. A person with intellectual limitations may know that he or she does not understand something but may not want to look incapable and so doesn't tell anyone. Teaching people with functional challenges how to best protect themselves, contributes to optimal development.

Living with limitations leads to frustration and anger. Such feelings lead to a higher risk of depression and suicide and may result in increased risk for violence. Youth may lash out against the inequity, or cause themselves harm in any number of ways, when they do not receive adequate support for managing both physical and emotional pain that may come with disabilities. Additionally, they may have difficulty both understanding and communicating about the range of challenges these issues bring up. **Practically speak-**

ing, if a youth does not understand how rules and consequences relate to each other, and doesn't know how to talk about it, adults may think the youngster knows what he or she should be doing and is purposefully defying rules. This may not be true.

Sophia is a single parent of four children who has never behaved violently. She has some intellectual limitations, as do her children. Her oldest daughter, Kate, has significant developmental disabilities and has been verbally violent and physically assaultive and has behaved in sexually harmful ways. Sophia's oldest son, Mike, has mild limitations, was on probation for theft, and has been physically abusive toward one of his toddler brothers. The little ones have been receiving specialized services since birth in order to support optimum development.

Sophia's family received a range of services geared toward youth violence prevention in addition to public services for individuals with developmental disabilities. The family received intensive home-based family therapy to address the violence. The clinician, a family therapist, specializes in trauma, youth violence, and developmental disabilities. As a highly specialized service provider, that professional was designated to facilitate a formal family systems and ecological evaluation with detailed recommendations that served as a map for the treatment team, and promoted Sophia's leadership.

Intervention addressed Sophia's inability to support her daughter after Kate's biological father and the father of her three brothers sexually abused her. Family and individual therapy focused on stopping all violent and criminal behavior. Education focused on teaching the two teenagers sexual health as a foundation to stop sexual harm. While the work took about 18 months, the family has been free of violence for years and everyone is doing well. Team members from several service agencies and juvenile probation and representatives from the state department of social services collaborated effectively throughout the entire process.

Given that people with limitations often experience feelings of frustration and anger, it is important that service providers have knowledge about how to best address such important feelings. Interventions facilitated with sensitivity about the issues people with disabilities face promote both healing pain and stopping violence.

Culture

So many cultural issues impact youth violence it is hard to make sense of them all. Skin color plays a huge part. African American and Latino youth are disproportionately represented in the juvenile justice system (Piquero, 2008). Ethnicity, which means being a part of a large group of people who have a common race, nationality, or tribal or religious background, can also influence the experience of youth violence. Some nationalities or tribes have strong values and beliefs about the use of violence and may oppose it or promote it in rituals and rites of passage for young people.

Political and religious beliefs also can impact decisions about behaving violently. Sometimes people in politics are referred to as "hawks" or "doves." Hawks refer to those who promote aggression in resolving conflict, and doves are those who promote diplomacy and peacekeeping. Some religions preach messages from the Bible such as "an eye for an eye, and a tooth for a tooth," which means to strike back in kind when something has been taken. Another Bible passage that influences religious beliefs is "turning the other cheek." which implies that people should respond to violence by refusing to engage in it.

Geography is another important component of evaluation and assessment. Availability and access to services varies depending on where a child lives. Typically cities offer more services than rural areas. However, in crowded housing complexes in large cities there is a higher probability of crime and violence than in rural communities where less people are likely to congregate. Geography also reflects socio-economic status, or class. Wealthy people more often live in safer communities where there is less visible youth violence. However, the children in these wealthier communities who have less parental supervision or structure in their lives may be prone to using their access to larger amounts of money to buy drugs and engage in other risk-taking behaviors, thus moving themselves into a subculture promoting harm to self and others. People with less money, who are more likely to be African American, Hispanic, and/or immigrants, are more likely to live in areas with higher incidences of visible youth violence that may appear to be accepted as part of the community's culture. The Future of Children publications from the Woodrow Wilson School at Princeton University and publications from the Brookings Institute provide more details about these concerns.

Family values influence youth violence. When families promote violence to manage conflict, such as intimate partner violence or physical punishment, young people are likely to develop values and beliefs that promote harm.

All service providers committed to youth violence prevention are expected to demonstrate cultural competence and sensitivity. The federal government and professional licensing boards require it through continuing education.

Prevention Strategies

Once again when all children learn to respect all living things primary prevention is successfully accomplished. Parents, caregivers, and all service providers can promote acceptance and model ways to embrace diversity. Schools and religious, athletic, and leisure organizations can all provide consistent messages about acceptance and tolerance. When adults provide enthusiastic messages about diversity and enrichment through cultural understanding everyone's life is improved.

Secondary prevention strategies build on those identified in the previous section. They involve zero tolerance for any type of demeaning or discriminatory behavior. When adults witness such practices it is imperative that they respond immediately and effectively. Simply telling youth when behavior is offensive and that it will not be tolerated may be enough to stop it. All child-serving settings are required to train staff to provide a culturally sensitive protective response whenever discrimination rears its ugly head. All adults who have a role in guiding children should closely consider the words and attitudes they use to communicate so they are promoting only respectful and kind messages.

Tertiary prevention requires competent intervention. Licensed mental health professionals are required to obtain continuing education on cultural competence. Therapy should address youth violence in the context of a young person's life and day-to-day experiences. Supporting youth involves creating a safe and stable setting in which they can address experiences of discrimination in order to explore potential solutions for managing it without resorting to harm directed at self or others. Helping youth learn to take a stand against violence enables them to decide how they want to promote non-violent cultural experiences as they create a vision for their future.

Gender

Stereotypes about violence have historically focused on male perpetrators and female victims. This is not necessarily the case. Statistically, the vast majority of both perpetrators of violence and crime victims are male. Boys, by far, perpetrate the majority of youth violence, and are the vast number of victims of youth violence. Does that mean girls should just be ignored when it comes to youth violence prevention? Not at all! Services addressing both victimization and perpetration of youth violence should be equally available to all children.

Recent reports on juvenile justice bring up serious concerns not only about an increase in female aggression and violence, but also the lack of services for young women in the juveniles justice system (Cauffman, 2008). While girls and boys have similar childhood experiences, such as trauma and difficult family experiences, that place them at risk of youth violence, the impact on girls greatly influences both their adult lives and the lives of their future children. Young women are also likely to require continued support, possibly long after any violent behavior.

Prevention Strategies

As with all children, primary prevention occurs when girls grow up in a stable, loving, and nurturing environment. Optimum elements of child development are thoroughly addressed in Chapters 2 and 7.

Secondary prevention with girls should focus on effective responses to early warning signs such as bullying, negative temperament, and impulsivity. Addressing issues of trauma, victimization, and the unique mental health

Risk Factors for Youth Violence

The Future of Children, 2008

- Early puberty
- Developmental disabilities
- Mental health problems
- Lower levels of empathy
- Heightened sensitivity to rewards and stimulation
- Dysfunctional families and anti-social socialization
- Harmful pre- and post-natal biological experiences
- Poor parental monitoring
- Early interpersonal victimization
- Negative temperament
- Deviant peers
- Poverty
- Impulsivity
- Low IQ

The following risk factors are more pronounced for girls:
- Adversarial interpersonal relationships
- Mental health problems
- Lower levels of empathy
- Poor parental monitoring
- Early interpersonal victimization

Girls involved in the juvenile justice system are more likely to experience the following in adulthood:
- Higher mortality rates
- Psychiatric problems
- Dysfunctional and violent relationships
- Poor educational achievement
- Less stable work histories
- Lower occupational status
- Substance abuse
- Poorer physical health
- Reliance on social assistance
- Victimization by, as well as violence toward, partners

needs of each young girl integrates information from the previous section on developmental disabilities. Such a process enhances a holistic approach for healing pain and preventing future harm both for these youth and for future generations.

Diverting female offenders with mental health problems to community-based treatment programs is a recommended foundation for tertiary prevention. Due to mental health and developmental disabilities only the most dangerous should be placed in juvenile justice facilities.

Lesbian, Gay, Bisexual, and Transgendered Individuals

Sexual identity is a highly controversial issue in the United States. People who openly acknowledge being gay, lesbian, bisexual, or transgendered risk being victimized through discrimination or hate crimes. Others who are suspected of being so are also at risk of being bullied, harassed, tormented, assaulted, or murdered. Young people who are treated in such ways may also be at risk for acting out their pain through violence, particularly harm to self or suicide. Support for these youth and their families is tremendously important.

Providing access to services involves awareness of organizations such as PFLAG, a national alliance that stands for Parents, Families, and Friends of Lesbians and Gays, and the Human Rights Campaign; these organizations and others like them provide a broad array of vital services for these youth and families.

Supporting youth and families with gay, lesbian, bisexual, or transgendered members can be a complex process. First of all individuals may not be clear about their own sexual identity development. Clinical support of such important exploration requires specialized training. Licensed mental health professionals can obtain such training through their professional affiliations, such as the National Association of Social Workers (NASW) and the American Association for Marriage and Family Therapy (AAMFT). These websites are also provided at the end of the chapter.

It is very important to understand that adolescent sexual development is a fluid process and that adolescence is a time of developmental exploration in all facets of life. Just because a youth expresses a range of sexual interests does not mean his or her sexual identity is fully realized. Providing a great deal of patience and support for potentially high levels of confusion and possible frustration allows youth to gain education, understanding, and insight into the complex reality of human sexuality. Warm, genuine, nonjudgmental, and empathic support enhances potential for a successful outcome indicating lifelong sexual health and well-being.

Risk for Violence with Lesbian, Gay, Bisexual, and Transgendered Youth
Centers for Disease Control and Prevention, 2010

Many Lesbian, Gay, Bisexual, and Transgendered (LGBT) youth are happy and thriving. However, LGBT youth without supportive parents and a supportive school environment are more likely than other adolescents to experience difficulties in their lives, such as violence.

Negative attitudes toward LGBT youth put them at higher risk for bullying, teasing, harassment, physical assault, suicide, and substance use.

Personal experiences of trauma influence sexual identity development. When youth have experienced child sexual abuse it can wreak havoc on their sexual identity. If someone of the same sex abused them they may have questions about their own sexual identity development. If someone of the opposite sex abused them, they may not feel safe expressing themselves sexually with others of the opposite sex for fear the same thing will happen again. Young people may not understand how their body could experience sexual pleasure, and possibly orgasm, at the same time they may have been hurt and terrified through experiences of sexual abuse. It can be very confusing for young people. It can also be very challenging for family members and service providers dedicated to helping these youngsters heal the pain.

Other types of child abuse can also impact sexual identity development. Young people who have been physically abused or witnessed intimate partner violence may not feel safe to express themselves sexually for fear of being assaulted or raped. Verbal and emotional abuse such as using derogatory sexual terms or hearing family members promote hatred toward those who are gay, lesbian, bisexual, or transgendered may prevent young people from safely exploring sexual identity development. Clinicians addressing these challenges should specialize in both trauma and sexual identity development. These issues are addressed in the *T.O.P.* Workbook for Sexual Health*, which can be a resource for both youth and their family members (Schladale, 2010).

When a youth clearly identifies as gay, lesbian, bisexual, or transgendered, he or she may not feel safe to come out to family members for a variety of reasons. Therapy with these youth should address the pros and cons of coming out and should carefully address any potential danger in doing so. Service providers may meet separately with designated family members in order to see if the youth's fears are accurate and how to best support both the youth and his or her family members.

Youth who are confused or who struggle with their own and/or family members identifying as gay lesbian, bisexual, or trans-gendered may be at risk of violence. They may mistakenly direct confusion by lashing out through harmful language and insulting words and bullying. Hate crimes committed by youth can be extremely serious. A young man incarcerated for attempted murder told his therapist that he tried to kill a man he thought was gay because his father was gay and he hated his father for it and wanted to get back at him. Everyone involved in youth violence prevention has responsibility for preventing such grievous crimes.

Prevention Strategies

As mentioned before, primary prevention begins when all children are taught to respect all living things. Parents, caregivers, and educators can provide information about sexual identity development and the range of ways humans express their sexuality. Additionally youth can participate in school and extracurricular program activities that promote human rights. Evidence-based sexual health curricula address sexual identity development as a part of comprehensive education.

Secondary prevention strategies with these youth and families involve zero tolerance for discriminatory practices or hate crimes. When school personnel are notified of any harmful behavior indicating any elements of sexual identity, staff can adhere to policies and protocols created to provide immediate and effective intervention. Staff in all child-serving settings can be trained to provide a protective response any time the need arises.

Finally, tertiary prevention requires knowledgeable intervention. When youth identifying as gay, lesbian, bisexual, or transgendered behave violently, it is critical for service providers to explore all aspects of the experience in order to understand everything that influenced a youth to commit acts of harm to self and/or others. Therapy focuses on exploration of healthy coping strategies for buffering the possibly lifelong discrimination these youth risk facing. Helping them learn to celebrate their sexuality and obtain love, support, and understanding are vital elements of health and well-being.

Substance Use

Underaged substance use is a huge problem in the United States. Young people are bombarded with messages about substance use, and teenage partying often involves binge drinking, use of illegal drugs, and misuse of prescription drugs. Schools have also become a primary location for obtaining illicit substances.

The *Journal of General Psychiatry* (Wu et al., 2011) published findings from a National Survey on Drug Use and Health involving 72,561 teens aged 12 to 17. According to the research, 37% of the youth surveyed used drugs or alcohol in the past year, and 7.9% met the criteria for a substance-related disorder. The most widely used illicit drug was marijuana (13%) followed by narcotic painkillers, which were used by 7% of the teens surveyed. A 2010 report from the Office of Applied Studies found that almost one-third of American teens used alcohol; one-fifth used an illicit drug; and almost one-sixth smoked cigarettes. These studies accentuate the continued ease of access to substances at an early age in the United States.

Underaged substance use influences bad decision-making. When youth are drunk, or high, they are vulnerable to behaving violently and/or being victimized. The media is filled with stories of victimization and perpetration in which illegal substances were involved. The connection between substance use and violence documents a need for improved screening methods, early detection, and diversion services.

Prevention Strategies

When adults model responsible substance use, primary prevention occurs. It also involves childhood education. While the Substance Abuse and Mental Health Services Administration (SAMHSA) continually supports research on this topic, challenges remain in primary prevention. One program, DARE (Drug Abuse Resistance Education), was used in schools across the United States but was found to be ineffective. It is extremely important that community collaboration require evidence-based practices. While it is awesome that schools and law enforcement are collaborating to teach kids about the dangers of substance use, it's a waste of time, effort, and money if it doesn't show positive results.

> Sometime after participating in a school-based DARE program, 10-year-old Miguel was vacationing with family and having dinner in a pizza parlor. When the youngster's aunt, who seldom drinks alcohol, ordered a beer, the little rascal responded in surprised horror by loudly stating, "Tia Juanita, you're not supposed to do drugs!" While entertaining to other restaurant patrons, Miguel's education did not adequately prepare him to distinguish between drug and alcohol abuse and moderate, and legal social drinking by responsible adults.

Primary prevention must be developmentally congruent. Programs for young children should be concrete with simple messages. Middle and high school substance use curricula provide more detailed information and address decision making. For youth with developmental disabilities, curricula need to be presented in a way that meets individual learning styles.

Primary prevention for substance use also involves screening. Pediatricians, early childhood development programs like Head Start, childcare programs, and schools can all provide very simple effective screening in order to identify potential vulnerabilities.

When universal screening for children identifies vulnerabilities toward substance use, secondary prevention involves early detection. Child-serving agencies can create policies and protocols outlining a uniform response for addressing concerns. Agencies can provide written information that includes facts and resources. Staff can be trained to confidentially provide resources and services for both youth and family members.

When detection indicates serious concerns, tertiary prevention can initially focus on diversion. Diversion is the process of keeping youth away from juvenile justice and from more restrictive levels of care, in order to reduce potential for further harm. Court diversion programs are used when youth come before a judge for the first time, or for minimal problems that can best be served through less restrictive services. Diversion is very important when substance abuse services can be used to help youth understand the dangers, address the problems, and enhance motivation for change. Substance abuse services can be effective in helping youth to both stop substance use and stop all harm to self and others.

Only when youth are not successful in stopping harm should criminal justice services be implemented. A continuum from least to most restrictive services can provide youth with services that best meet their unique situation and motivation for change.

> Alex struggled with a high level of drug-seeking behavior and was placed in residential treatment for crimes he committed while under the influence. His transition plan included referral for substance abuse services in addition to other therapeutic activities. He returned to the community and immediately started using again. Attempts were consistently made to monitor his participation in diversion services but he was unsuccessful. He was getting high at school, leaving classes, and endangering others. Finally his probation officer, in collaboration with his treatment team, remanded him to a state juvenile facility where it was determined he will remain until he turns 19.

Foster and Adoptive Families

Foster and adoptive families seldom have adequate information about a child's pre-natal, physical, and emotional experiences with their biological parents. In additional to being removed from home, these youth sometimes have a host of special needs relating to many other topics addressed in this chapter.

While many states and private agencies work diligently to provide adequate training and resources for foster and adoptive families, fiscal limitations can greatly restrict such important efforts. In focus groups many of these parents report high levels of concerns about their children's life experiences and resulting violent behavior. They identify feeling inadequately prepared to support the youth effectively.

Prevention Strategies

Primary prevention for adopted youth and those in foster care involves all of the same things identified in all previous primary prevention sections of the book. Along with all other children, we want these youth educated about health and well-being.

Children who have been adopted or placed in foster care have been removed from their family homes because of parental abuse or neglect, and thus primary prevention didn't work. These children automatically require secondary prevention.

Secondary prevention for these youth may require additional monitoring through pediatric visits that provide additional screening for physical and mental health needs, and other early childhood services that assess development. These youth may be at risk of developing attachment disorders so it is important to support youth, parents, and siblings in maintaining healthy relationships.

Public and private agencies providing adoptive and foster care services often have resources to help both youth and foster or adoptive families adapt to placement. It is critical that all youth and families have easy access to such resources. **Practically speaking, youth in foster care will be at higher risk for violence in their life if they are not given additional services and support to address their complicated life circumstances.**

In addition to evidence-based violence prevention services, tertiary prevention for these youth addresses additional challenges they may face in coming to grips with being in foster care or being adopted. They may struggle with differing levels of pain about being removed from their families. The age and circumstances under which they were removed greatly influence their ability to make sense of and manage the experience. Issues of grief, loss, and shame may be overwhelming. These youth are more likely to have developmental disabilities and to struggle with complex trauma-related symptoms.

Pregnant and Parenting Teens

Hope is a powerful contraceptive.
The way you help young people avoid pregnancy is by providing them
with real evidence that good things can happen in their lives.
Michael Carrera

Teen pregnancy changes the lives of young parents forever. As mentioned in the book's introduction, unplanned and unwanted children are more likely to be involved in youth violence as they grow. Young people who have been in foster care are 71% more likely to experience unplanned pregnancy than are other young adults (Thiessen Love et al., 2009). But this section is not just about pregnant and parenting teens who have been in foster care. This section is about all pregnant and parenting teens and the risk of their being involved in youth violence.

We know a lot about the lives of pregnant and parenting teens. According to renowned specialist Claire Brindis, (2011), many come from multiple generations of teen parents who have experienced poverty and other risk factors in their family backgrounds that include inadequate health care. Young teen parents have often been exposed to substance abuse and violence; have experienced child abuse, sexual assault, or early sexual activity with numerous sexual partners; and have been involved in child welfare. They often struggle academically and drop out of school. Risk factors for teen fathers include: school dropout, delinquency, substance abuse, aggression and violence, unemployment, and lack of involvement in service provision (Brindis, 2011). We also know that the children of teen parents are more likely to end up in prison and become teen parents themselves.

Many young parents have experienced significant trauma and are at risk of passing this legacy on to the next generation. Trauma can result in multiple domains of impairment that include problems with: affect regulation, anxiety, addictions, aggression, social problems, eating disorders, physical health, sexual disorders, and revictimization.

According to the National Child Traumatic Stress Network (NCTSN), an optimal response involves supporting teen parents in developing healthy relationships with supportive adults, partners and peers, and their children. This is how violence with this population can be stopped.

> Camilla, 19, is the mother of two-month-old Leah. Leah's father, Graham, is also 19. Both parents struggle with drug addiction. During Camilla's pregnancy she assaulted Graham during a fight they were having. The police were called and the parents were ordered to have no contact until the designated court date several months away. They violated the court order and began living together at Camilla's mother's home. Camilla decided to participate in therapy in an attempt to stop using drugs, to stop the violence, and to become the best mother she can be. Camilla and Graham both continue to struggle with drug use and the relationship is very unstable. Leah is being detoxified through specialized medical services since she became drug addicted in utero. Camilla continues to participate in all therapeutic activities and hopes to begin college in the fall. If she remains drug free and does not behave violently for six months the charges will be dropped.

Prevention Strategies

Primary prevention for teen pregnancy and youth violence involves sexual health curricula for school-aged children of all developmental levels. The federal government and organizations such as the Sexuality Information and Education Council of the United Stated (SIECUS), the Healthy Teen Network, the Annie E. Casey Foundation, Planned Parenthood, and the Guttmacher Institute all work diligently to prevent teen pregnancy.

Secondary prevention with this population involves working closely with teen parents to stop the intergenerational experience of premature, unplanned, and unwanted pregnancies. It also includes supporting young fathers in a variety of ways that reduce vulnerabilities for involvement in any type of violence.

According to the Children's National Medical Center (2011) expert policy recommendations involve:

- Creating comprehensive medical homes for adolescent parents and their children.
- Adapting counseling to the developmental level of adolescent parents.
- Encouraging positive parenting.
- Closely monitoring development of both parent and child.
- Encouraging positive involvement of baby's father and extended family.
- Providing family planning services.
- Encouraging educational achievement.
- Serving parents in their home, school, community, and medical settings.

Tertiary prevention for pregnant and parenting teens can be quite complex and challenging. It can be hard to engage teen fathers in service provision, especially when either or both parents have behaved violently. In addition to everything needed for optimal young parenting, violence prevention must be included in a trauma-informed approach for services. The federal government is supporting such service delivery through demonstration projects funded by the Department of Health and Human Services, Office of Population Affairs, and Office of Adolescent Pregnancy Programs.

Conclusion

What you are shouts so loudly in my ears
I cannot hear what you say.
Ralph Waldo Emerson

Youth with disabilities and others who have historically experienced discrimination are particularly vulnerable to being targeted as potential victims of youth violence. Gay, lesbian, bisexual, and transgendered youth are also at high risk of internalizing their pain and causing harm to themselves. Statistics indicate these youth are at high risk for suicide. Youth with learning disabilities are also vulnerable toward behaving violently toward others.

Additionally, African American and Hispanic youth are at high risk of experiencing crime and are disproportionately represented in the juvenile justice system. While girls are increasingly at risk for violent behavior, systems of care may not be serving them adequately. Violence increased vulnerabilities for substance use and abuse. Foster and adoptive families face a range of challenges relating to a youth's history of trauma and to symptoms that may surface years later and that place youth at higher risk of harm to self or others and for unplanned pregnancies.

While taking all aspects of uniqueness into consideration can make service providers feel overwhelmed, a clearly defined comprehensive approach for youth violence prevention can help individuals, organizations, and communities share a balanced approach that does not overload any single service, or the youth and families themselves.

A broad range of service providers specialize in all sorts of unique characteristics in youth and families. When these folks provide leadership, supervision, and training, everyone involved can understand how to provide effective services for all youth and families. The best outcomes are achieved when everyone is happy to work collaboratively in order to streamline services, maximize outcomes, and have a little fun along the way.

While everyone can interact respectfully when addressing uniqueness, it is also vitally important to support people with developmental disabilities or any designated special needs according to federally established best practices.

Recommendations

- Celebrate diversity and uniqueness!
- Abide by the golden rule (treat others as you want to be treated).
- Provide training for all service providers to address uniqueness in youth and families.
- Maintain cultural competency and sensitivity.
- Follow the leadership of youth and family members in service delivery.

Resources

American Association for Marriage and Family Therapy (AAMFT): www.aamft.org

American Psychological Association (APA): www.apa.org

Future of Children: www.futureofchildren.org

Guttmacher Institute: www.guttmacher.org

Healthy Teen Network: www.healthyteennetwork.org

Human Rights Campaign: www.hrc.org

National Association for the Advancement of Colored People: www.naacp.org

National Association of Social Workers (NASW): www.socialworkers.org

National Organization for Women: www.now.org

Parents, Families, and Friends of Lesbians and Gays: www.pflag.org

National Campaign to Prevent Teen and Unplanned Pregnancy: www.teenpregnancy.org

Youth Communication: www.youthcomm.org

Sex Education Library: www.sexedlibrary.org

Sexuality Information and Education Council of the United States: www.siecus.org

Stop Underage Drinking: www.stopalcoholabuse.gov

Chapter 9

When All Else Fails...
Out of Home Placement

There is no failure except in no longer trying.

Elbert Hubbard

Overview

Thank goodness the vast majority of youth behaving violently are no longer placed out of home, a long distance from where they live, for long periods of time. After years of incarcerating youth, or placing them in residential treatment facilities, policy makers in the United States are taking action to prevent ineffective practices. During the last ten years out of home placement has decreased considerably across the country and children are being served much more successfully in their homes and local communities.

There are still times when violent behavior continues despite all community efforts. Sadly there are times when youth and/or family members are not ready, willing, or able to maintain safety with the youth at home. When this happens, team members are faced with difficult decisions about how to best meet a youth's needs for support and prevention. In this chapter we address decisions about out of home placement when all efforts fail to influence safety and stop youth violence.

Objectives

By the end of this chapter we hope you will be able to:

- Recognize out of home placement only as a short-term stabilizing component of a full continuum of care.
- Understand why out of home placement is an option of last resort and not a remedy for stopping harm.
- Create a system of effective communication and collaboration when youth must leave home.
- Minimize negative effects when youth require out of home placement.

When all else fails...

What a sad state of affairs it is when a youth has to leave home because he or she cannot be safe. When this occurs family members are often overwhelmed, worn out, and demoralized. Youth feel out of control and haven't succeeded in behaving pro-socially. Team members often grapple with frustration and an inability to identify any more creative ways to address the problem.

When violence meets a criminal code, police may be called and youth may be placed in detention or a crisis facility. *Criminal codes are the state, federal, or Bureau of Indian Affairs laws that describe what behavior constitutes a crime.* Whether or not identified violence meets a criminal code, youth may be placed in a locked psychiatric facility or a secure residential treatment setting in order to prevent harm to self or others. When all else fails it is still important for everyone to stay on track to stop the violence.

Out of Home Placement

Out of home placement is tertiary prevention. It should only be considered as a last resort when a youth and/or his or her family members are clearly unable to maintain safety after violence has occurred. There are a variety of out of home placement options when youth are unable to be safe. They may involve short-, mid-, or long-term services. These services are typically licensed by the state they are in and must adhere to state regulations and policies. Out of home program options differ from state to state. Historically, some youth have stayed in programs for months and months when communities have not considered alternatives. Sadly, without ever addressing serious problems in service delivery, some children end up with long-term stays in short- and mid-term facilities.

Short-term interventions involve crisis stabilization in settings like detention, psychiatric facilities, or designated group homes. Depending on each community's protocol, families may be instructed to call the police or a designated community crisis telephone line. Sometimes they are instructed to go directly to a designated location, often a local hospital. Job number one is always safety and stabilization. Additional goals may include helping youth, family members, and witnesses to calm down after a violent episode. Sometimes a goal is to detain youth for criminal investigation. Other times it may be to stabilize them physically after harm to self. Short-term interventions usually last no more than 48 hours.

Mid-term programs range from 7 to 90 days and may be combined with short-term services. While all have similar goals, they can be quite different, and it is easy to get confused about them. Some may involve assessment or diagnostic centers, foster care, or group homes. Unfortunately cities and counties with inadequate community-based resources are at risk of having too many children in out of home placements, far from home, for too long.

Long-term services involve any out of home placement lasting six months or more, and include foster care, group homes, and residential treatment and juvenile justice facilities. Research findings clearly prove that residential services do not stop youth violence (ATSA, 2000; Chaffin, 2008; Office of the Surgeon General, 2001). While Multidimensional Treatment Foster Care (MDTFC) is an evidence-based practice, other long-term services may not be based on research. This is why only one chapter of this book addresses out of home placement. Don't do it unless safety is really threatened! It's much harder work, with limited benefits, often creating more barriers to success. Please, only consider this option when all else really has failed! Here's why...

Challenges

First, let's get the money issue out of the way. Out of home placement costs a lot more than home-based services. When money is spent on ineffective practices those dollars are taken away from effective practices. What a waste! Resources are tight enough and money for youth violence prevention should be well spent.

The worst thing to do in an effort to stop youth violence is to place youth with others behaving violently. Violence is highly contagious. Put a group of youth with violent histories together and what are they likely to do... brag about violence in an effort to be seen as "tough enough" or "man enough" and give each other ideas about more ways to be violent. We certainly don't want that!

Youth come into treatment with a variety of strengths, needs, influences, learning styles, and abilities, which is why individualized treatment is so important. Youngsters engaged in deliberate self-harm or suicidal behavior may have very different needs from those involved in physical violence toward others. When any of these youth are using illegal substances another layer of complexity is introduced into the mix. Sometimes youth are behaving violently in quite a number of ways through harm to self and others at the same time.

Personality and mental health are important factors in developing individualized services. Youth who feel and express guilt, shame, and embarrassment have different needs from those with little regard for the feelings of others or a willingness to accept accountability. Youth are vulnerable to being viewed, or seeing themselves, as victims or perpetrators within a residential peer group. Such experiences jeopardize safety and create more problems. **Practically speaking, if out of home placement does not provide a safe environment for youth, they are not receiving the one thing we hoped to achieve by removing them from home.**

A large multi-program agency in one state hires one therapist per program and calls the therapists "generalists." When youth have needs that exceed a generalist's skill base, the state contracts with specialists to additionally serve the youth and family. Such situations create complex challenges when youth and families have multiple therapists. Youth, family members, residential staff, and therapists can all get confused and begin to wonder who is supposed to be addressing what behavior with whom and when.

Children in out of home placement are often homesick. Be it ever so humble, there's no place like home. Even when serious problems exist at home most children miss family members and a sense of place. Such pain and confusion create significant challenges in treatment.

Parents may experience their child's out of the home placement as an implied message that someone else is now in charge and they have little or no decision-making power in their child's life. When parents feel unimportant, or that they failed in some way, they may resist participation in treatment. Such behavior may look like abandonment. Another challenge occurs when youth and/or families develop an "us against them" attitude toward service providers when they perceive that family loyalty is at stake.

While Stephen was in residential treatment he got into trouble a lot for running away. After many incidences of going "AWOL," a graduate student conducting research at the facility asked him where he went, and he replied, "To the cornfields." When asked why, he said, "I miss my family and all the noise here makes me crazy. At least in the cornfield it's quiet and I can think."

Children taken out of their home often feel like failures. They may think they've let their parents down and were a bad role model for younger siblings. Even with therapeutic activities, it's harder for positive youth development to occur when a youth feels ashamed, embarrassed, demoralized, and hopeless about being locked up. It's hard to maintain positive youth development when children have additional struggles with self-esteem and hopelessness relating to out of home placement.

Cultural attitudes about out of home placement often include negative opinions about juvenile correctional facilities, psychiatric hospitals, residential treatment centers, and foster care. Some youth struggle to come to grips with such attitudes. Out of home placement creates yet another hurdle for youngsters to jump over in the quest for a positive self-image and a belief they can do better. When youth are given messages that lock-up or the psychiatric hospital are the only places that can handle them, a positive self-image is tough to conger up. They feel locked up no matter how much good treatment is offered.

Another hurdle residential service providers sometimes have to overcome is a tough guy image that being bad is cool. If being locked up is seen as a badge of honor, engaging youth in positive youth development can be quite difficult.

When children are placed away from home, services have to double up to help the youth in placement and help the family at home so things will be better when the youth returns. Collaboration and service delivery become more complex and challenging. When residential program budgets are cut, family involvement and aftercare services are often the first to be reduced or eliminated. Family and community services are often seen as expendable, yet treatment has to address the violence that led to out of home placement without being able to solve the problem where it occurred, at home.

Solutions

When all else seems to be failing, when information from other chapters in this book and from the wealth of information provided on identified websites have not solved the problem, here are some ways to manage out of home placements most efficiently.

- Consider the least restrictive settings that can maintain safety.
- Obtain services as close as possible to the family's home.
- Make sure programs are dedicated to listening carefully and following the family's lead in identifying goals for placement.
- Consider placements that have a reputation of collaborating with youth, families, and community service providers.
- Hold programs accountable for such important collaboration.

- Commit to services for short amounts of time.
- Maintain continuity of service provision as much as possible.
- Minimize duplication of efforts through collaborative decision-making.
- Hold regularly scheduled informal and formal team meetings to closely assess, monitor, and document treatment progress.
- Consistently focus on reconciliation, reconnection, and reunification at all times a youth is out of his or her home.

At age 16, Amelia, had to spend time in a group home after physically assaulting her grandfather, crashing his car in the school parking lot, getting suspended from school, and committing burglary and theft by breaking into a neighbor's house and stealing alcohol. Her grandparents, with whom she lived, were offered the best services available by the state, but they still lived in almost constant fear. Amelia consistently expressed a high level of motivation to continue getting in trouble this way. Whenever she got mad, her immediate response was, "I wanna punch 'em in the face." It didn't matter whom she was angry with.

During her time in residential services, she continued to be violent and received even more criminal charges. After several months she finally engaged in therapy and decided to stop harm. She still struggles a great deal but Amelia is living with her mother and trying to finish her senior year of high school.
Did the residential placement make a difference? Who knows? Would she have eventually stopped on her own at home? Some youth stop violence simply through maturing. Could her grandma have taken any more? The team did not think so.

Was service delivery harder while she was in placement? You bet! Her individual and family therapist worked hard to collaborate with the residential treatment team, but they had some differences in values and beliefs about how to best serve this family. Disagreements challenged effective collaboration but most service providers worked diligently to stay focused on solutions.

Local substance abuse services had to be terminated and new ones started in the town where the group home was located. Then different substance abuse services had to be found when she left residential treatment, as she was unable to continue with the original program. Whew, what a lot of extra work and a lack of continuity in service delivery.

That's a long list of information to take into consideration. Here's some additional information that may be helpful.

All states have government social services named something like Department of Health and Human Services, Children and Families Department, Department of Human Services, etc. These organizations usually have information on the state government website that designates types of care and protocols for placing children away from home. Treatment teams can obtain such information to streamline decision making. Designated case managers often take the lead in this process.

Once a child is removed from home, many teams are required to assess the situation weekly, monthly, or quarterly. Some states have managed care organizations that monitor progress and allocate funds for services. In such cases all service providers are responsible for adequately documenting all required information. This can also help prevent duplication of efforts.

Deciding on Placement

Out of home placement often involves a painful, frightening, confusing, and frustrating process. First, youth may be placed in a stabilization unit, detention facility, or hospital either during, or immediately after, behaving violently. When they cannot return home safely decisions are made about longer-term placement. Teams often come together with urgency or in emergency situations to make quick decisions. Hopefully a desired placement is available and a safe and smooth transition occurs.

Sometimes children are required to return home to await placement even when it is unsafe to do so. There may not be space available, or the program may be waiting on required information. A waiting period may be required even after placement has been decided. This can be a confusing time, especially when the youth settles down and does not behave violently. Teams may decide not to pursue out of home placement only to be reminded of the need when violence erupts again.

> Vince was violent toward his younger brother and children in the neighborhood. He had received psychiatric services since he was a very young child and was diagnosed with bipolar disorder at age five. When he was a toddler Vince witnessed his father assaulting his mother. Vince was placed in detention after his violence escalated and community services were not successful. A family systems evaluation determined that safety could not be maintained in the community and Vince remained in detention. A court-appointed community-based family therapist provided individual and family therapy. The detention facility was local so Vince's mom and stepdad could attend weekly family sessions along with regular visitation. The family therapist contacted extended family members who either participated in treatment or received progress reports. Family communication involved continuous brainstorming about accessing community resources and exploring support for Vince to return home.

Decisions about out of home placement are most effective when done collaboratively. Families are often at a loss about what to do or where to turn. Case managers and seasoned service providers often know a great deal about community resources and the range of reasonable options. Plus, they know the family and can help assess the best potential "fit" for placement. Well-written program documents, site visits, and staff interviews can go a long way to aid in the decision-making process. School and community resources should also be addressed.

This is a time when thoughtful service delivery can go a long way in helping youth and family members to feel supported and cared for. Patiently acknowledging and addressing a range of emotions that often surface during such difficult times can contribute to safety and stability. Clarifying the roles of both established and new service providers can help youth and family members understand what to expect and how to plan accordingly.

Whew, what a lot of work! As mentioned in Chapter 1, when collaboration occurs, everyone's job is a whole lot easier. Most everyone providing out of home services is dedicated to youth violence prevention. Bringing new folks into the picture and helping them get a running start with all the complex dynamics that lead to out of home placement can be mind-boggling. Treatment teams may be working together cohesively and welcome new participants who know very little about the current situation. It is important to support new team members as ongoing violence can cause frustration and added strain to treatment team dynamics. However residential service providers join the ongoing team, thoughtful consideration of additional challenges can go a long way to promoting harmony and successful outcomes.

When a youth is removed from home it is important for new services to be consistent and adhere to research-based practices that form the basis for all youth violence prevention. These are provided in Chapter 6. Current treatment team members are responsible for giving new service providers any information that can streamline progress and aid family reunification.

Relationships that youth and families have with community-based service providers should not be dismissed when youth are placed out of their home. A plan for the youth to return home and/or transition back to community services after out of home placement is optimally considered right at the beginning of placement. Previously established community-based services may be available when the youth returns home. Having continuity of service providers and support in the community aids in a smoother transition home. The rest of this chapter focuses on additional issues that must be considered when out of home placement occurs.

Reconciliation, Reconnection, and Reunification

Reconciliation means to make friendly again, to settle or bring into harmony. It is a process of supporting families in this effort when any family members have behaved harmfully. The goal is healing emotional wounds caused by family violence and abuse. This can occur without reunification.

Reconnection is the ability of family members to visit in a way that ensures physical and emotional safety for everyone involved. Family visits should be consistently monitored and/or supervised in order to assess for safety and the potential for reunification.

Reunification means to unify again after being divided. Family reunification represents the physical rejoining of family members with a youth who has been placed away from home. It is a complex process that requires reconciliation in order to be successful.

Reconciliation, reconnection, and reunification are critical issues unique to out of home placement. Decisions to remove children from their homes requires attention to all three in order for families to heal and begin life anew. The following information can assist family therapists in addressing initial concerns after removal occurs.

Preliminary Preparation for Family Reconciliation

- Identify anyone willing to consider participation in family reconciliation and create a roster of these people.
- Talk with each person about how family discussions about reconciliation might go.
- Identify the resistance or ambivalence each person has about family reconciliation, reconnection, and/or reunification.
- Explore how past family discussions have been facilitated successfully, and how future ones might go well.
- Support all participants in planning for successful participation.
- Allow each person to imagine what questions others will have and how the questions might best be addressed.
- Encourage each participant to plan how to get their questions answered.
- Create a plan to address problem behavior if it occurs during a meeting.
- If any victims want to participate, make sure that protocols for restorative justice, victim apologies, and making amends have been completed and safety plans are established and maintained (making amends are addressed in Chapter 6).
- Teach everyone to manage difficult feelings respectfully (affect regulation) throughout the process.
- When all preparations are made, schedule family meetings for reconciliation.

A Process for Family Reconciliation

- Family meetings are facilitated in any location providing physical and emotional safety and confidentiality.
- They include family and any social support network members everyone agrees on.
- All participants do not have to attend every meeting.
- Family members not previously willing to participate are welcomed if they change their mind and go through preliminary preparation.
- Goals for reconciliation are established collaboratively in the first session.
- Family members create a vision of what reconciliation will look like for them.
- Once goals and a vision are established, discussion moves to reestablishing safety by planning for reconnection through visitation.
- Preliminary discussion about consideration of reunification may occur.
- Assessment of progress toward established goals is addressed at the beginning of each session. This can be formally documented or addressed informally by asking, "How are things better since we last met?"
- Individual session goals are identified at the beginning of each meeting and achievement measured at the end of each session. This can be formally documented or addressed simply by asking, "How has our time together today been helpful?"
- Ongoing assessment of progress influences discussion about possibilities for reunification.
- If victim/s are in the home, have been participating in reconciliation, and want the youth to return home, reunification is addressed.
- If victim/s are not in the home, and if the youth and all family members want reunification, the process can begin.
- If victim/s are in the home, do not want the youth to return home, or the treatment team (including family members) thinks it is unsafe for the youth to return home, other living arrangements are explored and plans for continued family contact are made.

A Process for Family Reunification

- Everyone involved has full knowledge of a youth's strengths and needs and plans for continued success.
- All family and social support network members have documented plans for how to intervene if the youth is struggling to remain non-violent.
- All family and social support network members are committed to report any potentially harmful behavior to the designated service providers or local authorities.
- Home visits are scheduled in accordance with court orders and licensing or credentialing protocols.
- Responsibility for supervision and monitoring is clearly assigned, documented, and assessed on a continuous basis.
- Designated family members and service providers "debrief" following each visit

---

Debriefings should include the following topics:
- Highlights of the visit (activity, participants, what made it a highlight, etc.)
- Low points of the visit (activity, participants, what made it problematic, etc.)
- Reporting protocols for any criminal behavior that is revealed.
- Coping strategies used for handling any stress and conflict.
- Strategies for reducing conflict during future visits.
- Challenges regarding any urges to behave violently. If so, what were the specific crimes; what were the vulnerable situations; and, most importantly, what self-intervention was used to prevent harm?
- Planning for continued success during future home visits.

- Assess level of service needed in the community before return home.
- Collaborate to provide a smooth transition of services and avoid a gap in meeting youth and family needs for safety and continued success.
- Celebrate completion of out of home placement.

- Discharge from residential services.
- Maintain contact with placement staff as needed.
- Monitor progress toward goals for maintaining continued success.
- Notify service providers immediately if successful outcome is threatened.
- Reassess for level of service needed on an ongoing basis.
- Participate in follow-up tracking.

If victim/s are in the extended family, neighborhood, school, church, or broader local community and contact is allowed:
- When indicated, designated service providers meet with victim/s and victim's caregivers for community notification and preparation for any contact with youth.
- Victim/s, and victim's caregivers, are notified and instructed to contact authorities if any potentially harmful interaction with the youth occurs.

If a no-contact order is in effect:
- Inadvertent contact with a victim is reported immediately and discussed with pertinent family and service providers.
- Contact by a victim is reported immediately and discussed with pertinent family and service providers.
- Any attempt to contact a victim is reported immediately and discussed with pertinent family and service providers.
- If victim contact is discovered, visits are halted until the youth demonstrates contrition, makes amends (real or symbolic), and recommits to honest communication with the treatment team, family, and social support network members.

What to Do When Youth Can't Go Home?

To say it is disappointing when a youth cannot return home is an understatement. Many consider it tragic. When such a situation occurs most everyone struggles with having to accept such a difficult and often disappointing state of affairs. Some youth and parents may feel devastated. A lot of people struggle with feelings of hopelessness and failure. It's very tough when children can't live at home for any reason, let alone violence. The inability to return home implies an ongoing lack of safety and stability. How sad is that?

Stan's violent behavior toward his younger siblings occurred in his home over a period of two years. His mother and grandmother who both lived in the home did not acknowledge the violence when it was occurring. As a working single mother, Keri was away from home or exhausted when she was there. She was a victim of child abuse that went untreated and she suffers from depression. Grandma Helen favored Stan over the other children. In grandma's eyes, Stan could do no wrong. Helen still has a hard time acknowledging Stan's violence even after he admitted it, took responsibility, and successfully completed residential treatment.

Helen now lives in a senior citizen center and Keri is alone raising the younger children. Throughout treatment, Keri has minimally improved her skills in observing interactions among the children. With community services, she is doing all she can to keep the two youngest children safe and to develop skills needed to move forward in life. Although the younger children want Stan to be a part of their lives again, Keri is not capable of assuring safety in the home if Stan lived with them. Looking for a place to live began while Stan was in residential treatment. He was 17 when he was ready for discharge and was not ready for independent living. No foster home was available. He had a year of high school to finish and needed to develop independent living and job readiness skills.

While exploring adult services a team member contacted a local homeless shelter and resource center for men. The director of the facility committed to supporting Stan through his senior year of high school. Stan enjoyed the camaraderie of the other men, and some of the more established ones mentored him. The program provided meals, household services, support with homework, and structure based on shelter rules. In order to live there, Stan agreed to mandatory wakeup times; curfews; set mealtimes; activities such as school, job searching, and work; and substance abuse treatment. With support from the director, the men at the shelter, his therapist, his mentor, the juvenile probation officer, school support personnel, and his mother, Stan established a successful routine of school, work, and enrichment activities and transitioned back into the community safely. His daily needs were met and he began saving money to move into his own apartment.

When youth cannot go home, their treatment team should be able to access the family's initial evaluation and revisit recommendations about creating a permanency plan. *A permanency plan is usually a brief document, or notation, about where a child will permanently reside.* It simply addresses a long-term, or "permanent." vision for a youth's future living arrangements. When a youth is unable to return home it is time to activate an established alternative permanency plan that should be on record in the youth or the family's case file. If one has not been made it is time to do so. Alternative living arrangements have to be made for permanency planning.

When youth are treated in or near their home community it is a lot easier to develop natural supports that may be with them for life. Permanency planning involving only paid help does not work for the long term. Having youth in out of home placement attend local community activities such as those at church and school provides continuity in their life. Connection with community is a part of long-term success.

Regardless of whether a permanency plan is available, decisions have to be made about where a youth can live indefinitely. All of the considerations in the section labeled "Determining Placement" should be addressed at this time in the same way.

Open and respectful acknowledgment of the youth and his or her family experiences can help reduce confusion and ease potential pain caused by permanency decisions. Treatment teams can support everyone's needs about managing logistics such as transportation, school changes, and decisions about family visits and community resources. Flexible service provision and collaboration can reduce barriers to success and help youth and family manage such a challenging transition.

Conclusion

We like to feel we can get out of trouble
quicker than we got into it.
                                        Donald Sutherland

Youth violence prevention is tough enough when evidence-based services are provided in a youth's home and community. When the situation deteriorates so much that out of home placement may be indicated, things get a whole lot trickier. Treatment teams considering out of home placement should use EXTREME CAUTION!

When emergency removal for crisis stabilization, foster care, group home, or residential treatment are indicated it is vital to consider any such options only as short-term stabilizing components within a full continuum of care. The Office of the Surgeon General (2001) determined residential treatment to be an ineffective practice for youth violence prevention. No current information indicates otherwise. It should therefore be an option of last resort and not pretend to be a remedy for stopping harm. When youth must be removed from home collaboration is even more challenging and can strain treatment team efficiency. Minimizing potentially negative effects can be done through effective communication that promotes family reconciliation, reconnection, and reunification. Everyone involved can work hard to minimize negative effects when youth have to leave home.

Recommendations

- Stay current on research findings about out of home placement for youth violence prevention.
- Know what options are locally available for youth crisis stabilization.
- Provide crisis protocols for all team and social support network members.
- Monitor use of these protocols when violence occurs.
- Consider out of home placement with extreme caution and only as tertiary prevention when all else has failed.
- Collectively review placement options and use least restrictive settings.
- Keep the family involved in the process.

- Choose out of home placement based upon the unique needs of each youth and family.
- Assess "fit" through program documents, site visits, and staff interviews.
- Welcome new service providers onto the treatment team and promote optimum collaboration.
- Hold out of home placements accountable for using documented and research-based interventions in accordance with those identified in Chapter 6.
- Focus on family reconciliation, reconnection, and reunification at all times.
- Get the youth home as soon as possible.
- If they can't return home activate an established alternative permanency plan.

Resources

Office of Juvenile Justice and Delinquency Prevention: www.ojjdp.gov

Office of the Surgeon General: www.surgeongeneral. gov/library/youthviolence/

Parkside Family Counseling, LLC: www.parksideforfamilies.com

Resources for Resolving Violence, Inc.: www.resourcesforresolvingviolence. com

Chapter 10

Taking Good Care of Ourselves

Do not be daunted by the enormity of the world's grief.
Walk humbly now. Do justly now. Love mercy now.
You are not obligated to complete the work.
But neither are you free to abandon it.

The Talmud

Overview

We live in a society with a lot of mixed messages about taking good care of ourselves. On one hand there is a lot of information about health and well-being, and on the other hand we are bombarded with messages about unhealthy indulgence. Additionally, youth violence prevention is extremely hard. This chapter addresses challenges and solutions for addressing the impact of youth violence prevention on personal and professional development.

Objective

By the end of this chapter we hope you will be able to:

- Have a clear understanding of how youth violence prevention impacts you.
- Commit to a holistic approach for lifelong self-care.
- Have fun in life doing things you love to do!

Looking for Shade in America

Joann

Last year I took a ten-week leave of absence from my work to ride my bicycle across the United States. I work too hard. I know that about myself. I needed a break. For several years I played with the idea and everything came together in 2010 to make it happen.

For thirty years I have been listening to stories of violence and abuse. Some horrific, some not as bad. All are painful. I thought perhaps the repetitive motion of bicycling that I find tremendously soothing might help me pedal the stories out of my system. I envisioned letting them go as I rode from California to Maine. I wanted to ride home. Bring it on home. Work it out. Saddle up and ride with it.

The trip was brutal and the actual bike riding was the easiest part. One hot afternoon in nowhere North Dakota the voice inside my head screamed out that "everything is a %#@*ing metaphor!" It is. There is nothing easy about working to stop violence. It's brutal. As we shared in the introduction it can suck the ever lovin' life out of amazing people.

I'm thrilled to report that violence has not sucked the ever lovin' life out of me. I remain passionate about the work I do. I am devoted to my family and friends. I am thrilled to ride a bike or paddle a kayak. I adore most of the people I work with. I love to read and watch movies. I even watch a few television shows. I am amazed by nature and the world we live in.

So I get up every day and spend my time with unsung heroes. Youth who struggle to take a stand against violence. Parents who find energy to not give up on their little rascals whose violent behavior tests their love and devotion every day. I have the tremendous honor of working with and training professionals who show up on the job every day and seldom receive thanks for a job well done, or get paid an adequate wage to take good care of themselves and their families.

I collaborate with professionals who piss me off and make my job harder. I navigate systems with policies and procedures that sometimes defy understanding and seem to work against violence prevention. I face off against social messages and media that sensationalize and glorify all aspects of violence and abuse. I work in a country whose statistics on violence surpass many others and that is almost continuously involved in violence around the world.

While riding my bicycle across the Nevada desert in triple digit August temperatures I literally could find no shade, no respite from the searing heat. I kept riding. I rode and rode. In desperation I kept on. At mile 63 shade appeared. I was so thrilled I took a picture of the shady road surface. For the rest of the trip I kept looking for shade in America. Shade made everything about the ride so much easier. Every time I see that picture I still think about looking for shade in America.

Working in youth violence prevention is like looking for shade in America. A lot of the time the work feels like searing heat. It's brutal and all participants desperately want some relief. Taking a stand against violence is like looking for shade on a relentlessly hot day. Respectful behavior is the solution for violence prevention. Respectful behavior is the shade. Only it brings relief.

Respectful behavior begins with each and every one of us. It begins with self-respect and self-care and ends with genuine, warm, nonjudgmental, and empathic interactions with all others. Even when we don't feel liking behaving this way!

So I think I'll go take a bike ride and hope for some shade along the way...

Taking Care of Me

Please take a few minutes to check all of the following statements that apply to you.

❑ I understand the difference between a problem-focused approach and a strength-based collaborative model for youth violence prevention.

❑ I know how to maintain my core values without being deterred by negative forces.

❑ I collaborate and maintain good communication with others.

❑   I surround myself with people who want me to succeed.

❑   I'm comfortable talking about my strengths and talents.

❑   I model the behavior of other successful people.

❑   I, myself, am a good role model.

❑   I have regular contact with people who listen and can give me good advice.

❑   I am excited about my future.

❑   I organize my life to include a balance of work and play.

❑   I focus adequate time on things I am passionate about.

❑   I exercise regularly.

❑   I eat healthy foods.

❑   I have fun.

❑   I maintain mental health and well-being.

❑   I take good care of myself spiritually.

❑   I know well-being depends on staying motivated over time, and I maintain short-, medium-, and long-term plans that help me stay healthy.

I am doing the following things to enjoy life on a regular basis:

Personal and Professional Challenges
in Youth Violence Prevention

In her book, *Trauma Stewardship*, Laura van Dernoot Lipsky states that "trauma stewardship refers to the entire conversation about how we come to do this work, how we are affected by it, and how we make sense of and learn from our experiences" (2009, p. 6). The entire book provides compelling information about both the impact of constantly addressing trauma in our lives and comprehensive solutions for managing it. She describes stewardship as "the careful and responsible management of something entrusted to one's care" (p. 6). In this case, the "something entrusted to one's care" is ourselves. How we take care of ourselves while dedicating efforts to youth violence prevention defines who we are. Lipsky maintains that "stewardship involves: our intention in choosing our work; our philosophy of helping others; the tone our care giving takes; [and] daily decisions about how we live our life (p.11).

Given that most people working in this field could make more money doing other things indicates that money is not a primary motivation for preventing youth violence. Reference was made in the introduction of this book to Tina Turner's song, "What's Love Got to Do with It?" and here it is again. Love has a great deal to do with it. Parents love their children even when they choose to behave violently. Within a family, love for each other helps motivate people to stop being violent.

Dedication to safe communities motivates many working in this field. People with personal experiences of violence are motivated to help others as they were helped, or to prevent it from happening to others. Sometimes motivation is a combination of all of the above. For whatever reasons people are involved in youth violence prevention, self-care is critical.

> Grace and Angie made a pact with themselves and each other to give up smoking and the sweets that were left in the staff lounge to munch on. What they didn't give up was their cigarette break time. Each day Grace and Angie motivated each other to take a 5 to10 minute walk around the block, mid-morning, at lunchtime, and again at mid-afternoon. Other co-workers in the agency were impressed and soon an informal walking club developed.

People learn to take care of themselves throughout their lives. How a person addresses self-care may come from cultural experiences, friends and role models, or seemingly insignificant habit-forming behaviors. Our values and beliefs greatly influence how we take care of ourselves while working in such an emotionally charged field as youth violence prevention. Our aptitude for self-care will determine what kind of toll this work will take on each one of us.

Community support for this difficult work and access to resources make a huge difference in how we manage stress throughout our lives. Even professional orientation for those working in this field influences personal decisions about health and well-being. When professionals receive messages about being tough at the expense of addressing personal needs they may struggle to acknowledge the importance of trauma stewardship. Personal histories of violence and/or abuse, racism, sexism, homophobia, and any types of oppression and/or discrimination shape, and possibly distort our worldview and our behavior.

> *Our deepest fear is not that we are inadequate.*
> *Our deepest fear is that we are powerful beyond measure.*
> *It is our light, not our darkness, that most frightens us.*
> *We ask ourselves, who am I to be brilliant, gorgeous,*
> *   talented,and fabulous?*
> *Actually, who are you not to be?*
> *You are a child of god.*
>
> *Your playing small doesn't serve the world.*
> *There's nothing enlightened about shrinking so that other*
> *   people won't feel insecure around you.*
> *We were born to make manifest the glory of god that is within us.*
> *It's not just in some of us, it's in everyone.*
> *And as we let our own light shine, we unconsciously give*
> *   others permission to do the same.*
> *As we are liberated from our own fear, our presence*
> *   automatically liberates others.*
>
> Marianne Williamson
> *A Return to Love*

Mental health literature can guide self-care. Parallel process, transference, and counter-transference are defined and discussed at length in Chapter 4. These experiences are important to be aware of as we work to build relationships with youth and families as well as in our efforts to take care of ourselves. Each is defined again here along with examples of situations that, if left unaddressed, could get in the way of effective self-care.

A parallel process is the simultaneous experience of similar feelings, attitudes, and behaviors in two or more situations. Caregivers and service providers may have weathered so many acts of violence that they parallel each other in a way that they all start to feel the same. When left unattended, such experiences can lead to a numbing effect that negatively impacts personal health.

Transference is a reproduction of emotions in which a client substitutes a service provider for another person in the youth's or family member's life. For example, a young person may begin to treat a service provider as a close family member.

Counter-transference occurs when a service provider reproduces emotions and substitutes a client for another person in the worker's life. This happens when service providers view a particular youth as their own instead of a client.

All of these experiences are a normal part of service delivery. However, the way these experiences are dealt with will make them something that can be easy to address or a barrier to self-care and good services for youth and families. Interactions with youth and family members, as well as co-workers, can be reminders of a multitude of personal experiences. Clinical supervision and consultation are the easiest professionally established ways of addressing experiences that influence thoughts, feelings, and behaviors toward clients.

It's so important to stay clear about who we are, and what we're doing in youth violence prevention. Many amazing and heroic people have personally experienced youth violence and dedicate their lives to prevention. This is an absolutely awesome thing to do as long as self-awareness and self-care are Job Number One. If they are not, service providers are vulnerable to counter-transference and to treating youth and/or family members in ways that are not genuine and can hurt the working relationship and create barriers to successful outcomes.

> Michaela, a licensed mental health professional, was having a weekend lunch with a valued colleague with whom she sometimes interacted socially. All of a sudden Michaela felt like she was providing therapy for the other person. The thought was, "oh no, this feels like therapy." She felt disappointed and burdened. Her physiological reaction was a desire to get away. After leaving her colleague Michaela decided she was not going to initiate future social contact with the other person.
>
> Self-care involves paying attention to thoughts, feelings, and physiological reactions that influence behavior (affect regulation). Mindfully observing such internal experiences allows people to identify a parallel process. For Michaela the relationship no longer felt balanced, or reciprocal. She felt burdened by the experience of planning a fun time with a colleague that was not work related, and instead felt like she was on the job. The lunch became a parallel to Michaela's work, instead of a fun break from it.

Vicarious traumatization is a term used to describe trauma symptoms service providers are at risk of developing when helping others who have experienced trauma. People who spend a great deal of time in close proximity to youth violence may develop symptoms themselves even if they have never personally experienced youth violence. *Burnout is an experience of being overwhelmed and overloaded by the burdens of youth violence prevention.* It may impact any or all facets of personal and professional life. Exploration of burnout should address all holistic domains. They are the physical, social, psychological, and spiritual elements of life. Burnout is an experience that usually builds over time and is influenced by multiple situations related to difficult experiences. Vicarious traumatization might also be confused with burnout. The two experiences can be interwoven. and vicarious traumatization could be one of the factors resulting in burnout when left unaddressed. Experiencing a parallel process, transference, or counter-transference and leaving it unaddressed can also factor into burnout.

Claudette is 62, works in youth violence prevention, and adopted 14-year-old Patty when she was 4. For many years they lived happily together and fondly watched delightful videos that Claudette made of Patty throughout her childhood. A year and a half ago Patty began lying, stealing, and assaulting Claudette. Patty was placed in short-term residential care and returned home with intensive home-based services. Additionally the family receives Wraparound and specialized therapy from another source. Patty continues to struggle with violent behavior, the police have to be called periodically, and she is taken to the local hospital for crisis stabilization where they wait very long hours for services.

Claudette has had to take off a great deal of time from work, which has compromised her upcoming retirement. Claudette's parents are aging and dependent upon Claudette for financial, physical, and emotional support. Recently while Claudette was looking for Patty after Patty ran away from home, Claudette's sister called to complain about Patty and about Claudette's problems in managing her.

Claudette recently described herself as "crispy," which is her term for burnout. She is working closely with her therapist to address her own needs for self-care while devoting herself to her daughter and parents. Claudette periodically gets out to play golf but not much else. Her selfless devotion to others is greatly testing her ability to take good care of herself at a time when she needs it the most. Her therapy focuses on finding a balance while juggling all of the challenges that place a tremendous amount of stress on her.

Claudette's therapist also works diligently to balance the intense services needs of this family. During every emergency call she constantly assesses Patty's needs, Claudette's needs, and her own needs to optimally serve the family in a way that honors their autonomy and decision making without promoting dependency.

Experiences relating to all of the terms defined here are commonplace in youth violence prevention. Experiencing any or all of them does not imply that someone is bad, or something is wrong. They are all normal responses to the abnormal challenges of youth violence prevention. A situation with any one of them only becomes problematic when it is not addressed in ways that decrease problems and increase feelings of well-being. Ignoring the challenges of youth violence prevention is irresponsible and harmful.

Stressors Impacting Self-Care

Stress is a given in youth violence prevention. The intensity of challenges in this effort stems from a variety of sources. They include but are not limited to:

- Demands for successful outcomes creating heightened pressure to succeed when problem behaviors have potentially grave consequences.
- Limited resources causing people to feel undervalued and overworked.
- Frustrations in trying to prevent violence resulting in decreased patience and tolerance to get the job done.
- Disrespect, coercive confrontation, and/or abusive use of power and control being used to obtain compliance.
- An "us against them" attitude developing between groups. Youth and family members may not trust service providers. Service providers may not trust or value other service providers. Public and private entities may view themselves at odds, or in opposition to each other.
- Dereliction of duties, failure to follow policies and protocols, and/or granting undeserved privileges causing divisive team membership.

Such stressors can create a domino effect of bad feelings, dissatisfaction, and impaired performance, all of which negatively affect outcomes. Historically, youth violence prevention was based on a correctional model of intervention, and service providers used power and control in detrimental ways. In order to promote evidence-based practices, programs are challenged to openly address trauma stewardship, which includes parallel processes, transference, counter-transference, vicarious traumatization, and burnout. The following material can be helpful in exploring solutions to these problems.

Personal and Professional Challenges

Anyone committed to youth violence prevention can feel vulnerable when he or she experiences:

- Self-doubt
- Anxiety about the violence
- Resistance in any number of ways
- Frustration with limitations of services
- Team divisiveness
- Personal and/or professional isolation
- Hopelessness and/or helplessness
- Feelings of fear, anger, powerlessness, and loss of control
- Difficulty managing personal challenges

Individuals who ignore or lack an awareness of the impact of parallel processes, transference, counter-transference, and vicarious traumatization risk creating barriers to client success in the following ways:

- Negative interaction with other team members
- Disconnection, and disenfranchisement from other team members
- Secrecy and collusion that harm communication
- Breaking confidentiality and discussing others in harmful ways
- Misuse of power and control
- Demanding, yelling, or shouting
- Attempting to "get back" at others for a perceived offense
- Denial and rejection of personal accountability for behavior

When collaboration truly occurs, self-care becomes contagious, and everyone interacts respectfully and with thoughtful consideration.

Solutions

Solutions for managing all related challenges occur in ways that enhance personal satisfaction, treatment team cohesion, and successful outcomes. They include, but are not limited to:

- Learning all about trauma stewardship
- Openly acknowledging all challenges
- Regularly scheduling venues for addressing everyone's concerns
- Communicating in ways that embrace and honor diversity
- Mentoring and ensuring personal guidance for everyone
- Developing team leadership and cohesion based upon multidisciplinary representation of all service providers, youth, and family members
- Collaborating among everyone across the full continuum of care
- Adhering to evidence-based practices
- Providing consistent training for all service providers and families when applicable
- Addressing individual and collective affect regulation
- Interacting respectfully at all times
- Promoting sensitivity and tolerance for differences and uniqueness
- Ensuring there is a trauma-informed approach for everyone
- Modeling desired behavior at all times

Sometimes solutions for self-care involve decisions to stop being involved in youth violence prevention. There are a variety of experiences that can lead people to stay away from youth violence prevention all together, get away from it periodically, or leave it permanently. It's not for everyone.

Violence has a profound effect on those who experience it personally. As previously quoted in Chapter 2, Betsy McAlister Groves said, "exposure to violence changes the landscape of childhood forever" (2002, P.2). Such an important statement does not just pertain to children we serve. Many people dedicated to youth violence prevention have experienced it firsthand. Some have only been victims, but others have gone on to cause harm to self or others. All have potential to survive without additional harm.

Survival may include the realization that true self-care involves stepping away from it as much as possible. Just because people are very knowledgeable about it does not mean it is always in their best interest to work in close proximity to it.

For service providers, making a decision to get some distance from youth violence prevention may mean leaving the field temporarily, or permanently. Many wonderful service providers struggle with such a decision for a variety of reasons. They may think taking a leave of absence and changing jobs is a weakness or indicates they have not come to grips with the impact of violence on their life. They may incorrectly think they have to prove something. They may be so used to it that they think it is normal, and they can't imagine life without it. How frightening is that?

Both service providers and family members may realize that taking a stand against youth violence also means taking a stand against it in their personal lives. Many adults working valiantly to stop youth violence are secretly involved in it. Some may be involved in intimate partner violence, as a perpetrator, victim, or both. Some may be harming children, or animals. Others may be involved in acts of violence toward themselves through smoking, eating disorders, sexual harm, deliberate self-harm, and/or substance abuse.

Still others may be in relationships that don't involve blatant or physical violence, but cause harm nevertheless. Maintaining relationships with partners who cause harm in other ways, such as their own substance abuse or criminal behavior, causes great distress. Stopping youth violence might require ending highly valued relationships that are not in a person's best interest.

Ending harmful relationships or leaving jobs in youth violence prevention are extremely important decisions and may prove to be life saving. There is a lot of good to be done in this world and people can choose to do so in a variety of ways. When you think about it, any good work may help to prevent youth violence. Good work is about improving the world for everyone! When that occurs there is less youth violence.

> *We can make a difference without suffering;*
> *we can do meaningful work in a way that works for us and*
> *   for those we serve...*
> *We can leave a legacy that embodies our deepest wisdom and*
> *   greatest gifts instead of one that is burdened with our*
> *   struggles and despair.*
>
> *Laura van Dernoot Lipsky*

Conclusion

Do what you love. The rest will work itself out.
                                        Grace Schladale

Having a clear understanding of how youth violence prevention impacts everyone involved requires thoughtful consideration. There are ways to identify its influence and take action to prevent or minimize any negative symptoms. Acknowledging how powerfully violence can intrude on daily life provides a foundation for addressing it and taking a stand for lifelong self-care.

Everyone involved in youth violence prevention can experience satisfaction for a job well done, even when violence continues. When youth are not motivated to stop, everyone else can still commit to excellence in service provision and practice self-care regardless of outcome. Maintaining a commitment to self-care care pays off in a multitude of ways. Health and well-being are maintained through commitment to physical health and exercise, loving and caring relationships, optimal mental health, and embracing the human spirit. Learning to balance activities with rest and relaxation helps everyone to practice holistic self-care that takes into consideration the physical, social, psychological, and spiritual needs of all human beings. Have fun in life doing things you love to do! And Stop It (violence that is)!

Be patient toward all that is unsolved in your heart
And try to love the questions themselves.
Do not seek the answers that cannot be given you
Because you would not be able to live them.
And the point is to live everything.
Live the questions now.
Perhaps you will gradually without noticing it
Live along some distant day into the answers

Rainer Maria Rilke

Recommendations

- Get enough sleep
- Eat well
- Have fun!
- Move your body
- Nourish your soul
- Play!
- Learn
- Take a break
- Travel
- Slow down
- Relax!
- Love
- Forgive
- Celebrate
- Take time for self-reflection
- Use clinical supervision or a trusted friend to talk about the effects trauma has on you
- Take charge of your life
- Respect yourself as much as you respect others

Resources

Authentic Happiness: www.authentichappiness.sas.upenn.edu

Parkside Family Counseling: www.parksideforfamilies.com

Resiliency in Action: www.resiliency.com

Resources for Resolving Violence, Inc.: www.resourcesforresolvingviolence.com

Trauma Stewardship: www.traumastewardship.com

"Joyous playing and singing"

Appendix

The documents in the Appendix are provided in the order they were discussed in the book. First is a list of document titles by chapter indicating when the document was introduced. All documents are available at www.resourcesforresolvingviolence.com and can be downloaded in useable formats. The documents follow.

Chapter 5. Assessing Family Strengths and Needs

Elements of Optimum Child Development
Protective Factors for Youth Violence Prevention
Vulnerabilities in Families at High Risk of Youth Violence
Core Competency Domains

Chapter 6. Working Toward Success

T's Plan for Success (and example of a school safety plan)

Chapter 7. Stopping Violence for Good

Exploring a Pattern of Behavior

Elements Of Optimum Child Development*

On a 1 to 5 scale (1= not at all, 5 = very well) how well do you think your family is meeting the needs of each child being served?

Physical and Psychological Safety:	1 2 3 4 5
Appropriate Structure:	1 2 3 4 5
Supportive Relationships:	1 2 3 4 5
Opportunities to Belong:	1 2 3 4 5
Positive Social Norms:	1 2 3 4 5
Support for Efficacy and Mattering:	1 2 3 4 5
Opportunities for skill Building:	1 2 3 4 5
Integration of Family, School, and Community Efforts:	1 2 3 4 5

Now, please identify what might be done to improve efforts in each of the designated areas.

Physical and psychological Safety:

_____

Appropriate Structure:

_____

Supportive Relationships:

_____

Opportunities to Belong:

_____

Positive Social Norms:

_____

Support for Efficacy and Mattering:

_____

Opportunities for Skill Building:

_____

Integration of Family, School, and Community Efforts:

_____

* National Research Council and Institute of Medicine (2001, November 1). Community programs to promote youth development. Committee on Community-Level Programs for Youth. Washington, DC: National Academy Press.

Protective Factors for Youth Violence Prevention*

Internal Protective Factors

On a 1 to 5 scale (1 = not at all, 5 = very) how resilient do you find this youth?

Feelings of self-worth and self-confidence	1 2 3 4 5
Gives of self in service to others and/or a cause	1 2 3 4 5
Uses life skills, including good decision-making,	1 2 3 4 5
Assertiveness, impulse control, and problem-solving	1 2 3 4 5
Sociability/ability to be a friend	1 2 3 4 5
Ability to form positive relationships	1 2 3 4 5
Sense of humor	1 2 3 4 5
Internal locus of control	1 2 3 4 5
Autonomy/independence	1 2 3 4 5
Positive view of personal future	1 2 3 4 5
Flexibility	1 2 3 4 5
Capacity for and connection to learning	1 2 3 4 5
Self-motivation	1 2 3 4 5
Is "good at something"/personal competence	1 2 3 4 5

Environmental Protective Factors

On a 1 to 5 scale (1 = not at all, 5 = very) how resilient do you find this youth's environment (parents, guardians, extended family, school, and community)?

Promotes close bonds	1 2 3 4 5
Uses high warmth/ low criticism style of interaction	1 2 3 4 5
Sets and enforces clear boundaries (rules, norms, and laws)	1 2 3 4 5
Encourages supportive relationships with many caring others	1 2 3 4 5
Promotes sharing of responsibilities, service to others, "required helpfulness"	1 2 3 4 5
Has access to resources for basic needs of housing, employment, health care, recreation, nutrition, etc.	1 2 3 4 5

Expresses high, and realistic, expectations for success   1 2 3 4 5

Encourages goal setting and mastery   1 2 3 4 5

Encourages pro-social development of values and   1 2 3 4 5
   life skills

Provides leadership, decision-making, and other   1 2 3 4 5
   opportunities for meaningful participation

Appreciates the unique talents of each individual   1 2 3 4 5

* Henderson, N., Benard, B., & N. Sharp-Light (Eds.) (1996). Resiliency in action: Practical ideas for overcoming risks and building strength in youth, families and communities. Retrieved from www.resiliency.com.

Vulnerabilities in Families at High Risk for Youth Violence*

❏ Poor interactions between parents and children as early as the first year of life
❏ Emotionally distressed parents involved in anti-social behaviors
❏ Marital conflict and poor communication
❏ Parental criminal and violent behavior
❏ Alcohol and substance abuse
❏ Child abuse and neglect
❏ Harsh inconsistent discipline
❏ Poor parental supervision
❏ Violent neighborhoods
❏ Witnessing violence
❏ Learning problems
❏ School absenteeism
❏ Bullying, or being the target of bullying
❏ Being arrested before age 14

*Thornton, T., Craft, C., Dahlberg, L., Lynch, B., & Baer, K. (rev. ed., 2002). Best practices of youth violence prevention: A sourcebook for community action. Atlanta: Centers for Disease Control and Prevention, National Center for Injury Prevention and Control.

Core Competency Domains*

On a 1 to 5 scale (1 = never, 5 = always) how often does this youth?

1. Pro-social Skills:
Interaction (discreet observable social behaviors and assertiveness skills):

Initiate greetings or interactions: 1 2 3 4 5
Listen well: 1 2 3 4 5
Resist peer pressure: 1 2 3 4 5
Deal with positive and negative feedback: 1 2 3 4 5
Negotiate: 1 2 3 4 5
Accept criticism: 1 2 3 4 5
Effectively disagree and handle conflict: 1 2 3 4 5

Cognitive (thinking skills, particularly problem-solving skills applicable to a variety of situations):

Recognize, define, and clarify a problem: 1 2 3 4 5
Connect cause and effect: 1 2 3 4 5
Identify solutions: 1 2 3 4 5
Set realistic goals: 1 2 3 4 5
Predict and evaluate consequences: 1 2 3 4 5
Engage in step-by-step planning: 1 2 3 4 5
Anticipate pitfalls in carrying out solutions: 1 2 3 4 5

Self-Control (interaction and cognitive skills that help prevent an individual from displaying aversive or anti-social behavior):

Delay gratification: 1 2 3 4 5
Display impulse anger and aggression control: 1 2 3 4 5
Engage in emotional self-awareness: 1 2 3 4 5
Use positive self-talk: 1 2 3 4 5
Self-monitor: 1 2 3 4 5

2. Moral Reasoning Skills (making the right decisions for the right reasons):

Make good decisions: 1 2 3 4 5
Identify pro-social reason for decision: 1 2 3 4 5
Acknowledge pro-social outcomes: 1 2 3 4 5

3. Academic Skills (advancing in school to the highest possible level of academic achievement):

Engage in academic pursuits:	1 2 3 4 5
Express motivation to succeed:	1 2 3 4 5
Pass classes:	1 2 3 4 5

4. Workforce Development Skills (economic self-sufficiency):

Participate in pro-social employment activity:	1 2 3 4 5
Express motivation to succeed:	1 2 3 4 5
Participate in vocational training:	1 2 3 4 5

5. Independent Living Skills (self-sufficient living):

Successfully complete activities of daily living:	1 2 3 4 5
Manage money adequately:	1 2 3 4 5
Identify and use community resources:	1 2 3 4 5
Engage in pro-social leisure activities:	1 2 3 4 5

* Torbet, P. & Thomas, D. (2005). Advancing Competency Development: A White Paper for Pennsylvania. Pittsburgh, PA: National Center for Juvenile Justice.

T's Plan for Success at School!
(School safety plan for middle school)

I am a wonderful young man.
I want to be successful and not get kicked out of school.
This is my plan to make it happen.

I will eat lunch and have recess in the resource room.
I will try to hook up with Ms. C. to do activities like reading, computer activities, walking, or planning for sports activities, or I go to Mr. McL's room.

When I get upset I will:
1. Check in with a teacher I like, and get a sticker in my planner.
2. Help teachers at recess.
3. Call mom before lunch to tell her how I'm doing.

When I'm upset at school I will:
1. Give the teacher a hand sign (thumbs up, "I'm out of here") and go to Ms. K's first, and if she's not in go to Ms. C's room.
2. Let my teacher know by saying "I'm having a hard time and I'm going to see Ms. K."
3. I will then go to Ms. K's room to calm down.
4. If I can't stay calm I will call Mom from Ms. K's room.
5. If I'm still upset after talking to Mom, I will ask to take a walk with Ms. R or Ms. C, or with Mr. C if they are available.

I know it is bad to make threats and I will not:
• Tell anyone I want to hurt them, beat them up, or kill them.
• Talk about killing myself or wishing I'd never been born.
• Run away from school.
• Swear.

My name and signature are here as proof that I want to be successful.

T: _____

A lot of people like me and want to help me succeed. Their names and signatures are here so I can remember that they support me and my good behavior.

Mom: _____

Walter: _____

Ms. R: _____

Ms. C: _____

Mr. C: _____

Mrs. H: _____

Joann Schladale: _____

Mrs. K: _____

Exploring a Pattern of Behavior

Please write down exactly what pops into your brain after reading each question. You do not have to share your answers with anyone else if you don't want to.

1.   Please write down the problem that's bothering you?

2.   What comes to mind as you think about it?

3.   How are you feeling about it?

4.   Where in your body do you experience it?

5.   What are your fantasies about managing the upsetting experience?

6.   How does it remind you of anything from your past?

7.   How is being upset about it affecting your actions?

8.   How does it impact the way you are with others?

9.   What helps you to calm down while thinking about the upsetting experience?

10. How can you manage being upset without causing any harm?

Glossary

Affect regulation: A person's ability to manage emotions without causing harm.

Ally: A person or organization that cooperates with or helps another in a particular activity.

Appropriate structure: Ideal organization of a child's daily life. It involves predictable daily activities and timetables allowing for periods of activity and rest that promote physical and emotional growth.

Arousal: To evoke or awaken a feeling, emotion, or response.

Assessment: An ongoing process of face-to-face interactions and observations of youth and family members in order to collect information for ongoing service delivery. Assessment is the continuous process of monitoring a youth's status in order to thoughtfully plan and intervene in the most effective manner across all service delivery. Objective measures, when available, should be used.

Assessment scales: Scientific tools used for identifying specific information to help understand strengths and needs. Assessment scales must be valid and reliable (as proven through research) in order to accurately show what they claim to measure. Examples include topics such as intelligence levels, depression, assertiveness, etc.

Attachment: An instinctual biological bond that a child has with significant caregivers.

Autism: A mental condition that comes about in childhood and causes great difficulty in communication and connection with others.

Barriers: Anything that impedes progress toward, or completion of, established treatment goals.

Best practices: A term used to describe widely recognized and recommended models.

Burnout: An experience of being overwhelmed and overloaded by the burdens of youth violence prevention.

Cognitive: Brain processing that has to do with thinking, reasoning, and remembering.

Cognitive restructuring: Learning to think in a different way.

Collaboration: Exchanging information; sharing resources as a means for altering a youth's activities to prevent violence; and enhancing the capacity of everyone involved to create safer communities.

Community: The ecological structure in which a youth lives.

Community-based: Services and resources provided in a youth's home and community in order to minimize disruption of the youth's daily living and to provide participation by the youth's family and social support network.

Competency: Established criteria for adequate education, training, experience, and skills required to perform a specific task.

Competency development: The ability of youth to increase their knowledge and skills in order to become "productive, connected, and law abiding members of their community" (Torbet & Thomas, 2005, p.3).

Continuum of care: A broad range of interventions allowing service delivery to best meet the needs of a youth and his or her family in the least restrictive manner, based upon an initial holistic evaluation and ongoing assessment.

Conventional wisdom: Service delivery that is not founded in scientific evidence. It is based on what is generally done and believed without question.

Core values: Essential and enduring tenets of an organization, task force, or group of individuals united by a common purpose or goal. These core values are a small set of timeless guiding principles that require no external justifications. They have intrinsic value and importance to those individuals within the organization, task force, or work group (CARF: The Commission on Accreditation of Rehabilitation Facilities, 2001).

Counter-transference: When a service provider reproduces emotions and substitutes a client for another person in the worker's life.

Criminal codes: State, federal or Bureau of Indian Affairs laws that describe what behavior constitutes a crime.

Culture: Personal attributes and characteristics socially and biologically acquired; encompassing but not limited to gender, race, ethnicity, sexual orientation, religion, nationality, and financial status.

Family system: Everyone a youth considers family.

Disturbance of arousal: Thoughts, feelings, and physiological reactions people get when they are upset that influence their behavior. Behavior then influences outcomes.

Dynamic: Something that can change.

Dysregulation: Managing emotions or feelings in ways that cause harm to self or others. It is the inability to manage feelings in pro-social ways.

Ecology: Relationships between a youth and his or her physical and social environment.

Efficacy: An ability to make things happen.

Empirical: Something that is verified by observation.

Empirically driven: An effort to integrate scientifically based studies into practice. This is a broad term used to identify interventions based on scientific study as opposed to conventional wisdom, which has no foundation in research.

Engage: Establishing a meaningful contact or connection with someone.

Engagement: A continuous process of respectful communication that addresses the identified concerns and goals of the youth and his or her family.

Evaluation: A process of documenting a comprehensive review and accumulation of information regarding a specific youth's status at a given time. The process involves face-to-face interviews with youth, family members, and designated others such as pertinent extended family and service providers. The purpose is to collect information for initial or transitional service planning. Objective measures, when available, should be used. Holistic evaluation includes all areas of a youth's life.

Evidence-based practices: "The competent and high-fidelity implementation of practices that have been demonstrated safe and effective, usually in randomized controlled trials (RCTs)" (Chaffin, 2006, p. 661). A term used to identify the highest level of research supported by multiple, controlled, randomized outcomes studies.

Family: "Two or more persons who share resources, share responsibility for decisions, share values and goals, and have commitments to one another over time. The family is that climate that one 'comes home to,' and it is this network of sharing and commitments that most accurately describes the family unit, regardless of blood, legal ties, adoption, or marriage" (American Home Economics Association, as cited in Friedan, 1981, p. 78). This may include other family or social support network members not previously involved in the youth's life.

Family system: Refers to everyone a youth considers family.

Family therapy: A modality of treatment in which the interrelationships of family members are examined in order to identify and alleviate problems of one or more family members. Family therapy may include any individual who has an important connection to the youth, regardless of blood or legal ties.

Focus on parents and family: Active and consistent involvement of the family as the core of all service delivery.

Forensic evaluation: An evaluation designed to assist the legal system in the decision-making process.

Harm reduction: A positive, health-promoting approach for youth learning to manage their lives in ways that no longer cause harm to self or others.

Holistic: All parts of a person's life, including all physical, social, psychological, and spiritual aspects.

Home visiting: Providing services to youth and families in their own homes.

Human ecology: The study of individuals in relationship to others and the environment.

Indicated prevention: Providing interventions when violence has occurred.

Individualized treatment: Treatment that ensures that all services are flexible and based upon the unique individual strengths and needs of each youth and family.

Individual therapy: Therapy that is prescriptive and provided by a specially trained and credentialed therapist. It is used as a forum for addressing personal concerns, family issues, and for providing crisis intervention.

Ineffective strategies: Interventions that according to research do not work and may have potential to do harm. These practices have been identified in at least one study demonstrating harmful effects.

Integration of family, school, and community efforts: Effective coordination of activities among all parts of a child's life in order to optimize health and well-being.

Making amends: A process by which people take responsibility for harm they have caused and commit to never doing it again.

Manualized approach: A model that has a specific manual or guide to follow in order to standardize services and promote successful outcomes.

Mattering: The understanding that something is important.

Mentoring: An adult-child relationship in which an experienced adult role model, usually not a family member, is available to a youth in an informal setting on a regular basis.

Multi-modal: A term used to describe a combination of treatment modalities to include multidisciplinary meetings; individual, group, and family therapy; and psycho-education. Multi-modal simply means using more than one method, or modality of treatment

Multi-sensory activities: Coping strategies involving any of the five senses to address difficult feelings as a way to manage pain and calm down.

Multi-sensory self-soothing: A way of using any of the five senses (sight, sound, smell, taste, and touch) to remain calm in difficult situations.

Opportunities to belong: Activities that make it possible for a child to develop a sense of connection and fitting in with a positive group or community.

Parallel process: The simultaneous experience of similar feelings, attitudes, and behavior in two or more situations.

Permanency plan: A brief document, or notation, about where a child will permanently reside.

Physical safety: The condition of being protected from harm.

Physiology: The way in which body parts function. Arousal is a response to a stimulus.

Physiological arousal: The way in which the human body responds to a stimulus.

Positive social norms: How society expects people to act and get along. Such behavior promotes respect and law-abiding behavior. Positive social norms are behaviors that reflect pro-social values based on respect for all living things and the environment.

Practices: The actual application of a method identified as a strategy.

Primary prevention: Focusing on public education to prevent involvement in any type of violence.

Psychological safety: An emotional experience of feeling safe and protected from harm.

Program: Any clinical entity providing home- and/or community-based service to youth and their families.

Promising practices: Interventions supported by empirical studies but that require more investigation to meet standards for evidence-based practices.

Protective factors: Characteristics that can diminish potential for violence, or stop it after it occurs.

Protocol: A specific procedure and/or process required by research findings, organizations, and legal entities.

Qualified mental health provider [QMHP]: An individual who holds a master's degree or doctorate from an accredited program in a mental health field. This person adheres to all licensure/certification requirements that are mandated by the state where services are being provided. Nationally, QMHPs are generally considered to be psychiatrists, psychologists, social workers, marriage and family therapists, mental health counselors, and clinical nurse specialists.

Reconciliation: To make friendly again, to settle or bring into harmony.

Reconnection: The ability of family members to visit in a way that ensures physical and emotional safety for everyone involved.

Reunification: To unify again after being divided.

Resilience: The ability to bounce back after something bad happens.

Restorative justice: A process to involve, to the extent possible, those who have a stake in a specific offense and to collectively identify and address harms, needs, and obligations in order to heal and put things as right as possible (Zehr, 2002).

Risk assessment: A process of classifying or categorizing individuals according to indications of likelihood of engaging in future harmful behavior. This is done on the basis of subjective clinical impressions, objective actuarial methods, and valid reliable risk assessment instruments (Chaffin, Bonner, & Pierce, 2003).

Screening: A systematic way of looking at an identified population in order to consider needs for intervention. This is primary prevention.

Secondary prevention: Identifying youth at risk of acting violently and directing specific efforts toward preventing such involvement.

Selective prevention: Focusing on groups believed to be at risk of behaving violently.

Service providers: Employees who deliver services to youth and families in conjunction with therapists and/or other involved QMHP.

Services: Any research-based activities that influence youth violence prevention. This may include therapy, community service, mentoring, physical fitness activities, and expression through art drama, dance, or music.

Sexuality: Anything having to do with a human being's experience of being sexual. This includes sex roles, gender identity, and sexual expression.

Social-cognitive interventions: Therapeutic techniques that focus on changing thinking and interactional patterns of behavior. Any activities that promote social skill building and cognitive restructuring.

Social support network: Any non-related persons who are seen as important to the youth and are assessed to provide positive role modeling.

Skill building: Competency development.

Specialized training: An educational process, based upon empirically based practices that prepares all service providers to respond competently to the special needs of youth and families.

Staff: Employees who deliver services to youth and families in conjunction with therapists and/or other involved QMHP.

Static: Something that cannot change.

Support for efficacy and mattering: A youth's understanding that he or she is important and can impact change.

Strategies: Plans of action or policies designed to achieve a major or overall aim.

Supportive relationships: Connections with others that promote optimum growth, health, and well-being.

Systems of care: All professional, public, and private entities brought together to serve youth and families in an organized, integrated manner.

Tertiary prevention: Efforts to stop violence from reoccurring after any acts of harm toward self and/or others.

Template: A preset format for a document.

Therapeutic engagement: A shared commitment between service providers and family members to actively support a child's effort to stop harm.

Therapist: Any qualified mental health professional licensed to provide psychotherapy. This generally includes psychiatrists, psychologists, marriage and family therapists, social workers, clinical nurse specialists, and mental health counselors.

Transference: A reproduction of emotions in which a client substitutes a service provider for another person in the youth's or family member's life.

Trauma: A deeply distressing or disturbing experience that has lasting effects.

Treatment: A research-based approach for addressing change.

Therapy: Specific, research-based, therapeutic models, or practices that influence youth violence prevention. This may involve evidence-based practices such as Multisystemic Therapy (MST) or Trauma-Focused Cognitive Behavioral Therapy (TF-CBT).

Treatment fidelity: The process of adhering to an evidence-based intervention or approach to therapy that monitors compliance with all components of the model to ensure successful outcomes.

Universal prevention: attempts to stop violence from ever happening in the general population.

Vicarious traumatization: A term used to describe trauma symptoms service providers are at risk of developing when helping others who have experienced trauma.

Violence: Any behavior involving intention to hurt, damage, or kill someone, or something.

Youth: Any person under the age of 18 or 21, depending on legal age as defined by state statute, for which services are being provided.

Youth violence: intentional harm committed by any person under the age of 18 or 21, depending on legal age as defined by state statute. It includes harm to self or others.

Wraparound: A collaborative, strengths-based model of family- and community-centered practice anchored in ecological and systems theory. The process is designed to bring social support network members of a youth and family together for the purpose of keeping the youth within the family system.

References

Abbey, A. (2005). Lessons learned and unanswered questions about sexual assault perpetration. Journal of interpersonal violence, 20, 39-42.

Americans with Disabilities Act (1990). www.ada.gov/

Applegate, J. & Shapiro, J. (2005). Neurobiology for clinical social work: Theory and practice. New York: W. W. Norton.

Association for the Treatment of Sexual Abusers (ATSA). (2000, March 11). The effective legal management of juveniles sex offenders. Retrieved January 9, 2008, from http://www.atsa.com/ppjuveniel. html.

Beck, A., Steer, R., & Brown, G. (1996) Manual for the Beck Depression Inventory-II. San Antonio, TX: Psychological Corporation.

Borduin, C., & Schaeffer, C. (2001). Multisystemic treatment of adolescent sexual offenders: A progress report. Journal of Psychology & Human Sexuality, 13:3/4, 25-42.

Bowlby, J. (1988). A secure base: Parent-child attachment and healthy human development. New York: Basic Books.

Brindis, Claire. (2011). Taking a Pulse: State of the State – Adolescent Pregnancy and Parenting Field. Promoting What Works: A Symposium of Promising Approaches for Supporting Pregnant and Parenting Adolescents. Department of Health and Human Services, Office of Adolescent Pregnancy Programs: Washington, D.C.

Butts, J., Mayer, S., & Ruth, G. (2005). Focusing Juvenile Justice on Positive Youth Development. Issue Brief, October. Chicago: Chapin Hall Center for Children at the University of Chicago.

Cauffman, E. (2008). Understanding the female offender. In The Future of Children: Juvenile Justice, 18:2. Woodrow Wilson School of Public and International Affairs at Princeton University and the Brooking Institute.

Centers for Disease Control and Prevention (2010). www.cdc.gov.

Center for the Study and Prevention of Violence, Institute of Behavioral Science. (2011) University of Colorado at Boulder. Blueprints for violence prevention.

Chaffin, M. (2008). Our Minds are Made Up – Don't Confuse Us With the Facts: Commentary on Policies concerning Children With Sexual

Behavior Problems and Juvenile Sex Offenders", Child Maltreatment, 13:2.

Chaffin, M. (2006). Can we develop evidenced-based practice with adolescent sex offenders? In R. Longo & D. Prescott (Eds.), Current perspective: Working with sexually aggressive youth and youth with sexual behavior problems. (pp. 661-681). Holyoke, MA: NEARI Press.

Chaffin, M., & Bonner, B. (1998). "Don't shoot, we're your children": Have we gone too far in our response to adolescent sexual abusers and children with sexual behavior problems. Child Maltreatment, November, 314–316.

Chaffin, M., Bonner, B., & Pierce, K. (2003). NCSBY Fact Sheet: What research shows about adolescent sex offenders. Oklahoma City, OK: Center on Child Abuse and Neglect, University of Oklahoma Health Sciences Center.

Children's National Medical Center. (2011). www.childrensnational.org

Chorpita, B., Yim, L., Donkervoet, J., Arensdorf, A., Amundsen, M., McGee, C., Serrano, A., Yates, A., Burns, J., & Morelli, P. (2002). Toward Large-scale Implementation of empirically supported treatments for children: A review and observations by the Hawaii Empirical Basis to Services Task Force. Clinical Psychology, 9(2), 165-190.

City Voices and Perspectives. (2011). Minneapolis Blueprint for Action. www.preventioninstitute.org.

Cochran, C., Mayer, L., Carr, T., Cayer, N., McKenzie, M., & Peck, L. (2012). American Public Policy: An Introduction (10th Edition). Boston, MA: Wadsworth Cengage Learning.

Cook, A., Blaustein, M., Spinazzola, J., & van der Kolk, B. (2003). Complex trauma in children and adolescents. White paper from the National Child Traumatic Stress Network Complex Trauma Task Force. www.nctsn.org

Cornell University Family Life Development Center. (2011) Cornell Research Program on Self-Injurious Behavior in Adolescents and Young Adults. www.crpsib.com

Damon, 2004, quoted in Evans, D., Foa, E., Gur, R., Hendin, H., O'Brien, C., Seligman, M., & Walsh, T. (2005). Treating and Preventing Adolescent Mental Health Disorders: What we know and what we don't know. A research agenda for improving the mental health of our youth. Oxford, U.K.: Oxford University Press.

Dennis, K. & Lourie, I., Everything Is Normal until Proven Otherwise (2006) CWLA Press, Washington, D.C.

Diagnostic and Statistical Manual of Mental Disorders, Fourth Edition DSM-IV-TR (Text Revision). (2000). American Psychiatric Association.

Dishion, T., McCord, J., & Poulin, F. (1999). When interventions harm: Peer groups and problem Behavior. American Psychologist, 54 (9), 755–764.

Dodge, K. Pettit, G., & Bates, J. (1997). How the experience of early physical abuse leads children to become aggressive. In D.T. Cicchetti (Ed.), Rochester symposium on developmental psychology, 263 Rochester: Rochester University Press. (P.277).

Duncan, G., Magnuson, K., Boyce, T. & Shonkoff, J. (2010). The long reach of early childhood poverty: Pathways and impacts. Boston, MA: Center on the Developing Child, Harvard University. Retrieved November 7, 2010 from www.developingchild.harvard.edu.

Duncan, B., Miller, S., Wampold, B., & Hubble, M. (Second Edition). (2010). The heart and soul of change, delivering what works in therapy. American Psychological Association.

Ferber, T., & Pittman, K., with Marshall, T. (2002). State youth policy: Helping all youth to grow up fully prepared and fully engaged. Takoma Park, Maryland: The Forum for Youth Investment. www.forumforyouthinvestment.org.

Finkelhor, D. (2009). The prevention of childhood sexual abuse. In The Future of children: Preventing child maltreatment. 19:2, Fall.

Ford, J., Chapman, J., Hawke, J., & Albert, D. (2007). Trauma among youth in the juvenile justice system: Critical issues and new directions. National Center for Mental Health and Juvenile Justice Research and Program Brief.

Friedan, B. (1981). The second stage. New York: Summit Books.

Grealish, M. (2011) Community Partners, Inc. www.wraparoundsolutions.com

Groves, B. (2002). Children who see too much. Boston, MA: Beacon Press.

Hamilton, J. (2005). Clinicians' guide to evidence-based practice. Journal of the American Academy of Child and Adolescent Psychiatry, 44:5, May.

Harrendorf, S., Heiskanen, S., & Malby, S. (2011) International Statistics on Crime and Justice. United Nations Office on Drugs and Crime. HEUNI Publication Series No. 64.

Henderson, N., Benard, B., & Sharp-Light, N. (Eds.) (1996). Resiliency in action: Practical ideas for overcoming risks and building strength in youth, families and communities. Retrieved from www.resiliency.com.

Henggeler, S., Schoenwald, S., Borduin, C., Rowland, M., & Cunningham, P. (2009). Multisystemic treatment of antisocial behavior in children and adolescents. New York: The Guilford Press.

Hodges, K. & Kim, C. (2000). Psychometric study of the child and adolescent functional assessment scale: prediction of contact with the law and poor school attendance. Journal of Abnormal Child Psychology, 28 (3), 287-297.

Kagan, R. (2007). Real Life Heroes: A life storybook for children. New York: Routledge.

Kagan, R. (2004) Rebuilding attachments with traumatized children. New York: The Haworth Maltreatment and Trauma Press.

Jenkins, Alan. (1990). Invitations to Responsibility: The Therapeutic Engagement of Men Who Are Violent and Abusive. Adelaide, South Australia: Dulwich Centre Publications.

Judicial Education Center (1999). Key principles for permanency planning for children. In Child Welfare Handbook. Reno, NV: National Council of Juvenile and Family Court Judges.

Kauffman Foundation Best Practices Project (2004). Closing the quality chasm in child abuse treatment: Identifying and disseminating best practices. www.capacitybuilding.net.

LeBuffe, P. & Naglieri, J. (1999). Devereux Early Childhood Assessment DECA. Lewisville, NC: Kaplan Press.

Levitt, S. & Dubner, S. (2005). Freakonomics: A Rogue economist explore the hidden side of everything. New York: William Morrow.

Martinson, F. (2010). Sexual development in infancy and childhood. In G. Ryan, Leversee, T. & S. Lane (Eds.), Juvenile sexual offending: Causes, consequences, and correction. Hoboken, NJ: John Wiley & Sons, Inc.

McMackin, R., Leisen, M., Cusack, J., LaFratta, J., & Litwin, P. (2002). The relationship of trauma exposure to sex offending behavior among male juvenile offenders. Journal of Child Sexual Abuse, 11 (2), 25–40.

Miles, P. & Franz, J. (2011), www.paperboat.com

Miller, W. & Rollnick, W. (2002). Motivational interviewing. New York: The Guilford Press.

Mulvey, E. & Iselin, A-M. (2008). Improving professional judgments of risk and amenability in juvenile justice. In The Future of Children: Juvenile Justice, 18:2. Woodrow Wilson School of Public and International Affairs at Princeton University and the Brooking Institute. www.futureofchildren.org.

Mrazek, P. & Haggarty, R. (Eds.) (1994). Reducing risks for mental disorders: Frontiers for preventive intervention research. Washington, D.C.: Institute of Medicine, National Academy Press.

National Research Council and Institute of Medicine (2001, November 1). Community programs to promote youth development. Committee on Community-Level Programs for Youth. Washington, DC: National Academy Press.

Office of the Surgeon General (2001). Youth violence: A report of the surgeon general. www.surgeongeneral.gov.

Olds, D., Hill, P., Mihalic, S., & O'Brien, R. (2006). Nurse-Family Partnership: Blueprints for Violence Prevention, Book Seven. In Blueprints for Violence Prevention Series. Elliott, D. (ed). Boulder, CO: Center for the Study and Prevention of Violence, Institute of Behavioral Science, University of Colorado.

Office of Applied Studies Report (2010, April) A day in the life of American adolescents: substance use facts update. www.samhsa.gov

On the Right Track. (2004). Sexuality Information and Education Council of the United States.

Piquero, A. (2008). Disproportionate minority contact. In The Future of Children: Juvenile Justice, 18:2. Woodrow Wilson School of Public and International Affairs at Princeton University and the Brooking Institute. www.futureofchildren.org.

Prochaska, J., DiClemente, C. & Norcross, J. (1992). In search of how people change: applications to addictive behaviors. American psychologist. 47(9), 1102-1114.

Provence, S., Erikson, J., Vater, S., & Palmeri, S., (1995) Infant-toddler developmental sssessment. Chicago: Riverside Publishing.

Rasmussen, L., Burton, J., & Christopherson, B. (1992). Precursors to offending and the trauma outcome process in sexually reactive children. Journal of child sexual abuse, 1 (1), 33-48.

Ryan, G., Leversee, T. & Lane, S. (Eds.) (2010). Juvenile sexual offending: Causes, consequences, and correction. Hoboken, NJ: John Wiley & Sons, Inc.

Saunders, B., Berliner, L., & Hanson, R. (Eds.) (2004). Child physical and sexual abuse; Guidelines for treatment (revised report: April 26, 2004). Charleston, SC: National Crime Victims Research and Treatment Center

Schladale, J. (2010). The T.O.P.* workbook for sexual health. Freeport, ME: Resources for Resolving Violence, Inc.

Schladale, J. (2008). Empirically driven assessment of juvenile offenders. The sex offender, Vol. 6: Offender evaluation and program strategies. Kingston, NJ: Civic Research Institute.

Schladale, J., Langan, T., Barnett, P., Nunez, J., Fredricks, K., Moylan-Trigiano, J., & Brown, D. (2007). Community based standards for responding to sexual harm by youth. Freeport, ME: Resources for Resolving Violence, Inc.

Schladale, J. (2006). Family matters: The importance of engaging families in treatment with youth who have caused sexual harm (493-514). In Longo, R. & Prescott, D. (Eds.) Current perspective: Working with sexually aggressive youth and youth with sexual behavior problems. Holyoke, MA: NEARI Press.

Schladale, J. (2002). The T.O.P.* workbook for taming violence and sexual aggression. Freeport, ME: Resources for Resolving Violence, Inc.

Schore, A. (2003). Affect regulation and the repair of the self. New York: W.W. Norton & Company.

Scott, E. & Steinberg, L. (2008). Rethinking juvenile justice. Boston: Harvard University Press.

Siegel, D. (1999). The Developing mind: How relationships and the brain interact to shape who we are. New York: The Guilford Press.

Stien, P. & Kendall, J. (2004). Psychological trauma and the developing brain. New York: The Haworth Press.

Steinberg, L. (2008). Introducing the issue. In The Future of Children: Juvenile Justice, 18:2. Woodrow Wilson School of Public and International Affairs at Princeton University and the Brooking Institute.

Substance Abuse and Mental Health Services Administration, (2011).

www.samhsa.gov

Szalavitz, M. (2006). Help at any cost: How the troubled-teen industry cons parents and hurts kids. New York: Riverhead Books.

Thiessen-Love, L., McIntosh, J., Rosst, M., & Tertzakian, K. (2009). Fostering hope: Preventing teen pregnancy among youth in foster care. Washington, D.C.: The National Campaign to Prevent Teen and Unplanned Pregnancy.

Thornton, T., Craft, C., Dahlberg, L., Lynch, B., & Baer, K. (2002). Best practices of youth violence prevention: a sourcebook for community action (rev.). Atlanta: Centers for Disease Control and Prevention, National Center for Injury Prevention and Control.

Torbet, P. & Thomas, D. (2005). Advancing Competency Development: A White Paper for Pennsylvania. Pittsburgh, PA: National Center for Juvenile Justice.

University of Colorado Blueprints for Violence Prevention. www.colorado/edu/cspv/plueprints.

van Dernoot Lipsky, Laura (2009). Trauma Stewardship. San Fransisco: Berrett Koehler Publishers, Inc.

van der Kolk, B. (1994). The body keeps the score: Aproaches to the psychobiology of posttraumatic stress disorder. In B. Van der Kolk, A. McFarlane, & L. Weisaeth (Eds.), Traumatic stress: The effects of overwhelming experience on mind, body, and society. (pp.214-241). New York: Guilford.

Van der Kolk, B. (2004). Frontiers of Trauma Research. Cape Cod Institute, MA: July 12–16. Conference Presentation.

World Health Organization (2010). Sexual health: Working definitions. www.who.int/reproductive-health/gender/sexual-health.html.

Worling, J. & Langstrom, N. (2006). Risk of sexual recidivism in adolescents who offend sexually: Correlate and assessment. In Barbaree, H. & Marshall, W. (Eds.). The juvenile sex offender. (pp. 219-247). New York: The Guildford Press.

Wu, L-T., Woody, G., Yang, C., Pan, J-J. & Blazer, D. (2011) Racial/Ethnic Variations in Substance-Related Disorders Among Adolescents in the United States. Journal of general psychiatry, 68:11, 1176-1185.

Zehr. H. (2002). The little book of restorative justice. Intercourse, PA: Good Books.

Joann Schladale

Joann is a licensed marriage and family therapist who has been working in the field of trauma, child abuse, and interpersonal violence since 1981. As founder and Executive Director of Resources for Resolving Violence, Inc., she provides extensive consultation, program development and evaluation, clinical supervision, and staff development and training on emically driven and evidence-based practices. She works closely with public and private agencies on prevention, mental health and protective services, juvenile justice, and teen pregnancy prevention.

Joann has received professional awards and made hundreds of presentations throughout North America, Europe, and Africa focusing on childhood trauma, sexual harm, youth violence, and teen pregnancy prevention and positive youth development. She has written chapters in numerous scholarly books; she is the author of the T.O.P.* Workbook for Sexual Health (2010), and The T.O.P. Workbook for Taming Violence and Sexual Aggression (2002); and she collaborated in the creation of Community-Based Standards for Addressing Sexual Harm by Youth (2007).

She enjoys a bit of heaven living in the Maine woods, gardening, jogging, biking, and kayaking whenever she can.

Therese Langan

Therese Langan is a licensed master's level social worker and has been working in the field of trauma, child abuse & neglect, mental health, and juvenile justice since 1985. As owner and lead clinician of Parkside Family Counseling, LLC, she runs this small private agency serving children, adolescents, adults, and families with emotional, behavioral, or relationship problems that get in the way of their overall success. She supervises clinicians and other service providers who serve youth and families through services offered in the office, home, school, and community. Therese provides family therapy to youth and their families primarily through a home-based family therapy model of service. She is involved in community collaboration efforts that are working to reduce youth violence and provide evidence-based services in Lenawee County, Michigan, where she works. She collaborated in the creation of Community-Based Standards for Addressing Sexual

Harm by Youth (2007).

Therese lives in Ann Arbor, Michigan, where she enjoys running, biking, and live music in small venues. She travels when she can and has a list of places to explore that only gets longer.

Acknowledgments

Most sincere thanks go to all the young people and their families who showed us that genuine concern and individualized services offered with a good dose of hope really does work.

Wow, does it take a lot of amazing people to get a book written! While our names are on the cover it is so important to publicly credit others who made this effort possible. Joann thanks family members: John Zink; Erin and Canaan Schladale-Zink; Gayle and Gabriella Schladale; and best friend, Penny Howard.

Therese's family is huge and full of supportive and wonderful people. They include Emma and Jack Langan; Anne Marie Langan; Bruce and Ian Campbell; Mary Beth Langan; Ted and Andrew Coutilish; Carol Ann Martinelli and Michael Goler; Maureen Boucher; Michael, Genevieve, and Owen Randazzo; Moira Duclos; Jackie Duclos; Karen, Paul, Caitlin, and Ben Moser; Audrey and Alana Hensley; Ivan, Andrew, Nevaeh, and Sidney Currie; Reggie Green; Regi Christian; and Donell Mitchell. Some of Therese's friends who supported her through this project are: Anne Kramer, Fred Bayoff, Drew Hart, Britta Kallmann, Leslie Keane, Scott Simon, Judy and David Carmein, Cynthia Koch, Chris Gardiner, and Paul and Diana Crossley.

Maureen Boucher, our graphic designer (and Therese's cousin), is a creative delight, and Marcia LaBrenz a wonderful editor. Thanks to Ari Weinzweig for putting Therese back in touch with Jim Reische and to Jim for recommending Marcia. Ari and team Zingerman's not only provided inspiration, but delicious sustenance as we were writing.

We profoundly thank everyone who read drafts at different points along the way, sometimes more than once. Peter Barnett, Penny Howard, Anne Kramer, Laurie Raymond, and Gabriella Schladale were steadfast in reviewing almost every chapter and providing critical feedback. Patricia Campbell, Cynthia Koch, Mary Beth Langan, and Daniel Okonkwo provided excellent feedback about some early drafts. Thank you also to Joanne Claflin, Shannon Elliott, Bob Gauthier, Leslie Keane, and Donell Mitchell for every word of encouragement. Tami Johnson helped with so many details that it would be difficult to list them all. Special thanks to Lotta Olvegard and Blair Carlson who graciously offered their home in Sweden for a week of intensive writing. And thanks to John Zink for the index.

Sandie Worthington, Rick Meaghar, Marjorie Kosalski, and Erica Deering, have been Joann's steadfast colleagues in the State of Maine Department of Health and Human Services, Children's Behavior Health Services. I adore you guys!

A team of diverse, energetic, and generous service providers at Huron Services for Youth, Inc., Vaughn House in Ann Arbor, demonstrated real collaboration during my first post-graduate work experience. Anne Evans, Jim Vassal, Drew Hart, Gabby Thompson, Rich Casteels, Bil Aarons and Phil Schieble were the foundation of that team. They taught me to pay attention to the boys' needs and how to see their unbelievable strengths. The teenage boys taught me the essence of survival. Vaughn House provided the opportunity to be a foster parent to Ivan, Reggie, Regi, and Donell.

Many highly valued professionals across this country have contributed enormously over the years, many without knowing it. This special group includes Beth Abbott, Joe Abel, Howard Adler, Kim Alaburda, Barbara Altadonna, Randy Barnett, Steve Bengis, Jim Beougher, Brian Bill, Mike Bishop, David Braccialarghe, Cynthia Brock, Triste and Lawrence Brooks, Laura Burns, Julia Cabral, Mary Ann Campbell, Greg Carman, Paul Castaldi, Mario Chavez, Toby Chavez-James, Randall Cherry, Princess Coleman, Lyn Cordova, Elizabeth Cote, Dan Cressman, Maria Cristalli, Penny Cunningham, Phyllis Denton, Al Dickson, John Druhushak, Anne Evans, Nikole Fether, Ellen Ford, Stella Gallegos, Ellen Gatewood, Mark Gomez, Tina Goodby-Ware, Jerry Gregory, Diane Gutierrez, Tom Hall, Bruce Hawkins, Judge Gregg Iddings, Jeffrey Konigsberg, Kelly Landaker, Diane Langelier, JoAnne Lenahan, Ted Lovato, Donna Lucero, Ruby McClesky, Jeannie McClung, Claire McGinn, Maryann McRobert, Judi Magder, Marilyn Martin, Steve Meyers, Libby Mills, Joe Mirabel, Mike Mohler, Joan Moylan-Trigiano, Theresa Nez, Jim Parshall, Anne Pascale, Toby Pina, Bryce Pittinger, David Prescott, Shawn Proudfoot, Kathleen Roe, Gail Ryan, Peggy Ryder, Margaret Schultz, Jim Scorch, Mary Seabloom, Celeste Siebel, Tim Slover, David Stanifer, Larry Sutton, Kathryn Szewczuk, Joann Tabachnick, Jeff Tidd, Terry Tideman, Maggie Vincent-Poehlman, Susan Voight, Claudia Wallace, Katy Weiks, Floyd Wells, Elizabeth Williams, and Beverly Wilder.

And then there are those people who don't know us or our work but have provided a wealth of inspiration. People like Geoffrey Canada, Mark Chaffin, Barry Duncan, David Finkelhor, Judith Hermann, Mark Hubble, James Garbarino, Betsy McAlister Groves, Joshua Kendall, Michael Patrick MacDonald, Scott Miller, Luis Rodriguez, Phyllis Stien, Douglas Thomas, Patricia Torbet, Bessel van der Kolk, and many others whose important publications contributed to the foundation of this book.

We can gush on and on so it's probably way past time to stop. If anyone we know feels hurt by accidentally being excluded here please let us know and we'll give you a free copy of the book.

Index